124

CRITICAL ESSAYS IN MODERN LITERATURE

Critical Essays in Modern Literature

THE METAFICTIONAL MUSE

THE METAFICTIONAL MUSE

The Works of ROBERT COOVER,
DONALD BARTHELME,
and WILLIAM H. GASS

Larry McCaffery

UNIVERSITY OF PITTSBURGH PRESS

Published by the University of Pittsburgh Press, Pittsburgh, Pa. 15260
Copyright © 1982, University of Pittsburgh Press
Feffer and Simons, Inc., London
Manufactured in the United States of America

Library of Congress Cataloging in Publication Data

McCaffery, Larry, 1946–
  The metafictional muse.

  (Critical essays in modern literature)
  Bibliography: p. 281.
  Includes index.
  1. American fiction—20th century—History and
criticism.   2. Coover, Robert—Criticism and interpretation.   3. Barthelme, Donald—Criticism and interpretation.
4. Gass, William H., 1924–   —Criticism and interpretation.   I. Title.   II. Series.
PS379.M33   813'.54'09   82-1872
ISBN 0-8229-3462-0   AACR2

Portions of this book were previously published, in slightly different form, in "Donald Barthelme's
Snow White: The Aesthetics of Trash," *Critique* 16 (April 1975); "The Art of Metafiction: William
Gass's *Willie Masters' Lonesome Wife," Critique* 18 (August 1976); "Literary Disruptions: Fiction in a
'Post-Contemporary' Age," *boundary 2* 5 (Fall 1976); "Robert Coover's Cubist Fictions," *Par Rapport* 1
(Winter 1978); the Robert Coover and William H. Gass entries in *Dictionary of Literary Biography*
(Detroit: Gale Research Co., 1979); "Meaning and Non-Meaning in Barthelme's Fictions," *Journal of
Aesthetic Education* 13 (1979); and "Donald Barthelme and the Metafictional Muse," *Sub-Stance* 27
(1980).
  Grateful acknowledgment is made for permission to reprint passages from the following works:
Pricksongs and Descants by Robert Coover, copyright © 1969 by Robert Coover, reprinted by per-
mission of E. P. Dutton, Inc. and Jonathan Cape Ltd. *The Public Burning,* copyright © 1977 by Robert Coover, reprinted by permission of the Viking Press and Penguin Books Ltd. *The Origin of the
Brunists,* copyright © 1965 by Robert Coover, reprinted by permission of the Viking Press and
Georges Borchardt, Inc. *The Universal Baseball Association, Inc., J. Henry Waugh, Prop.,* copyright
© 1968 by Robert Coover, reprinted by permission of Random House, Inc. *Come Back, Dr. Caligari*
by Donald Barthelme, copyright © 1961, 1962, 1963, 1964 by Donald Barthelme, reprinted by permission of Little, Brown and Company and ICM. *Snow White* by Donald Barthelme, copyright ©
1967 by Donald Barthelme (New York: Atheneum, 1967), reprinted by permission of Atheneum Publishers. *Fiction and the Figures of Life,* copyright © 1970 by William H. Gass, reprinted by permission of the author. *Omensetter's Luck,* copyright © 1966 by William H. Gass, reprinted by permission of the New American Library, Inc. and the Sterling Lord Agency, Inc. *Willie Masters' Lonesome
Wife,* copyright © 1971 by William H. Gass, reprinted by permission of Alfred A. Knopf, Inc. *The
World Within the Word,* copyright © 1978 by William H. Gass, reprinted by permission of Alfred A.
Knopf, Inc.

CONTENTS

For Nina Baym, Sinda Gregory, and Jerry Klinkowitz,
in appreciation for what they contributed,
in their different fashions, to the completion of this book.

PREFACE

It is a curious anomaly that we listen to jazz, we look at modern paintings, we live in modern houses of modern design, we travel in jet planes, yet we continue to read novels written in a tempo and style which is not of our time and not related to any of these influences. The new swift novel could match our modern life in speed, rhythms, condensation, abstraction, miniaturization, X-rays of our secrets, a subjective gauge of external events. It could be born of Freud, Einstein, jazz and science.

Anaïs Nin, *The Novel of the Future*

Anyone trying to keep up with recent trends in fiction is sure to have noticed that the literary climate changed considerably from the early 1960s to the early 1970s. Back in the sixties, cries about the "death of the novel" and "literary exhaustion"—warnings common enough, really, since Cervantes' time—seemingly were being taken seriously by readers, critics, and even authors. In the United States the depressing appraisals of such influential French critics as Alain Robbe-Grillet (*For a New Novel*) and Nathalie Sarraute (*The Age of Suspicion*) were accepted by some, while others worried that the "new directions" left available to writers were dead ends, cop-outs, or—worst of all— just plain *boring*. Even John Barth, recognized by many as our most brilliant and promising young novelist, was spreading the word about "The Literature of Exhaustion."[1] Today, however, such worries seem as distant to our sensibilities as Day-Glo paint, protest rallies, and other relics of the period. Indeed, the period from roughly 1965 until 1975 produced a remarkable crop of serious, formally innovative writers and works; this burst of literary energy has resulted in what Jerome Klinkowitz has termed "The Death of the Death of the Novel."[2] Meanwhile, although fiction in America has been enjoying a boom that it hasn't experienced since the 1920s, both readers and critics have been hard-pressed to figure out exactly how to describe **ix** this new breed of fiction or how to account for its development. Since 1970, for example, a large number of scholarly books and articles have been devoted to the analysis of what has variously been termed "surfiction," "superfiction," "parafiction," "metafiction," and (the most popular phrase) "postmodern fiction." In addition to being unable to agree on the proper designation for this fiction, critics have found little to agree on concerning the nature of this new fiction except that contemporary fiction has been producing *some sort* of radically different works.

This study aims at clarifying some of the issues and problems faced by readers and critics of contemporary fiction by examining the works of three of the most significant writers to emerge from the "boom period" of the late 1960s. The works of these three writers— Robert Coover, Donald Barthelme, and William H. Gass—offer a wide but representative spectrum of the sorts of challenges that this new fiction has made to the fundamental assumptions which have dominated fiction for almost two hundred years: the traditions of the realistic novel. What this work intends to do is demonstrate that, despite the variety of styles and approaches to be found in the fiction of Coover, Barthelme, and Gass, their work also shares certain important tendencies. In particular, these writers share a "metafictional" impulse which is at the heart of much of the nontraditional fiction and popular culture of the past fifteen years. After an introductory chapter which examines and clarifies the key concepts, "metafiction" and "fiction-making," I discuss individual works by Coover, Barthelme, and Gass in detail, my discussion centering on the metafictional impulses which unify them. In trying to identify the peculiarly postmodern qualities of these works, I do not intend to suggest that their metafictional tendencies have arisen in a vacuum; indeed, my investigations actually suggest quite the opposite notion—that they have derived from a well-established tradition of avant-garde art which has evolved from a wide range of developments in painting, music, scientific and philosophic studies, and many other realms.

I have had much help while this study was evolving. Robert Coover, Donald Barthelme, and William Gass were all kind enough to talk with me on several formal and informal occasions. The editors of *boundary 2, Contemporary Literature, Critique, The Dictionary of Literary Biography, Fiction International, The Journal of Aesthetic Education,* and *Sub-Stance* allowed me the opportunity to express some of my thoughts about contemporary fiction in their pages; for the use of some of my material which appeared there, in much different forms, I am very grateful. Jerome Klinkowitz, Raymond Federman, Sinda Gregory, Campbell Tatham, Thomas LeClair, Edward Brandabur, Dan Majdiak, and Nina Baym all helped supply some of the ideas that are developed here. My copy editor, Jane Flanders, was invaluable in helping me prepare my manuscript. Finally, San Diego State University provided a summer fellowship and several units of release time which allowed me to complete this work.

THE METAFICTIONAL MUSE

FICTION MAKING AND 1
THE METAFICTIONAL MUSE

The literary disruptions witnessed in American fiction, beginning in force with the season of 1967–68 and continuing through the 1970s, signal not only a major development in the genre, but also its rebirth. The shock is not how far the disruptionists have gone, but how far we had let conventional fictionists desert the true ideals of artistic construction in favor of some wholly inappropriate documentation which was never really fiction at all.

Jerome Klinkowitz, *Literary Disruptions*

What a dreary way to begin a story he said to himself. . . . Another story about a writer writing a story! Another regressus in infinitum! Who doesn't prefer art that at least overtly imitates something other than its own processes?

John Barth, "Life Story"

To anyone who looks back on the literary events of the 1960s, it seems pretty obvious that many of the truly significant books to be published during that decade were almost totally ignored by the public and were often misrepresented by critics. The main reason that these works were greeted with bewilderment or misrepresentation is that they defied many of the accepted premises regarding what we had come to expect from fiction. These premises derived primarily from the conventions of the realistic novel which had come to so dominate our view of fiction that it was difficult for many readers and critics to realize that these premises were, in fact, only conventions and not givens. There were exceptions to this rule of anonymity, of course: after meager sales in hardback, Joseph Heller's *Catch-22* became in 1962 a huge bestseller in paperback; with the success of *Slaughterhouse-Five* in 1969, Kurt Vonnegut, Jr., became an instant celebrity and his previous books were rescued from the bus station and supermarket racks; meanwhile, although largely ignored by the public, the works of such nontraditional tal- 3 ents as Thomas Pynchon, John Barth, Jerzy Kosinski, and Donald Barthelme were being warmly received by many reviewers and critics. But the majority of significant innovative writers — writers such as Ronald Sukenick, Harry Mathews, Gilbert Sorrentino, Steve Katz, Ishmael Reed, Robert Coover, and Stanley Elkin — were either treated as literary eccentrics or, more frequently, totally ignored.

What has become obvious now from today's perspective is that these nontraditional works have a great deal more in common than they appeared to have at first. Many of these works, for instance, share a sense of playfulness and self-consciousness and are further unified by their willful artificiality and by their central preoccupation with metafictional concerns. Indeed, if we take a sampling of several of the major representative works of this period — say, Nabokov's *Pale Fire,* Vonnegut's *Slaughterhouse-Five,* Coover's *Universal Baseball Association,* Barth's *Chimera,* Sukenick's *Up,* Pynchon's *V.,* Gass's *In the Heart of the Heart of the Country,* Federman's *Double or Nothing* — we find that all develop basically the same pattern: a central character is presented who is lonely, alienated, disaffected, skeptical; these characters also feel themselves victimized by a repressive, cold social order to such an extent that their lives seem meaningless, drab, fragmented; in response to this powerful sense of personal isolation and violation, these characters decide to create or invent a system of meaning which will help to supply their lives with hope, order, possibly even some measure of beauty. The systems which these characters devise are sometimes obviously artificial in nature: Billy Pilgrim's Tralfamador, Stencil's quest, Henry Waugh's baseball game, the literary fictions of Kinbote's, Sukenick's, Federman's, or Gass's narrators; at other times, these systems are more subtly subjective, as with the creation of myth, religious systems, historical and political perspectives. One of the big dangers faced by many of these characters is a tendency to ignore their own roles as the creators of these fictional systems. Once they begin to lose sight of the fictional nature of their systems, they tend to become controlled by their creations rather than being able to use them as useful or even necessary metaphors. But despite the prospect of being manipulated by their own fictions, these characters usually give themselves over gladly to their artifices, for the depressing alternative is to resign themselves to the forces of entropy, nihilism, and boredom. The point seems to be that *any* system of order, whether derived from aesthetic principles, paranoia, madness, or superstition, is preferable to a life of emptiness and chaos (one thinks of Kinbote's pathetic but magnificently embodied Zembla, Waugh's baseball game, Oedipa Maas's Tristero conspiracy, Billy's Tralfamador).

In addition to focusing so often on the fiction-making process, this new fiction is quick to take advantage of the formal possibilities of the genre to help reinforce its point about the subjective nature of all systems. Thus these works tend to present themselves as self-conscious inventions and insist on the fact that every art form is merely another of man's imaginative creations. Fiction cannot hope to mirror reality or tell the truth because "reality" and "truth" are themselves fictional abstractions whose validity has become increasingly suspect as this century has proceeded. Consequently we find that these works usually include a reflexive irony which mocks the realistic claims of artistic significance and truth; they also insist that the reader accept the work as an invented, purely made-up entity. Such works therefore become metafictions—fictions which examine fictional systems, how they are created, and the way in which reality is transformed by and filtered through narrative assumptions and conventions.

Mas'ud Zavarzadeh has provided a useful starting point for an understanding of metafiction in his discussion of various new literary tendencies in *The Mythopoeic Reality*:

"Metafiction" is ultimately a narrational metatheorem whose subject matter is fictional systems themselves and the molds through which reality is patterned by narrrative conventions. . . . Metafiction more than other modes of transfiction is conscious of its own fictivity, and, in contrast to the interpretive novel, which operates with the aesthetic assumptions of verisimilitude, exults over its own fictitiousness, which it uses as the very terms of its narrative ontology—it is a "mask which points to itself." . . . This intense self-reflexiveness of metafiction is caused by the fact that the only certain reality for the metafictionist is the reality of his own discourse; thus, his fiction turns in upon itself, transforming the process of writing into the subject of writing. The credibility of fiction, therefore, is reestablished not as an illuminating commentary on life but as a metacommentary on fiction itself.[1]

As Zavarzadeh's discussion implies, the metafictionist focuses on literary forms, patterns, and conventions, and upon the language process itself. This is not merely the expression of a perverse sense of self-consciousness or narcissism; instead, the metafictionist begins with the assumption that we are forever locked within a world shaped by language and by subjective (i.e., *fictional*) forms developed to organize our relationship to the world in a coherent fashion. The primary impulse behind metafiction is therefore its awareness that our participation in the world involves the projection of our deepest hopes, fears, and needs onto reality in various fictionalized forms. These forms are embodied in cultural and ideological discourse, which play a crucial role in shaping the individual's response to reality. By implication, every significant human act carries with it a context of meaning which is directly a function of language and of the rules of transformation established *by the system itself* and not by any exterior, imposed meaning. The metafictionist, then, attempts to examine many of the same issues as have traditional writers: what is the meaning of personal identity and personal knowledge? To what extent is man shaped by his environment and by the systems he has devised to deal with reality? What is the nature of man's fears and needs and how do they find expression in a world which alternately seems threatening or utterly trivial? But in examining these familiar issues, the metafictionist implies that within the act of creation, of fiction making, we can find the key to unlocking the complexities of self-definition and the manner in which we project this definition through language.

This program of fictions-about-fictions is not limited to fictional interventions into established literary fictions, such as Barthelme's *Snow White*, Barth's *Chimera* or *Letters*, or John Seelye's *The True Adventures of Huckleberry Finn;* nor can it be explained as the familiar book-about-the-writing-of-a-book approach, a method which can be traced at least as far back as *Tristram Shandy* and which has recently been brilliantly used by writers such as Gide, Beckett, and Nabokov. Although these two metafictional approaches *are* often found in the works of recent metafictionists, a definition of metafiction must also include the kinds of works which focus on the creation of fictional systems of all kinds. It is important to broaden our definition thus because even with metafictional works which deal directly with the creation of a literary text—as with Gass's *Willie Masters' Lonesome Wife,* Sukenick's *Up,* Coover's "The Magic Poker" and "Klee Dead," Nabokov's *Pale Fire,* or Federman's *Double or Nothing*—we find that the author is using the writer/text relationship as a paradigm for all of human creative activity. By exploring how the writer produces an aesthetic fiction, the metafictionist hopes to suggest the analogous process through which all our meaning systems are generated. On the other hand, an important group of metafictional works may initially appear to have little to do with art or the nature of literary fictions but, upon close examination, suggest a rich variety of implications about the role of the artist and the artist's relationship to aesthetic constructs. Examples are Coover's *The Universal Baseball Association,* Pynchon's *V.,* and Gass's *Omensetter's Luck.*

Before beginning a detailed examination of the works of Coover, Barthelme, and Gass, I should discuss briefly the changing role of fiction in the 1960s and 1970s and suggest some of the reasons for this change. I will divide these introductory remarks into two sections: first, a broad discussion of some of the developments in philosophy and art that helped lay the groundwork for the literary experimentation that occurred in the 1960s; second, an examination of how the metafictional impulse fits into the context of specific literary tendencies characteristic of the period. These introductory remarks should provide a context which will enable us to approach the works of Coover, Gass, and Barthelme in a unified fashion.

The Fiction-Making Process

That man enjoys making fictions, and that he has done so for untold thousands of years, seems obvious. But it has taken the past two centuries and the work of a varied assortment of philosophers, psychologists, and scientists to make us understand the extent to which man relies on this process. In a recent interview, Robert Coover stated that his own concern with the concept of man-as-fiction-maker developed because of his sense that "we have come to the end of a tradition. I don't mean that we have come to the end of the novel or of fictional forms, but that our ways of looking at the world and of adjusting to it through fictions are changing."[2] Coover adds that this change has occurred because the fictions man has developed so painstakingly over the past several centuries have begun to lose their utility; we see this, for example, in the way that Euclid's geometry or Newton's concept of gravity has become outdated when confronted with the complexities of relativistic space. In explaining this process, Coover reveals that his concern with fiction making extends far beyond the categories of narrative or literary art to the fundamental systems through which we perceive and organize our knowledge of the universe:

> The question is not limited to how one produces narrative art; our basic assumptions about the universe have been altered, and so change has occurred in the broad base of metaphor through which the universe is comprehended. Our old faith—one might better say our old sense of constructs derived from myths, legends, philosophies, fairy stories, histories, and other fictions which help to explain what happens to us from day to day, why our governments are the way they are, why our institutions have the character they have, why the world turns as it does—has lost its efficacy. Not necessarily is it false; it is just not as efficacious as it was.[3]

By applying the term "fictions" to the products of such fields as philosophy, history, and science, Coover is directly expressing a viewpoint that lies at the center of his work, as well as at the center of Gass's and Barthelme's: that, partially due to human nature and partially due to the nature of the universe, we can never objectively know the world; rather, we inhabit a world of fictions and are constantly forced to develop a variety of metaphors and subjective systems to help us organize our experience so that we can deal with the world. These fictional systems are useful in that they generate meaning, stabilize our perceptions; such systems can also be appreciated as aesthetic objects apart from their utility functions. But when such systems lose their utility and become stale, they need to be overhauled or discarded completely. Unfortunately, our desire for permanency and order often tempts us to ignore the fictional nature of our systems; and as the works of Coover, Gass, and Barthelme often dramatically demonstrate, without this understanding, we tend to become trapped within our fictional systems, victims of our own decayed or obsessive creations. Indeed, all three writers are anxious to examine metafictionally how these systems are created and how they animate or deaden our relationship to the world. By focusing insistently on the creative process itself—especially upon the way our perceptions and methods of interpretation are influenced by our received language—all three writers hope to illuminate how man defines himself and his response to the world.

This view of the fiction-making process is heavily dependent upon the view of man-as-metaphor-maker which has been developed in so many fields of study since the Kantian revolution in philosophy. This view suggests that such pure notions as objectivity, absolute truth, or Kant's *Ding an sich* are forever beyond man's grasp because of the mediating effect of his own operations upon the world. Such an outlook, of course, could develop only after Kant helped to overthrow many of the metaphysical foundations on which empiricism had rested. These principles, put forth in Bacon's *Novum Organum* and summarized in J. S. Mill's methodological manifesto, *Canons of Induction,* rested on the assumption that all human knowledge is derived from experience and that our human senses supply us with reliable, objective reports about the real world. These principles were undermined by Kant's suggestion that subjective elements enter into all human operations and that perhaps even our sense data were from the outset primarily *symbols,* the product of a synthesis between matter and subjectively provided form. Once this subjective, symbolic relationship between the world and man's conception of the world is accepted, the notion of man-as-fiction-maker becomes an obvious extension. Ironically enough, acceptance of this notion also makes the legitimacy of realistic literary fictions, such as the realistic novel, seem more and more problematic.

The dilemma for the realistic novelist is that since the novel's beginning in the eighteenth century, empirical certainties formed the foundations of the conventions of realism. These conventions, as Ian Watt has persuasively argued in *The Rise of the Novel,* were intimately related to the optimistic, empiricist view that assumed the existence of a deterministic universe and the human ability to uncover the most intimate mechanisms of its operations. William Spanos has supplied a useful metaphor for this world view and the type of literature based upon it in his essay, "The Detective and the Boundary." As he explains it, until the rise of postmodernism most literature was based on a kind of "detective novel" premise: most writers assumed that man could solve the puzzle of nature—and of literature—if he examined the "clues" carefully enough. This problem-solving perspective is described by Spanos as having its ground in more than simply an acceptance of the susceptibility of nature to rational explanation:

Taking their lead from the existentialists, the post-modern absurdists . . . view the well-made play or novel . . . as the inevitable analogue of the well-made positivistic universe delineated by the post-Renaissance humanistic structure of consciousness. More specifically, they view the rigid deterministic plot of the well-made fiction, like that of its metaphysical counterpart, as having its source in bad faith.[4]

From this viewpoint, it is not at all accidental that the eighteenth century—the Age of Reason—was the century in which the realistic novel, with its logical, causal connections and linear development, began to flourish. This confidence in man's ability to know, to make sense out of the universe, reaches a high point in the nineteenth century, which was not coincidentally the age of the great realistic novel. By the mid-nineteenth century many assumed that science was very close to solving the puzzle of the material universe; a similar sort of ontological optimism is evident in the philosophies of Mill and of Hegel, whose totalizing claims for the human mind would help spark the existentialist revolt, beginning with Kierkegaard's *Concluding Unscientific Postscript.* This optimism can also be found in the historiographic approaches of Ranke, Taine, and Comte, in the linguistic investigations of Humboldt and Schleicher, in Freudian psychoanalysis, and in the theory and practice of the great nineteenth-century realistic novelists such as Stendhal, Zola, Eliot, and Tolstoi.

But we have come a long distance from that period of rigorously empirical outlooks. Indeed, even during the nineteenth century we see the development of the reverse process: the demolition of the

faith in rational, empirical investigation, the frank acknowledge-
ment of the subjective nature of our mental operations and their relationship to the world, and the injection of the concept of relativity
into the very fabric of the universe itself. We can certainly observe
this development as early as the literary theory and practice of the
romantics, with their emphasis on the creative imagination and its
constitutive powers. There were related developments in practically
every field of human investigation: Vaihinger and Nietzsche (and later, Croce and Cassirer) expanded and developed the Kantian imperatives in philosophy; Gauss, Riemann, and Lobachevski began
tinkering with perhaps our most trusted operation, mathematics,
and soon Poincaré had developed a categorical denial of geometrical empiricism; while Ernst Mach shook physics with his denial that
science could tell us anything about the world (it could tell us, he
suggested, only about the connections between our sense data), Mi-
chelson and Morley were conducting an experiment which would
eventually lead to Einstein's complete overthrow of our view of the
universe as a static, mechanistic entity.

Not surprisingly, the problem of analyzing the relationship between man and his metaphors, between objective and subjective
views of the world, has been one of the main topics of controversy in
this century. In a wide range of fields the notion of man-as-fiction-
maker has been put forward with impressive regularity, along with
the rejection of the concept of dogmatic, absolute truth. The importance of this idea can be found, for example, in such fields as the sociology of religion, historiography, anthropology, psychology, linguistics, and in practically all of the "metasciences."[5] Again and
again, study in these fields has arrived at a description of man locked
within his own forms, languages, and fictions which he creates and
manipulates as useful aids. Predictably, these epistemological revelations also began having a direct and profound effect on artists and
how they viewed their endeavors. The effect is probably most evident in painting and the plastic arts, with the introduction of cubism,
various forms of collage, and abstractionism. The effect on fiction
writing took longer to manifest itself, although there were some literary figures who quickly began incorporating the implications of
these discoveries into their works—figures such as the symbolist and

surrealist experimenters, and quirky individualists such as Alfred Jarry, Guillaume Apollinaire, Raymond Queneau, J. L. Borges, and Vladimir Nabokov.

As Frank Kermode has suggested in *The Sense of an Ending,* it was inevitable that literary fictions would be profoundly influenced by the discoveries of the fictional bases of other systems:

> There *is* a simple relation between literary and other fiction. . . . If we think first of modern fictions, it can hardly be an accident that ever since Nietzsche generalized and developed the Kantian insights, literature has increasingly asserted its rights to an arbitrary and private choice of fictional norms, just as historiography has become a discipline more devious and dubious because of our recognition that its methods depend to an unsuspected degree on myths and fictions.[6]

This view that literature is a free, consciously false construction is directly relevant to the literary approaches of Coover, Barthelme, and Gass; it also helps shed light on the literary theories of such poets as Mallarmé and Valéry. But it was almost fifty years before fiction really began to catch up with the other arts in terms of realizing the ultimate futility of the realistic, "slice-of-life" approach. By the early 1950s, a variety of influential literary figures such as Robbe-Grillet, Anaïs Nin, and Nathalie Sarraute were calling for an end to a narrowly conceived mimetic tradition in fiction and suggesting that a recognition of fiction's limits would also free writers to allow the genre to begin developing along the lines that most other art forms in this century had been following.

For the host of young, innovative talents that took up the challenge of exploring traditions more in keeping with the postmodern spirit, what ground rules could be taken for granted? Not too many, suggests author and critic Ronald Sukenick in an often-quoted passage from his own metafictional story, "The Death of The Novel":

> I will begin by considering how the world looks in what I think we may now begin to call the contemporary post-realistic novel. Realistic fiction presupposed chronological time as the medium of a plotted narrative, an irreducible individual psyche as the subject of its characterization, and, above all, the ultimate, concrete reality of things as the object and rationale of its description. . . . The contemporary writer—the writer who is acutely in touch

with the life of which he is part—is forced to start from scratch: Reality doesn't exist, time doesn't exist, personality doesn't exist. God was the omniscient author, but he died; now no one knows the plot, and since our reality lacks the sanction of a creator, there's no guarantee as to the authenticity of the received version. Time is reduced to presence, the content of a series of discontinuous moments. Time is no longer purposive, and so there is no destiny, only chance.[7]

The postmodernist fiction that began springing up in the United States, South America, and Europe during the 1960s took as its basic premise the fact that the mimetic approach of traditional fiction implies a naively dogmatic epistemology from the outset; concepts such as character and plot had to be reworked by writers who had grown skeptical about causal relationships, beginnings, middles, and ends (or progression in the old sense), and the existence of a coherent, meaningful world. Unable to feel any longer that they could present novels which depicted the true status of affairs in the world, postmodernist fiction writers decided to turn inward, to focus not on reality but on the imagination's response to reality—a response which became recognized as the *only* aspect of reality which could ever be known.

Works of the postmodern imagination often reflect this new epistemological orientation quite directly. Thus many new fictions deal openly with the hazards of knowing and with the systems we create to help us navigate through our daily experience. Widely differing structural devices helped reinforce the turn away from realistic norms: the use of multiple, contradictory perspectives (in Durrell's *The Alexandria Quartet* and in stories by Coover and Barthelme, for example), Burrough's "cut-out" methods, the increasing willingness of writers to use graphics and typography in their works, the deliberate confounding of fact and fiction, the general tendency of writers to flaunt their artifice—these may all be viewed as related strategies. Not surprisingly, many of these works focus on the mediating effect which language and literature have on man's relationship to the world; this is a central concern of Coover, Barthelme, and Gass, and is also evident in the works of Beckett, Borges, Ionesco, Barth, Nabokov, Cortazar, and Handke. These writers are all well aware that consciousness is embodied in a particular language and that it is our language which generates our response to the world. It is interesting that nearly all of these writers share a fundamental sense of *playfulness* in their roles as creators and manipulators of linguistic systems; by demystifying their role in the creative process and by insisting on the absolute freedom of the artist, they exhibit a liberating stance vis-à-vis their creations which underscores the potential we all share in opposing the repressive social and aesthetic values of our culture. Playfulness, then, becomes a deliberate strategy used to provoke readers to critically examine all cultural codes and established patterns of thought. Closely related to this reflexive play with literary forms is the proliferation of works which treat seriously such popular genres as the detective novel (in Nabokov, Borges, Stanislaw Lem, Manuel Puig, Butor), sports novels (Coover, Handke, Delillo, Roth, McGuane), and science fiction (Burgess, Calvino, Lem, Vonnegut, LeGuin, with Borges and Nabokov on the fringes).

What all these related developments suggest is that many of the best contemporary writers found themselves unable to write the kinds of social or psychological studies that dominated fictional tastes in America from 1930 to 1960. Not only did postmodern works tend to be more obviously artificial but also they became more formally outrageous and darkly humorous. A kind of bleak, absurdist comedy permeates the epistemological skepticism of most of the contemporary authors; they tend to treat ironically the attempts of their characters to settle on secure systems and truths. As a result, we observe their characters continually seeking answers and assurances, creating their own systems, and then becoming imprisoned within them, finally claiming that they can't go on in such a world and then going on anyway. At the same time, we are usually aware that the writers' irony is also *self*-directed, that their own efforts to organize elements into a work of art are as arbitrary and tenuous as those of their characters. Ronald Sukenick has provided a neat summary of how this metafictional focus illustrates something about the universal nature of fiction making:

Perhaps the fundamental assumption behind this line of fiction is that the act of composing a novel is basically not different from that of composing one's reality, which brings me back to a slogan I draw from Robbe-Grillet's criticism that the main didactic job of the contemporary novelist is to teach the reader how to invent his world.[8]

This statement helps demonstrate that the self-conscious, self-referential qualities of the metafictionists do not mean that they are inevitably self-indulgent, narcissistic, or minor writers — charges which have been consistently laid at their doorsteps by critics who feel more comfortable with the traditional, realistic literary forms.

The Literary Climate and the Metafictional Muse

In one of the many recent articles which attempt to outline the characteristics of postmodern fiction, Edward Said observes:

For such novelists as Thomas Pynchon, John Barth (particularly in *Chimera*), Donald Barthelme, fiction is a language with its own field and play, its own internal system of reference, its own sense of the opportunities available for inventiveness. Fiction is viewed not as an intervention into reality, nor as an addition to it — as was the case with classic realist fiction — but rather as an intervention in other fiction, or in other writing.[9]

William H. Gass makes much the same point about this type of fiction in his important essay, "Philosophy and the Form of Fiction," when he introduces the concept of the "metafictional novel":

There are metatheorems in mathematics and logic, ethics has its linguistic oversoul, everywhere lingos to converse about lingos are being contrived, and the case is no different in the novel. I don't mean those drearily predictable pieces about writers who are writing about what they are writing, but those, like some of the work of Borges, Barth, and Flann O'Brien, for example, in which the forms of fiction serve as the material upon which further forms can be imposed. Indeed, many of the so-called antinovels are really metafictions.[10]

Anyone who has closely examined the nature of the disruptive fictional experiments of the past fifteen years knows that both Said and Gass are right in suggesting that the themes, materials, and forms of *fiction itself* have served as the main objects of inquiry for many of the most important recent fictions. Gass's attempt to link up the metafictional impulse with the metasystems that have recently been developed in so many other areas of inquiry is especially interesting. As fields such as history, science, mathematics, linguistics, and logic have become more and more self-conscious about the nature of their investigations, it has naturally become necessary for them to develop systems and languages through which to deal with their own fields. But it is also crucial for these self-directed investigations to operate outside of the parameters of their own fields — to make sure that the system devised to examine the previous system is not infected with the same biases and premises used by the original system. In fields such as mathematics and logic, the necessity for a true *meta*system becomes absolutely essential, for, as Kurt Godel demonstrated, closed systems such as mathematical or logical systems can never be both complete and consistent. To take a familiar example, the famous paradox involving the statements "All Cretans are liars" and "I am a Cretan" can be solved only if we assume that the first statement is a "metastatement" which applies to all statements *except* itself and any other metastatements.[11]

For literary fictions, the necessity of having a truly "metafictional" system has not yet been demonstrated, although as yet there has been very little probing of the logical status of sentences within fictions. In a commonsense manner, it seems as if there is a difference between a work which tries to describe a condition which exists in the external world and a work which is either about itself or which uses previous fictional forms as the primary materials for its own formation. For our purposes, I will be using the term "metafiction" to refer to two related fictional forms: first, that type of fiction which either directly examines its own construction as it proceeds or which comments or speculates about the forms and language of previous fictions. Recent examples of this type of fiction are easy to spot and will be commented upon in more detail later in this chapter, but some representatives would include works such as Ronald Sukenick's *Up,* Steve Katz's *The Exagggerations of Peter Prince* and *Moving Parts,* Thomas Williams's *The Story of Harold Roux,* many of Borges's fables, Barth's *Chimera* — plus many of the works of Coover ("The

Magic Poker," "Klee Dead"), Gass ("In the Heart of the Heart of the Country," *The Tunnel),* and Barthelme (*Snow White* and many of the short fictions). A second, more general category refers to books which seek to examine how *all* fictional systems operate, their methodology, the sources of their appeal, and the dangers of their being dogmatized. Obviously this second category is potentially very large indeed, especially if we accept the idea that *all* systems are, in certain important aspects, fictional; this study will focus on the type of works which use their metafictional framework to make some sort of comment on the nature of artistic systems or literary fictions. Thus Robert Coover's *The Universal Baseball Association* uses an imaginary baseball game as its central metaphorical device, but it also illuminates a great deal about the role of an author and his relationship to a work of fiction; likewise, nearly all of William Gass's works can be viewed as metafictional examinations of the mediating effects of language and linguistic forms on his main characters.

What should be obvious from my definitions of metafictional works is that my categories are broad and will frequently overlap with more familiar fictional tendencies. To a certain extent, for example, any experimental novel is about fiction making; such a work suggests attitudes about the art of fiction by the very act of subverting or ignoring specific conventions and of introducing others instead. Often the metafictional aspects of a work play only a minor role in the book's development or operate harmoniously with other aspects of the work so efficiently that their presence is hardly noticed. Thus we can find metafictional impulses in a great many works that seem extremely conventional in form and content: it might not occur to us, for example, to label as metafictional George Eliot's discussion of realism in *Adam Bede* (and isn't Dorothea Brooke's problem in *Middlemarch* that of taking metaphors and fictional systems too literally?), or similarly to designate Hawthorne's "Custom House" section of *The Scarlet Letter.* What seems obvious to me, however, is that recent fiction—and especially recent American fiction—has allowed metafictional impulses to dominate its development in the past fifteen years. Thus I am in complete agreement with Edward Said's assertion that "American fiction, more than fiction generally, is a particularly apt *fictional* extension of past fiction. Just by being American . . . one can enter the discursive world of past fiction with notable ease."[12]

As I have already indicated, metafictional works are hardly a new phenomenon. In trying to find precursors, we can discover dozens of them, including Sterne's *Tristram Shandy* (written in the eighteenth century before realism had completely taken over the literary imagination of fiction writers) and even *Don Quixote* (which was developed both thematically and structurally in response to the literary traditions of the romance). But it has been the twentieth century that has seen metafictional works begin to appear with insistent regularity, in part because of the influences that I have outlined earlier in this chapter. The most important example of a metafictional work to appear early in this century is probably Gide's *The Counterfeiters,* taken together with the appended "Journal of *The Counterfeiters."* The period of 1900 until 1930 was, of course, a period of growth and experimentation for fiction, but with a few important exceptions (Gide, Roussel, and, above all, Gertrude Stein) most of the really significant experimentation tended to be largely extensions of realistic methods, especially the attempts of writers to develop methods of delving deeply into human psychology. Thus the great writers of the modernist period—Faulkner, the early Joyce, Virginia Woolf, Hemingway, Fitzgerald, Sherwood Anderson—were still operating primarily in the traditions of realism. From 1930 until 1950 the dominant mode, particularly in America, was still realism, although significant exceptions were emerging: Beckett, Witold Gombrowicz, Anaïs Nin, Djuna Barnes, Nathanael West, Céline, and, for our purposes, perhaps the two writers who were to have the most significant impact on the metafictionists of the 1960s—Vladimir Nabokov and J. L. Borges.

The movement toward radical and disruptive fictional forms was slowed down in America in part because of the social conditions of the times: the Depression, World War II, and the cold war of the 1950s. Unlike music or painting—which traditionally have never been required to make "socially significant" statements—literature in general, and fiction in particular, has long been viewed as having obligations to criticize the social and psychological conditions of its particular age. Thus with only a few significant exceptions (Barnes,

West, Hawkes, Patchen), American fictional approaches remained largely conservative during this period until the 1960s, when the literary climate—assisted by the radicalized social and political atmosphere—rapidly changed.[13] Virtually overnight, it seemed, our admiration for the important writers of the 1950s (Salinger, Mailer, Styron, Bellow, Flannery O'Connor, the early Roth, Malamud, and Updike) was transferred to a literary generation of a very different style and temperament indeed: Heller, Barth, Vonnegut, Coover, Barthelme, and Gass.

Needless to say, such a spectacular shift in literary sensibilities could hardly have occurred in a vacuum. For one thing, social conditions created an atmosphere of rebellious energy that had a widespread impact on nearly every segment of American life. The sixties were, above all, an age of revolution and developing self-awareness: spurred on by the musical revolution initiated by the Beatles and by a growing sense of unity created by opposition to the Vietnam War, the youth culture began to exert an influence on popular tastes as never before; black culture and the nascent women's movement developed a militant self-awareness while political disruptions were reported almost daily in the news. Meanwhile a new permissiveness was evident everywhere: in the classroom, in the new sexual morality, in the art world, and—thanks in part to court decisions favoring Nabokov, Henry Miller, William S. Burroughs, and others—in the world of fiction.

In addition to widespread transformations of values, there was also a whole series of specific literary factors that helped change writers' attitudes about fiction. For one thing, the important European criticisms of novelistic forms that had been written in the early 1950s and had generated so much excitement were finally translated and made available to American writers and critics. Probably the most important of these works was Alain Robbe-Grillet's brilliant study, *For a New Novel* (1965), which raised a number of significant questions about the validity of pursuing traditional methods in fiction. In his important essay, "On Several Obsolete Notions," Robbe-Grillet focused on the important differences between the way contemporary writers view their relationship to the world and the way in which realistic writers once did:

The narrative, as our academic critics conceive it—and many readers after them—represents an order. This order, which we may in effect qualify as natural, is linked to an entire rationalistic and organizing system whose flowering corresponds to the assumption of power by the middle class. In that first half of the nineteenth century which saw the apogee—with *The Human Comedy*—of a narrative form which understandably remains for many a kind of paradise lost of the novel, certain important certainties were in circulation: in particular the confidence in a logic of things that was just and universal.

All the technical elements of the narrative—systematic use of the past tense and the third person unconditional, adoption of chronological development, linear plots, regular trajectory of the passions, impulse of each episode toward a conclusion, etc.—everything tended to impose the image of a stable, coherent, continuous, unequivocal, entirely decipherable universe. Since the intelligibility of the world was not even questioned, to tell a story did not raise a problem. The style of the novel could be innocent.[14]

Robbe-Grillet goes on to anticipate the theoretical statements of such postmodernist spokesmen as William Gass and Ron Sukenick when he flatly states, "I do not transcribe, I construct. This had been even the old ambition of Flaubert: to make something out of nothing, something that would stand alone, without having to lean on anything external to the work; today this is the ambition of the novel as a whole."[15] He also suggests that the metafictional impulse is at the center of the contemporary novelists' concerns:

Lifelike, spontaneous, limitless, the story must, in a word, be natural. Unfortunately, even while admitting that there is still something "natural" in the relations of man and the world, it turns out that writing, like any form of art, is on the contrary an intervention. What constitutes the novelist's strength is precisely that he invents, that he invents quite freely, without model. *The remarkable thing about modern fiction is that it asserts this characteristic quite deliberately, to such a degree that invention and imagination become, at the limit, the very subject of the book.*[16]

Along with such critical pronouncements, translations of significant nontraditional works were also beginning to appear which helped further a growing sophistication and self-consciousness about the limits of realism and some possible alternatives for serious fiction. The works of many of the important French New Novelists (Michel Butor, Nathalie Sarraute, Robbe-Grillet, and their precursor, Raymond Queneau) began to appear in English translations during the late 1950s and early 1960s, for example; these works did not prove to be attractive to the American literary sensibility, but they did generate considerable controversy and provoked American writers and critics to reexamine many of their assumptions about fiction. As the 1960s progressed, the examples of other major nontraditionalists from other countries began to find their way into print—and even into readily available paperback editions. Especially important in this regard was the appearance of the translations of works by such writers as Günter Grass, Kobo Abe, Andrew Bely, Raymond Roussel, Peter Handke, and a whole series of magnificent South American writers (Garcia Marquez, Cabrera Infante, José Donoso, Manuel Puig, Vargas Llosa, Carlos Fuentes, Julio Cortazar, and several others). The most important translations to appear, however, were those of the two most influential figures in the metafictional outburst of the 1960s: the translation of Nabokov's Russian novels and of J. L. Borges's *Ficciones* (1962), a collection which may well have had more effect on the direction that American fiction was to take during the 1960s than any other single work.

The influence of Vladimir Nabokov, unquestionably the greatest metafictionist of all time, on the new generation of American writers is so pervasive that its precise limits are difficult to judge. Although the genius of such brilliant, nontraditional works as *The Gift, Invitation to a Beheading, Despair,* and *The Defense* went largely unappreciated by American audiences because they were not translated until the 1960s, his two American masterpieces, *Lolita* (1957) and *Pale Fire* (1962), offered immediate, lofty models for how metafiction could combine self-conscious, artificial, nonrealistic methods with a deep understanding of the human condition. Although published in America in 1957, *Lolita* was misrepresented for several years as a pornographic, largely realistic novel; only in the 1960s, when the intricacy of its word play and artifice began to be more fully understood, did it become recognized as the nontraditional classic that it is. *Pale Fire,* with its labyrinth of false scents, mirrors, and cross-references and with its playful but meticulously developed structure (consisting of introduction, poem, commentary, glossary), more immediately offered itself as a model for experimenters. Along with the pseudo-scholarly investigations of Borges, Nabokov's method in *Pale Fire* of creating a mock presentation which painstakingly imitates the forms of nonfictional works became one of the most familiar approaches of later American innovators (as, for example, with Stephen Millhauser's *Edwin Mullhouse,* Jerome Charyn's *The Tar Baby,* Alan Friedman's *Hermaphrodeity,* and many others). Likewise, the influence of Borges's *Ficciones,* which seemed to blend traditional literary and philosophic speculations with the methods of Kafka, detective novelists, and writers of fantasy and science fiction, became at once apparent in the short fictions of America's most talented and formally inventive writers such as John Barth (*Lost in the Funhouse*), Donald Barthelme (especially in his collections beginning with *City Life*), and Robert Coover (who even appended the subtitle, "Fictions," to his short story collection, *Pricksongs and Descants*).

American fiction's turn away from the conservatism of the 1950s was also greatly assisted by the arrival of several young writers of obvious genius who all published major nontraditional works in the early 1960s which helped set the tenor for the rest of the decade. Chief among these writers were John Barth, Thomas Pynchon, and Joseph Heller. Works such as Barth's *The Sot Weed Factor* (1960) and *Giles Goat Boy* (1965), Pynchon's *V.* (1963), and Heller's *Catch-22* (1961) served unmistakable notice that fiction in the sixties was going to pursue its own path. These works owed their unusual effects to a wide variety of nonstandard sources such as the absurdist theater, prenovelistic sources of myth and fairy tales, pop art, and the literary influences of such nonrealists as Nabokov, Céline, John Hawkes, and William Gaddis. The results were a peculiar blend of dark humor, literary parody, byzantine plots full of improbable coincidences and outrageous action, and one-dimensional, comic-book characters — attributes which would be evident in most of the important innovative works later in the decade.

One last important influence on the changing role of American fiction in the 1960s and 1970s was the almost inevitable emergence of sympathetic critics who could appreciate the efforts of contemporary innovators, articulate the nature of these experiments, and place the works into some sort of recognizable context. Needless to say, the works of many of the most exciting nontraditional talents had been roundly criticized, misrepresented, and often ignored by critics who had a stake in the continued dominance of their own area of interest. Thus even as late as 1967 Stephen Kock could make the following outrageous claim: "At the moment our literature is idling in a period of hiatus: the few important writers of the earlier generations are dead, silent, or in their decline, while the younger generation has not yet produced a writer of unmistakable importance or even of very great interest."[17] But as the sixties turned into the seventies, several critics were willing to take the plunge and accept the necessary challenge of trying to come to grips with what was variously being called "surfiction," "parafiction," and "superfiction." These critics included Richard Gilman (*The Confusion of Realms,* 1970), Ihab Hassan (*Paracriticisms,* 1974), Raymond Olderman (*Beyond the Wasteland,* 1972), Tony Tanner (*City of Words,* 1970), Jerome Klinkowitz (*Literary Disruptions,* 1975, and *The Life of Fiction,* 1977), and Raymond Federman (*Surfiction,* 1975). The most important single work of criticism to appear during the period, however, was William H. Gass's *Fiction and the Figures of Life* (1971), a study that provided the nontraditionalists with a manifesto which justified their efforts in terms of carefully established literary and philosophic principles. Gass's most often quoted phrase from this work was a remark which echoes both Paul Valéry and Robbe-Grillet: "There are no descriptions in fiction, there are only constructions."[18] What Gass goes on to examine in the important opening section of his book is the idea that fictional systems such as the novel are, in fact, *fictional*—they are symbolic systems of signs and relationships which are freely constructed and have no necessary connection to the world. This idea, which is the central concept from which contemporary fiction gathers its impetus, is also a key element in the metafictional impulse which we have already examined. Keeping these two related concepts of metafiction and the fiction-making process in mind, we can turn now to an examination of the individual works of three of the most important new talents to emerge during the "boom period" of the 1960s: Robert Coover, Donald Barthelme, and William H. Gass.

ROBERT COOVER 2
AND THE MAGIC
OF FICTION MAKING

The mind of man, when it is really at one with itself, shares this oneness with everything that is not itself, draws it into its own unity until mind and object are one.

> Goethe, in conversation with Riemer

All antiquity, all causality, every human principle, are fabulous inventions and obey the simple laws of invention.

> Paul Valéry, "On Myths and Mythology"

All of us, grave or light, get our thoughts entangled in metaphors, and act fatally on the strength of them.

> George Eliot, Middlemarch

Even before the publication of *The Public Burning* (1977) made Robert Coover famous, he had already achieved a solid reputation, mostly among academic and college audiences, as one of the most original and versatile prose stylists in America. In his three earlier book-length works of fiction—*The Origin of the Brunists* (1965), *The Universal Baseball Association, J. Henry Waugh, Prop.* (1968), and *Pricksongs and Descants* (1970)—Coover's ability to create and control a dazzling variety of styles and voices had been evident; indeed, *Pricksongs and Descants* is arguably the most significant collection of experimental fictions to appear anywhere since the "New Wave" period of the mid-1960s. But it was not until the appearance of *The Public Burning* that Coover's place as a major figure in contemporary fiction became assured.

Even more obviously than the works of Donald Barthelme and William H. Gass, the fiction of Robert Coover is tightly unified by its metafictional impulses. In examining the concept of man-as-fiction-maker, nearly all of Coover's works deal with characters busily constructing systems to play with or to help them deal with their chaotic lives. Some of these systems are clearly fictional in nature: we observe writers trying to create stories, men struggling to break the hold of mythic patterns, desperate people inventing religious explanations for a terrible catastrophe, a middle-aged man finding love and companionship among the imaginary players of a table-top baseball game. Yet Coover's work is filled with hints that other, less obviously artificial systems — such as mathematics, science, religion, myth, and the perspectives of history and politics — are also fictional at their core. Indeed, in most of Coover's fiction there exists a tension between the process of man creating his fictions and his desire to assert that his systems have an independent existence of their own. For Coover, this tension typically results in man losing sight of the fictional basis of his systems and eventually becoming trapped within them.

In developing this view of man-as-fiction-maker, Coover is hoping to illuminate not only the process through which narrative art is created but also the broad base of metaphor through which the universe is comprehended. His application points in the same direction as the study of the use of metaphor in so many other areas of investigation, such as anthropology, mathematics, linguistic analysis, the various metasciences, and so on. Each of these disciplines has tended to analyze its own structures as useful models or symbolic systems created by man — either consciously or through some sort of innate structuring agency within him — and then applied to the world. In his fascinating study, *The Myth of Metaphor,* Colin Turbayne has examined Descartes's mind-body dualism and Newton's universe-as-machine analogy as examples of the way in which metaphors gradually instill themselves as ontological verities. The process Turbayne describes for "undressing" such hidden metaphors is very similar to what Coover is aiming for in his fiction:

First, the detection of the presence of the metaphor; second, the attempt to "undress" the metaphor by presenting the literal truth, "to behold the deformity of error we need only undress it"; and third, the restoration of the metaphor, only this time with awareness of its presence.[1]

If we substitute Coover's concept of "fiction" for Turbayne's closely related term, "metaphor," we have a close approximation of Coover's method. For both Turbayne and Coover, the point is not at all *to do away* with metaphors and fictions; those forms that are still useful can continue to be applied and even admired as aesthetic objects — but this should be done *with awareness of their true nature.* This awareness does not hinder their utility, but it does permit us to break up more freely those forms which have lost their usefulness and to replace them with fresher, more vital constructions.

It is partially Coover's distrust of rigid, dogmatic attitudes of all kinds which leads him to dedicate his prologue to *Pricksongs and Descants* (perversely placed in the middle of his collection) to Cervantes. As explained by Coover, Cervantes's fictions "exemplified the dual nature of all good narrative art; . . . they struggled against the unconscious mythic residue in human life and sought to synthesize the unsynthesizable, sallied forth against adolescent thought-modes and exhausted art forms, and returned home with new complexities."[2] Mistrusting absolutes of any kind and feeling that the complexities of reality are as inexhaustible as the number of perspectives we bring to bear on it, Coover directs much of his work at breaking the hold of these "unconscious mythic residues" (themselves a form of fiction) over people. One strategy used for this purpose is to use "familiar or historical forms to combat the content of those forms" (*PD,* p. 79). Thus Coover often creates his fictions out of precisely the sort of familiar myths, fictions, cliché patterns, and stereotypes whose *content* he hopes to undermine. This undermining is achieved at times by overt parody or irony, and at other times by allowing the elements to freely engage and contradict one another. But at all times Coover hopes to deal with myth and fiction making on their own grounds (hence the metafictional character of all his works), and to use the energy stored within these mythic residues to break up the hold which they have and to redirect their forces.

Cervantes also represents for Coover a writer who felt the need to challenge the literary conventions of his age and who, in doing so, successfully created a narrative form capable of sustaining these challenges. Thus Coover observes, addressing Cervantes, "Perhaps above all else your works were exemplars of a revolution in narrative fiction, a revolution which governs us" (*PD,* p. 77). In *Don Qui-*

xote Cervantes combined what Coover calls "poetic analogy and literal history"—a combination which is usually credited with having given birth to the novel. Ironically, many of the conventions initiated in part by Cervantes have today become just as dogmatized as the stifling conventions of the romance in Cervantes's time. If Cervantes opened up a new world for narrative fiction, this world has alarmingly begun to shrink once more. As Coover says:

> But, don Miguel, the optimism, the innocence, the aura of possibility you experienced have been largely drained away and the universe is closing in on us again. Like you, we, too, seem to be standing at the end of one age and on the threshold of another. We, too, have been brought into a blind alley by the critics and analysts; we, too, suffer from a "literature of exhaustion." (PD, p. 78)

The modern writer, then, finds himself much in the same position as the Granny in the first story of Pricksongs, "The Door": he is "propped up there in the stale limp sheets once the scene of so much blood and beauty" (PD, p. 15). Like Granny, the writer has begun to see that what once seemed a "handsome well-lathed challenge to an old doxy" now "threatens to throw up walls between the posts and box [him] in." Trapped in their own "stale, limp sheets," contemporary writers may share Granny's wonder: "Where's my goodies? will I make it to the end?" (PD, p. 15).

Thus, like so many other contemporary writers and critics, Coover feels that relying on any one set of conventions (like those of realism) will lead inevitably to a dead end—much as relying on any single perspective will produce only a false perspective. Realizing that modern audiences have grown suspicious of many of the conventions of realism, Coover often adopts strategies which will allow him to deal with these suspicions openly. We find him experimenting with new or unusual narrative methods, but just as often we find him resurrecting the forms, techniques, and subject matter of past traditions which have lost their conventionality and staleness because of disuse.

One result of this insistence on form is that the metafictional quality of Coover's fiction derives as much from the *process at work* as it does from the content. His fiction can also be termed "self-reflexive" in the sense used by Roger Shattuck—that is, it "endlessly studies its own behaviors and considers them suitable subject matter. . . . It is not art for art's sake, but art about art . . . it strives to be its own subject."[3] This self-directed aspect of Coover's work means that it is not only possible to view many of his fictions—including his three novels—as allegories about art, but that in many specific passages we discover that the text is discussing itself as it proceeds. Thus even in his first novel, which of all his works seems the most realistic and concerned with social commentary, Coover's real subject remains the relationship between man and his invented creations—the creations we have broadly termed "fictions." We can now turn to *The Origin of the Brunists* and examine more specifically how Coover develops these concerns.

The Origin of the Brunists

Although flawed in certain respects, Robert Coover's first novel, *The Origin of the Brunists,* presents a clear, fairly comprehensive view of his metafictional impulses. Using the founding of the Christian religion as its primary analogue, *The Brunists* seeks to examine the hold which the fictions of religion and history maintain over men. Based in part on some actual experiences Coover had as a youngster in southern Illinois,[4] the plot of the book is built around a mining disaster which kills ninety-seven men. One of the survivors is Giovanni Bruno, a quiet, enigmatic man disliked by most of his fellow workers. Due to a variety of circumstances, coincidences, and local needs, Bruno becomes the unlikely center of a small religious cult, "the Brunists." The story climaxes when most of the participants gather together on the Mount of Redemption (a small hill near the mine) in a wild, orgiastic finale. Here they wait (unsuccessfully, as it turns out) for the end of the world or the coming of the White Dove—no one is quite sure which. As the book concludes, we discover that despite the failure of the predicted cataclysm, the Brunists have struck a responsive chord in the world's religious needs; their cult has spread to all the major areas of the United States, prospects for overseas recruitment look excellent, and scriptural books and records are topping all the best-seller lists. Meanwhile the faithful are solemnly being prepared to meet their maker "on the eighth of January, possibly next year, but more likely 7 or 14 years from now."[5]

Such a general plot summary gives little sense of what happens in the novel because apparent digressions and subplots dominate its development. More than any of Coover's other works, the strengths of this book are drawn from traditional fiction, especially the realistic novel. Thus The Brunists has more than twenty vividly drawn, realistic characters and provides most of the other elements of plot and setting familiar to conventional fiction. Indeed, it often seems as if Coover is using his first novel to polish up conventional narrative methods before he moves on to more ambitious, unusual approaches. He has acknowledged this in an interview with Frank Gado:

I thought of it, a bit, as paying dues. I didn't feel I had the right to move into more presumptuous fictions until I could prove I could handle the form as it now was in the world. In a sense, the trip down the mine was my submerging of myself into the novel experience and then coming out again with my own revelations.[6]

Yet if Coover is "paying his dues" to traditional fiction in The Brunists, his payments often seem to be made with ambivalent feelings. For example, he constantly undercuts the realistic impulses of the book by borrowing elements from the surreal, the fantastic, and the absurd. Like Thomas Pynchon and Herman Melville—V. and Moby Dick are the two books which most obviously influenced The Brunists[7]—Coover often halts his plot to present asides such as anecdotes, jokes, songs, and esoteric information. Such techniques make it obvious that Coover is more interested in exploring a complex idea through any fictional means than he is in following the conventions of realism.

The focus which holds the disparate parts of the novel together—and which ties this work firmly to Coover's other fictions—can be explained by some remarks he makes in the prologue to Pricksongs and Descants. The novelist, says Coover, should use "familiar or historical forms to combat the content of those forms and to conduct the reader . . . to the real, away from mystification to clarification, away from magic to maturity, away from mystery to revelation" (PD, p. 79). Thus in The Brunists, as in most of Coover's other works, we are presented with a plot founded upon a prior "mythic or historical" source from which we will eventually be released by what Jackson Cope has termed an "anti-formal revelation."[8] In other words, Coover hopes to use the familiar forms—be they the Christian analogues of The Brunists, the popular mythologies of sports (The Universal Baseball Association), fairy tales (Pricksongs), or the factual events of the Rosenberg case (The Public Burning)—to undercut the hold which the content of these forms still has on people. In The Brunists Coover uses the familiar, narrow Christian contexts but extends them so that the book becomes a metafictional commentary on the fictive process of history itself or, rather, on the ways in which human experience is conveniently translated and mythicized by chroniclers and historians.

By focusing The Brunists on religion and religious history, Coover provided himself with an obvious context in which to show the way that human intervention is imposed upon the world to give it meaning.[9] In times of crisis or chaotic disruption, religious and historical perspectives have always provided men with the attractive notion that events actually contain a recognizable order and meaning despite their apparent absurdity. Coover makes it clear that the initial impetus for the Brunist development is the desire on the part of the survivors of the dead miners to attribute some purpose to the catastrophe, to justify it somehow. Faced with a destructive event of such major proportions, the townsfolk find in the Brunist religion a fictional system which endows the terrible events they have experienced with an illusion of order and purpose.

After Bruno is found unconscious but alive in an area of the mine where most of the men were killed, Coover sets several subplots in motion which gradually converge. Although nearly every conceivable potboiler element can be found in these subplots (adultery, incest, adolescent sex play, sadism, voyeurism—all the usual soap-opera materials), none is gratuitous or included merely for sensation's sake. All of them in fact serve Coover's central purpose of establishing the wide range of elements which eventually contribute to the rise of the Brunist cult. Coover is well aware that it takes more than small-town religious fanaticism to start a major religion. Helpful circumstances, unlikely coincidences, unwitting and unwilling support, and just plain luck are all also essential. Perhaps most important of all, a religion needs an effective prophet or PR man to get the word out and drum up interest. Christianity, of course, had all of these factors operating in its favor; and so do the Brunists.

The original Brunists are mainly satirized as answer-seeking fanatics who see in Bruno the fulfillment of their various needs. Their cause attracts such crackpots as Eleanor Norton and Ralph Himebaugh who develop their own fictional systems in ways that illuminate the approaches of later Coover characters such as J. Henry Waugh and Richard Nixon. What all of these characters share is the tendency to rely on mythic notions of causality—notions which operate differently from the more recently developed views of science and logic.[10] Ernst Cassirer, who examines mythic thought in great detail in the second volume of his *Philosophy of Symbolic Forms,* remarks that for mythic thought "every simultaneity, every spatial coexistence and contact, proves a real causal 'sequence.' It has been called a principle of mythic causality and of the physics based on it that one takes every contact in time and space as an immediate relation of cause and effect."[11] It is easy to see how religious explanations of events grow very naturally from such mythic conceptions of reality. A similar mythic basis of thought underlies the numerological orientation of Norton, Himebaugh, and many of Coover's other characters.

Numerology relies in an obvious fashion on a mythic notion of causality. Like astrology—which also influences Mrs. Norton—numerology assumes that some sort of causal relationship exists between two entities (in this case, number and event) which do not have any logical or scientific (i.e., empirical) connection. Ela Norton, for example, tries obsessively to decipher hidden meanings in everyday events. In her frantic desire to discover these veiled implications, she relies on "divine dispatches" sent to her from a spirit called "domiron." Not surprisingly, one system of hidden order which she has uncovered is based on numerological inferences, especially relating to the number seven.

Lawyer Ralph Himebaugh is also a firm believer in numerology and is, as well, a parody of the mathematically oriented post-Renaissance scientist. Himebaugh's metaphysical notions amusingly parallel what has been called the "mathematical metaphysics" which developed after Galileo. Like Descartes, Galileo, Newton, and other formulators of the metaphysical foundations of modern science, Himebaugh is confident that all events can be explained in terms of mathematically determined forces and formulas:

Ralph's system was nevertheless for him a new science, and if he did not yet embrace the whole truth of the universe, it was only because he still lacked all the data, lacked some vital but surely existent connection—in short had not yet perfected his system.   (OB, p. 260)

Thus Himebaugh fills his spare time collecting and graphing statistical information, attempting to discover within the numbers before him a pattern, a basis for predictability. Ralph's theories, like those of the empirical scientist that Coover is satirizing, are "founded always in some concrete event in the world" and are "altered, revised with each discovery of new data" (OB, p. 259). Yet, despite his carefully formulated statistics and graphs, Ralph is also clearly a crackpot: not only does he devote most of his time to deciphering very un-empirical numerological signs, but also he is convinced that all events are controlled by a demonic force called "the destroyer."

Mrs. Norton's confident overview of events (from above by divine dispatches) and Ralph's slow assimilation of facts and numbers into a general framework seem to represent comic analogues of the two basic methods of achieving all knowledge—the rationalistic, deductive approach and the empirical, inductive method. In this case, as in the case of science itself, the two systems help support each other. As the novel's main character, Tiger Miller, summarizes at one point, "They shared, that is, this hope for perfection, for final complete knowledge, and their different approach actually complemented each other, or at least seemed to" (OB, p. 261). As we might expect of people who are seeking "final complete knowledge," their search for "final complete knowledge" ends in failure, just as all similar searches end in Coover's fiction. Thus Coover pokes a great deal of fun at both these methods and makes it obvious that Mrs. Norton and Ralph Himebaugh are simply projecting their own distorted personalities onto the world. Yet Coover also subtly undercuts this view by establishing a "real" numerological foundation in his own novel and thus indirectly creates an "objective basis" for the positions he mocks.

It isn't too difficult to uncover some sort of numerological pattern in the events of The Brunists. We probably laugh first at Ralph Himebaugh's analysis in the following passage, but further consideration may make us wonder if the pattern Ralph is describing isn't really there after all:

The number ninety-seven, the number of the dead, was itself unbelievably relevant. Not only did it take its place almost perfectly in the concatenation of disaster figures he had been recording, but it contained internal mysteries as well: nine, after all, was the number of the mine itself, and seven, pregnant integer out of all divination, was the number of trapped miners. The number between nine and seven, eight, was the date of the explosion, and the day of the rescue was eleven, two one's or two, the difference between nine and seven. Nine and seven added to sixteen, whose parts, one and six, again added to . . . seven!   (OB, p. 188)

Just as in a Nabokovian puzzle, certain patterns do mysteriously appear if we follow these numerological hints. If we take the number seven, for example, we find that Tiger Miller's high school basketball number was seven; the number of miners trapped was ninety-eight, which is itself composed of fourteen sevens (with fourteen itself being another multiple of seven); ninety-eight, if taken in a series leads first to seven (the number of miners trapped with Bruno) and then to six (the number who died); on the night of the mining disaster the basketball game is stopped with the score 14–11 (as noted above, fourteen is a multiple of seven; eleven is composed of two ones, the difference between nine and seven, and is also the date Bruno is rescued); Vince Bonali just happens to have seven children. After just a little of this sort of number-chasing, we sense that Coover is playing a joke on us—inducing us to establish fictional patterns in much the same way that we laughed at Ralph and Ela for doing. But Coover also seems to be demonstrating a more subtle point which is often made by Nabokov (most notable in Pale Fire): that seemingly ran-

dom appearances, under subjective human scrutiny, do often cohere into a pattern which can be applied to the world. And as we follow this game of creating a system from this series of elements, we
are inevitably pointed back to the original fiction maker of the
story—Coover himself. As he does in many of his stories, Coover begins by laughing at analytic machinery when used by his characters,
turns his humor upon our own tendency to dig up hidden meanings,
and all the while he mocks himself, the reader-critic within the
writer, the creator who can't resist exposing himself in his formal
strategies.[12]

If the fiction-making impulses of the original small cult of the
Brunists are fairly clear, it is even more evident that Giovanni Bruno
himself is nothing more than a befuddled pawn who is manipulated
by the religious needs of others. Certain that Bruno is "the One who
is to come" (*OB*, p. 132), Eleanor Norton becomes the unofficial
spokesperson and high priestess of a small group of devoted believers. Most of these believers are people like Clara Collins who are
desperately seeking some means of making sense of the recent tragedy at the mine. Bruno himself is brought home to sit in bed and
mutter bizarre, often incoherent remarks ("The tomb is its message";
"Baptize . . . light"), each of which is reverently noted and carefully
"decoded" by the message-hungry followers.

Coover's handling of the cult itself often seems one-dimensional
and at times slips into pure farce; his treatment of the response of
West Condon folk to Brunism, however, is more complicated and ultimately less sympathetic. Without exception the townspeople of
West Condon are shown to act solely in terms of their own selfish interests. Although these interests are not religiously motivated as are
those of the Brunists, they nonetheless all unknowingly aid the Brunist cause—and this is what ties their sections to the novel's primary
structure. Banker Ted Cavanaugh, for example, is never sympathetic
to the Brunist cause and in fact recognizes them for the crackpots
that they are. But because he is also concerned about the town's dismal economic situation and its inability to attract outsiders, he is
willing to use Bruno for a little free publicity. Thus when Bruno is
ready to leave the hospital, he sees to it that Bruno is brought home
in style:

Bruno's big homecoming was Ted Cavanaugh's idea. There was a national—
even international—focus on the man, why not put it to the whole town's ser-
vice? Already Bruno had emerged as something of a town hero, a symbol of
the community's own struggle to survive, so why not make the most of it?
. . . For the moment—no matter how arbitrary it might seem—he stood for
West Condon, and they all had to lift West Condon high!   (OB, pp. 143–44)

Even less sympathetic to the Brunists is preacher Abner Baxter,
who inherits his job when Ely Collins is killed in the blast. Uncertain
of his congregation's loyalty, Baxter sees the Brunist movement as a
threat to his own security. Hopeful of stabilizing his new position—
and supported with historical parallels to religious situations in the
past—Baxter declares a holy war on the Brunists and urges his pa-
rishioners to use any means to drive the new religion from their community. Thus begins the "Brunist Persecution" which, as was true
with Christianity and many other religions, only serves to draw the
Brunists together and publicize their cause. Baxter's children, after
making off with the disembodied hand of a charred miner, play cruel
and devilish tricks on the neighborhood (feeding ground glass to
dogs, placing excrement in the rival preacher's pulpit) under the
"Sign of the Black Hand"; the Brunists, who are willing to assimilate
anything which will fit into their pattern of beliefs, quickly interpret
these pranks as otherworldly messages or warnings. Like almost any
organism which hopes to prosper, the Brunists deftly take advantage
of whatever local conditions might aid in their development. Thus in
the process of establishing their creed—a purely arbitrary, invented
fiction—they provide an excellent example of why fiction making is
so useful to man.

By far the most important figure to aid the Brunists is the local
newspaper editor, Justin "Tiger" Miller. Miller's name supplies the
first clue about his role, for Justin was a second-century writer and
apologist for Christianity. But Miller and his newspaper The Chronicle are peculiarly modern sorts of religious apologists; although
Miller becomes the Brunists' public relations man, their historian,
prophet, and gospel-maker, he also is aware that they are a hoax. He
also introduces an important concept which is found in many of
Coover's fictions: the concept of game.

Tiger Miller's background may remind us of Updike's Rabbit Angstrom (in *Rabbit Run*), for it too is dominated by his legendary feats as a high school basketball player. In a revealing passage, we are told that games help provide some semblance of order in Miller's life:

Games were what kept Miller going. Games, and the pacifying of mind and organs. Miller perceived existence as a loose concatenation of separate and ultimately inconsequential instants, each colored by the action that preceded it, but each possessed of a small wanton freedom of its own. Life then, was a series of adjustments to these actions, and if one kept his sense of humor and produced as many of these actions himself as possible, adjustments were easier.   (*OB*, pp. 141–42)

This passage helps explain Miller's role in the book as a pseudo-historian or fiction-maker. It also offers a view of the world and man's position in it that seems to coincide with Coover's own view. The idea that life is a "loose concatenation of separate and ultimately inconsequential instants" directly opposes, of course, the historical view which attempts to explain and define meaningful relationships between events. Indeed, the notion that each moment possesses "a small wanton freedom of its own" opposes *any* concept of an *externally imposed* system of order. Once this view is accepted, the alternatives are evident: either man can adopt the despairing outlook that life is fundamentally and irrevocably absurd and chaotic; or he can consider the "freedom" of each moment as a sign that man can create his own system of order and meaning. If this latter alternative is accepted—and it is accepted by Miller, Waugh, and Nixon—the attraction of games, sports, and rituals of any kind becomes obvious—for here there is order, definite sets of rules to be followed, a series of signs that can be interpreted, noncapricious rewards and punishments, and a sense of stasis and repetition that seems somehow freed from the demands of process. The meaning and order of games are fictitious and arbitrary in the sense that they are invented subjectively and then applied to the transformational possibilities within the system. But unlike the equally fictitious sense of order provided by history, politics, or religion, games allow man to act with awareness of his position, without dogmatic claims to final truths and objectivity.

When the novel opens, Tiger Miller is presented as a game player without a "big game" to look forward to. Then when the Brunist controversy arises, Miller sees a chance to become involved in a new, potentially amusing game whose rules he is familiar with from his knowledge of the Bible and history—that is, the game of creating a religion. That Miller consciously conceives of his role in the Brunist affair as that of a player in a game is evident in the following passage:

> Their speculations amused Miller—who himself at age thirteen had read Revelations and never quite got over it—so he printed everything he thought might help them along, might seem relevant to them. . . . Once the emotions had settled down and the widows themselves had established new affairs or found mind-busying work, their eccentric interest of the moment would be forgotten, of course. Which, in a way, was too bad. *As games went, it was a good game, and there was some promise in it.*   (*OB*, p.141, emphasis added)

Late in the novel when Miller explains to a minister his own role in the Brunist affair, we discover that, for Miller, historians and theologians have always been engaged in the game of fiction making:

> "Exactly! It doesn't matter. Somebody with a little imagination, a new interpretation, a bit of eloquence, and—zap!—they're off for another hundred or thousand years." Miller passed his hand over the heap of manila folders on his desk. "Anyway, it makes a good story."
> Edwards gazes down at the folders. "But Justin, doesn't it occur to you? These are human lives—one-time human lives—you're toying with!"
> "Sure, what else?"
> *"But to make a game out of—"*
> Miller laughed. "You know, Edwards, *it's the one thing you and I have got in common."*   (*OB*, p. 264, emphasis added)

The point established here is crucial: Edwards recognizes that to Miller the process of creating a religion and presenting a historical version of it is a game, an arbitrary fiction conjured up by an imaginative mind. Miller agrees and adds that Edwards is likewise engaged in game playing. But while Miller is very much aware of the fictional basis of *his* game, Edwards and the Brunists are unaware of what they are doing (or at least they are unwilling to acknowledge it). This directly anticipates the situation that J. Henry Waugh (in *The UBA*) and most of the American public (in *The Public Burning*) find themselves in.

Ironically it is precisely Miller's game playing which enables the Brunists to develop and maintain their tenuous foothold in the community. As Miller has told Edwards, history has always been presented by men willing to embellish some here and add a little there to "make a good story." The fact that historical perspectives result from human intervention and selection is usually ignored by an uncritical public hungry for order and truth. Such a public is an easy prey for an "entertainer" such as Miller:

> Once a day, six days a week and sometimes seven, year in, year out, the affairs of West Condon were compressed into a set of conventionally accepted signs and became, in the shape of the West Condon *Chronicle,* what most folks in town thought of as life, or history. . . . That its publisher and editor, Justin Miller, sometimes thought of himself as in the entertainment business and viewed his product, based as it was on the technicality of the recordable fact, as a kind of benevolent hoax, probably only helped to make the paper greater. *(OB, pp. 150–51)*

This view of the historical procedure being "a benevolent hoax" is dramatized even more clearly early in the book: when Miller discovers that a United Press representative has considerably embellished a wholly falsified report that Miller himself dreamed up about the mine rescue, he laughs and comments, "Such are history's documents" *(OB, p. 99)*.

A good fiction promoter, Miller meets with great success in furthering the Brunist cause. Near the end of the novel, however, when Miller tries to remind everyone that the whole Brunist uprising has only been an amusing game, he discovers too late the tenacity with which people cling to their fictions and is nearly killed by an angry mob of Brunists. Like some of Coover's later characters who do not fully understand the appeal of arbitrary systems (the sheriff in *The Kid,* Lou Engels in *The UBA,* Julius Rosenberg in *The Public Burning*), Miller is underestimating the fanatical desire of people to cling to their illusions of order and meaning. When he encounters a frenzied mob of Brunists on the Mount of Redemption, an ironic reversal occurs as Miller-the-Tiger nearly becomes a sacrificial lamb.

The Brunists eventually go on to establish themselves as a major religion. They succeed in welding a creed and church hierarchy and set the foundations for precious and sacred traditions—all bearing considerable resemblance to the early stories, miracles, and wonders of Christianity. Naturally these parallels serve to parody the origins of Christianity; but as Leo Hertzel notes, Coover hopes to extend the range of the implications of this book into a "commentary on history, on the fantastic complexity and ignorance that lie at the root of all recorded and revered experience."[13] Coover also includes a brief, puzzling epigraph to his novel entitled "Return" which—like the final chapter to *The UBA*—throws into doubt many of the mythic and historical parallels and associations developed earlier. For example, we probably have identified Marcella Bruno's death with that of Christ, for it unites the Brunists and is even presented to us in a chapter entitled "The Sacrifice." But the last chapter invites us to see Miller's near-death as being the Christ parallel. Thus the first thing that Miller's girlfriend, Happy Bottom, says to Miller when he revives is, "And how feels today the man who redeemed the world?" (*OB*, p. 431). Later while Miller is delirious, he identifies himself on the cross: "He saw himself, crosshung, huge below, head soaring out of sight. . . . Something knocked against his cross: vibrations racked him and screaming, he fell" (*OB*, p. 432). But before these new parallels are firmly established, we are reminded that Miller also betrayed the new religion and helped cause the death of the first sacrificial victim, Marcella Bruno. Not surprisingly, then, Miller is also identified at times in this last section with Judas—a confusion of mythic parallels that continues when Miller considers his own role in the rise of the Brunists and decides that "crucifixion was a proper end for insurgents: it dehumanizes them" (*OB*, p. 436). The closest thing to a resolution of this mythic mixup comes in another ambiguous passage in which the Christ analogue vaguely seems to win out over that of the Judas:

Jesus, dying, disconnected, was shocked to find Judas at his feet. "Which . . . one of us," Jesus gasped, "is really He: I . . . or thou?" Judas offered up a hallowing, omniscient smile, shrugged, and went away, never to be seen in these parts again.   (*OB,* p. 437)

All this may be a metaphorical way of demonstrating the struggle going on within Miller to assess his role in creating the rise of the Brunists. Or it may be a puzzling diversion, included by Coover for reasons that Miller would appreciate: it makes a good story. At any rate, it is obvious that although Coover invites us to establish parallels and note associations, he also does not want us to create too many easy one-to-one relationships. As he continually reminds us, life just isn't as straightforward and easily interpreted as most fictions—including those of history, religion, and realistic novels— would like to make it seem. This brief epilogue thus tears down, or at least calls into question, some of the mythic and archetypal machinery that Coover has earlier set in motion. In doing so, it reminds us that such pattern making is useful in guiding our responses to both literary works and to life, but this utility is maintained only if we are aware that other perspectives are also possible. Only if we are able to develop an awareness of our own participation in the creation of fictions can we reject dogmatic attitudes and begin to take advantage of the fiction-making process. In short, we can be free only when we can distinguish our own creations from those which exist in the world. Kant began the overthrow of traditional philosophy by systematically developing this idea. This notion is also the point of departure for Coover's second, more complicated novel, *The Universal Baseball Association.*

The Universal Baseball Association, Inc., J. Henry Waugh, Prop.

Robert Coover's second novel takes up the concept of fiction making where *The Origin of the Brunists* left off. As one critic commented, "Myth, man's need for it and his creation of it from the inadequate fictions of his existence, is what the book is about"[14]—a remark which seems to summarize *The Brunists'* major concerns as well. But where his first novel's focus on religion tended to limit the scope of its probings, *The UBA* introduces a considerably broader spectrum of metafictional issues. Indeed, although *The UBA* deals with the fictions of religion and history—mostly in terms of satire and parody—its primary focus is on the more general fiction-making activities of myth and art.

The UBA actually evolved from a short story which Coover published in the *Evergreen Review* some five years before the publication of the novel. This story, "The Second Son," covers the action of what would later develop as the novel's second chapter. It tells a fairly conventional story of a fiftyish accountant who has become fanatically obsessed with a table-top baseball game which he has rigged up with an elaborate system of dice and charts (real baseball, he finds pretty boring). The complication arises when the hero, J. Henry Waugh, becomes so involved with the people and events of his game that he begins to believe in their literal existence. Specifically he grows so attached to one of the imaginary players (Damon Rutherford, who has become a sort of "second son" for him) that when the game decrees that Damon must die—struck by a pitched ball—Henry at first becomes enraged and then collapses into uncontrollable sobs.

In developing his novel, Coover decided to leave the basic framework of his story. As the puns in the title of the book tell us, J. Henry Waugh (JHWH, the Jehovah of his world) is a sort of deity presiding over a universe made up of baseball players—in effect, he is the "prop" upon which the universe rests because he has created this imaginary world and all the players in it. This universe—the "Universal Baseball Association" or the "UBA" for short—has been created by Henry partly because it provides him with many things which the real world does not, such as friendship, excitement, and love. Childless and long ago abandoned by his wife, Waugh takes little interest in his accounting job. Although he is genuinely fascinated by numbers, Henry finds his work and fellow workers boring and unimaginative; his boss, Mr. Horace Zifferblatt, is a "militant clock watcher"[15] (*Zifferblatt* means "clock face" in German) and is obviously unsympathetic to Henry's artistic temperament. The UBA is therefore created as an escape, a fantasy world to which Henry retreats when he is lonely or bored. It is also an outlet for Henry's strong imaginative and speculative tendencies which have been stifled by his humdrum, everyday routine. Into the foundations of his beloved Association Henry pours his wide-ranging ideas about mathematics, numerology, politics, history, philosophy, and various other disciplines. Thus, like the Brunist religion, Henry's Association can be seen as a fictional system created in response to specific needs and impulses.

The relationship between Henry and his Association is very complex and intricately developed, but on the most apparent level this relationship suggests an elaborate allegory about God and our own universe. Coover has explained that he specifically used the Bible as one of his basic structuring devices:

The Henry book came into being for me when I found a simple structural key to the metaphor of a man throwing dice for a baseball game he has made up. It suddenly occurred to me to use Genesis I.1 to II.3—seven chapters corresponding to the seven days of creation—and this in turn naturally implied an eighth, the apocalyptic day. Having decided on this basic plan, I read a lot of exegetical works on that part of the Bible in order to find out as much as I could which would reinforce and lend meaning to the division into parts.[16]

As the book develops Coover makes these biblical parallels evident and has a great deal of fun portraying his Jehovah as a befuddled, lonely old man who imagines beings into existence and then allows a set of dice—"heedless of history, yet makers of it" (p. 20)—to determine the events.[17] More important than these allegorical implications, however, is the fact that Henry's Association is a wonderfully clear example of a fictional system created by the human mind. As such it has certain obvious similarities to other blatantly fictional systems such as literature and myth. Indeed, Henry's Association is at its core mythically determined and derives its peculiar qualities from his own strong mythic orientation. This mythic orientation helps clarify some of the other relationships drawn by Coover between the UBA and other types of fiction—above all, the aesthetic fiction which we call the novel. The point is one familiar to many modern experts on myth: mythic impulses lie behind the creation of *all fictions.* Henry shares with mythic thinkers a variety of views; these notions, such as his ideas concerning names and his numerological speculations, are evident in the basic nature of the Association and derive from similar metaphysical views such as those which governed the thinking of Eleanor Norton and Ralph Himebaugh in *The Brunists*. But the most important tendency which Henry shares with mythic thinkers is his tendency to *believe literally in the fictions he has invented*. Although Coover creates Henry with more sympathy and understanding than the characters in his first novel, it is still this basic inability of Henry to accept the invented quality of his fiction that proves to be his undoing.

Like Tiger Miller, Henry has been drawn to games because his real life seems to provide little to stimulate his interests and ultimately provides no order or meaning to his existence. After discarding several other table-top games, Henry has finally settled on baseball because it provides a rich reservoir of tradition and mythology while still deriving its peculiar quality from statistics and records. Henry suggests that part of baseball's unconscious attraction for Americans lies in its containing "formulas for energy configurations where city boys come to see their country origins dramatized, some old lost fabric of unity" (p. 166). But its main attraction for him lies in the beauty and balance of its records, its developing sense of order and balance, and its comprehensive history. Of course, because he is an accountant, Henry's view of history is intimately connected with numbers; at one point Henry expounds a sort of neo-Pythagorean explanation of the sources of history to his friend Lou Engels: "History. Amazing how we love it. And did you ever stop to think that without numbers or measurements, there probably wouldn't be any history?" (p. 49).

Although it is Henry who creates the people of his universe, providing them with names and personalities, it is the dice, along with the charts, which actually decide what happens in the ball games. In a sense, then, the players are really only numbers (or, more generally, relationships) which gradually acquire a statistical history according to the dictates of pure chance (the dice). Just as with real baseball, these statistical histories accumulate into significant patterns of performance. Meanwhile Waugh mentally works out the details of what the players say and do other than the specific events occurring in the actual ball games — in effect, the players become personae of Waugh who brings to life what would otherwise be empty mechanics (or, as Arlen Hansen puts it, Henry "storifies numbers").[18] At times it is obvious that the players are extensions of Henry's own personality, as with his frequent barroom transformations into balladeer Sandy Shaw and his obvious adoption of the roles of Damon Rutherford, Sewanee Law, and happy-go-lucky Willie O'Leary. Yet at other times the ballplayers seem mysteriously to drift free of Waugh and adopt realities of their own while Henry becomes almost invisible. Most typically, however, the two worlds are blended, with neither establishing a clear dominance over the other. This free intermingling of Waugh's two worlds is one of the important structural features of the book, for it establishes the crucial point that the exciting fictional world of the Association is just as "real" for Henry as his banal, largely petty everyday world. The world of the Association, for all its rowdiness, crude humor, and violence, is also a personalized world where Henry finds friendship, love, and excitement. Thus the novel effectively demonstrates the appeal of literalizing our fictions just as did *The Brunists*.

One other important aspect of Henry's game is the way in which Henry names the ballplayers. Henry strongly feels that what keeps his game from being a collection of lifeless statistics is the act of giving his players names, an act which generates both form and meaning for his Association. We are told that "Henry was always careful about names, for they were what gave the league its sense of fulfillment and failure, its emotion. The dice and charts and other paraphernalia were only the mechanics of the drama, not the drama itself" (pp. 46–47). Waugh creates his ballplayers' names spontaneously from the events in his own life: "Everywhere he looked he saw names. . . . Bus stop. Whistlestop. Whistlestop Busby, second baseman. Simple as that" (p. 46). But Waugh's views about naming his players extend beyond simply trying to humanize them and give us a clear indication of how bound up his world view is with mythic thinking. Like all mythic thinkers, Waugh feels that names somehow determine a person's personality or essence. As he puts it, "Name a man and you make him what he is," and then quickly adds that "the basic stuff is already there. In the name. Or rather, in the naming" (p. 48). Ernst Cassirer has explained that it is characteristic of mythic thought to assume that a word or name does not merely have the function of describing or signifying someone:

Even a person's ego, his very self and personality, is indissolubly linked, in mythic thinking, with his name. Here the name is never mere symbol, but is part of the personal property of its bearer; . . . the name is not only a mark of the unity and uniqueness of the person, but actually constitutes it; the name is what first makes man an individual.[19]

As the following key passage indicates, Henry's view about the relationship between names and his players is remarkably similar to what Cassirer has described:

Now, it was funny about names. All right, you bring a player up from the minors, call him A. Player A, like his contemporaries, has, being a Rookie, certain specific advantages and disadvantages with the dice. But it's exactly the same for all Rookies. You roll, Player A gets a hit or he doesn't. . . . Sounds simple. But call Player A "Sycamore Flynn" or "Melbourne Trench" and something starts to happen. He shrinks or grows, stretches out or puts on muscle. Sprays singles to all fields or belts them over the wall. Throws mostly fastballs like Sewanee Law or curves like Mickey Halifax. . . . Not easy to tell just how or why. . . . *But name a man and you make him what he is.*

(Pp. 47–48, emphasis added)

The rich, complex relationship between Henry and his Association suggests a great deal about man and his fictional systems. If we examine the Association very carefully, for example, we discover that it closely resembles a novelistic world: like Waugh, writers are occupied in constructing imaginary worlds out of words and relationships; the combination of these elements into new shapes and patterns brings a new system into being which may be related to the world but is not necessarily descriptive of it. Also, in both cases "characters" are created by the act of giving an abstract relationship a name. This process is similar to that employed whenever man invents a fictional system, be it Henry's Association, a novel, a mathematical system, or a poem. All these activities involve concepts and relationships (like the "Player A" in Henry's Association or, say, the axioms of Euclid's geometry) which are named and then assigned *perfectly free but absolute definitions.* The systems which result are therefore constructions which are freely created. As is true of all fictions, these new systems can often usefully be applied to reality (this happens with mathematics and scientific models every day) or simply admired as aesthetic objects whose utility is minimal (as we regularly regard musical compositions and the creations of the plastic arts). But we should not confuse the logic, harmony, truth, or ontological status of our invented systems with those of the world. It is this sort of confusion which leads Henry to overcommit himself to the world of his ballplayers and gradually lose touch with ordinary reality. Much like the people who cried when Dickens's Little Nell died, Henry breaks down when Damon is killed—a clear indication that he, like the Brunists, has lost the ability to distinguish between fictional and factual truths and events.

In terms of the specific "materials" used by Henry to create his Association, we find that he relies mostly on the folklore, language, and mythology of baseball itself—along with his own prejudices, neuroses, and speculations about history, religion, politics, and philosophy. The players—like those of Philip Roth's *The Great American Novel*—are composites of several baseball stereotypes, mostly drawn from baseball's early, legendary period. The rules, strategies, and traditions of actual baseball are meticulously adhered to; indeed, some of the book's funniest and most convincing moments arise when Henry manipulates these familiar rules and traditions (as he does, for example, in the game with Lou Engel). Baseball also dominates the language of the novel, giving Coover an opportunity to show off his love of popular or unusual idioms.

Like his namesake, Henry created his league *ex nihilo* and designated the first season as Year I. Things went along smoothly for a while, and then in the year XIX Brock Rutherford came along with several other brilliant rookies and initiated the "Golden Age" of the Association. Since then, though, things have grown increasingly dull for Henry until suddenly—at roughly the point where the novel opens—a new excitement is brought back to the game in the person of Brock Rutherford's son, Damon. Damon—whose name suggests *daemon* or secondary divinity—is a brilliant rookie pitcher who helps Henry forget the memory of Brock's first son (who didn't pan out in the Association). From the outset it seems clear that Damon is the Association's version of Christ, a redeemer who can restore the Association to health and generate a new pattern of rebirth. Henry, who often identifies with Brock Rutherford (it is not a coincidence that Henry, Brock, and the UBA itself are all fifty-six years old when Damon arrives on the scene), thinks of Damon as a substitute for the son he never had; more directly, Henry identifies with Damon himself as the embodiment of the sort of heroic, self-assured, even sexually potent figure that he can never hope to be. Thus after Damon has pitched his perfect game, Henry asks Hettie the barmaid, "How would you like to sleep with . . . Damon Rutherford?" When she looks puzzled and asks who that is, Henry replies with a solemn, proud face, "Me" (p. 24). It is because of this sense of identification with and love of Damon and all he represents that Henry finds himself so awkwardly situated when Damon's life is threatened.

Soon after the novel opens, the roll of triple ones twice in a row places Damon in a potentially dangerous situation: when Henry refers to his "Special Occurrences Chart," he finds that another roll of 1-1-1 could mean that Damon would be killed by a bean ball. This is the novel's first crucial moment, for like the eighteenth century's deistic concept of God, Henry has always been reluctant to interfere with the actions on the ball field. Thus because of the rules he himself has established, Waugh cannot intervene in this situation, even to save his favorite player from possible destruction. "That was how it was," he says to himself. "He had to accept it, or quit the game altogether" (p. 40). Therefore he apprehensively rolls the dice once more, and when the dreaded combination comes up—1-1-1— Waugh can only look on in horror as his son and redeemer is killed.

After the death of Rutherford, the Association begins to deteriorate rapidly, and Waugh—now a broken, heartsick man—more and more lives only in the world he had created. Just after Damon's "funeral," Waugh experiences his own version of the dark night of the soul, patterned roughly after an epic descent into hell. Having lost most of his interest in the outside world, Henry is fired from his job but decides to keep things going in his Association, at least for a while. Angry and depressed, Henry momentarily considers destroying the Association one night; but as he considers his possible alternatives, he realizes that his own destiny has somehow become intimately connected to the system he has created:

So what were his possible strategies? He could quit the game. Burn it. But what would that do to *him*? Odd thing about an operation like this league: once you set it in motion you were yourself somehow launched into the same orbit; there was growth in the making of it, development, but there was also a defining at the outer edge.   (Pp. 141–42)

This passage is a good example of how Coover effectively brings together several levels of his book onto one plane. In addition to the obvious suggestion about Waugh's relationship to his unhappy cosmos and the equally evident parallels about God and his responsibility to our own universe, this passage is also showing what happens when man creates any sort of fictional system. The implication seems to be that after a system has been created, it attains its own status as an object in the world, hovering free of its creator but still capable of making demands upon him. Finally it also illustrates how dependent man is on his fictions and how difficult it is to lessen this dependency. Like the Brunist religion, Henry's Association has established itself as a new reality with impressive powers to resist dissolution.

Eventually Henry resurfaces briefly having dinner with his former officemate, Lou Engel. Although he shifts in and out of the persona of the fun-loving ballplayer, Willie O'Leary, Henry spends most of his dinner toying with the possibility of assuming total control of his universe. But at this point Henry remains unwilling to make this sort of absolute commitment and instead arrives at a compromise. In considering his previous lack of power within his Association—a condition that seems tied to Henry's feelings of sexual inadequacy—Henry thinks:

Impotent? not really. But sometimes total power was worse. Message of the Legalists: without law, power lost its shape. . . .Who said three strikes make an out? Supposing he just shipped Casey to the minors and to hell with the rules? He could at that. If he wanted to. Could explain it in the book. It wasn't impotence. Still, it might cause trouble. What trouble? The players . . . what players? Some kind of limit there, all right, now that he thought about it. He might smash their resistance, but he couldn't help feeling that resistance all the same. Their? mine; it was all the same.   (Pp. 157–58)

This passage shows the outlines of the battle which is raging within Henry; even now, at this late stage, Henry seems dimly aware at times that his Association is only a fiction and that the players are only extensions of himself ("the players . . . what players? . . . Their? mine; it was all the same"); but this distinction no longer seems to matter to him. His decision is to assume power but not to directly intervene; he will wield power but only within certain prescribed legal limits which the players can accept. For example, he won't send Casey back to the minors which would be illegal; but he will see to it that Casey always faces the toughest lineups under the most trying of circumstances. In other words, Henry wants to establish some measure of control but realizes that "without law, power lost its shape. . . . Some kind of limit there."

After Henry makes a date with Lou to show him his Association, he again goes home with Hettie. This time he adopts the persona of Sewanee Law whom Damon, the life force, had earlier defeated and whose name helps clarify Henry's decision.[20] Bent on achieving justice for Damon's death, Henry begins the next day to interfere subtly with the games, mostly in an effort to bring Jock Casey and the hated Knicks to their knees. By thrusting his own presence into the Association, however, Henry also begins to lose contact with the players, who seem to resent such intrusions:

He was destroying the Association, he knew that now. He'd kept no records, hadn't even logged a single entry in the Book. Didn't know if all the players had their required at-bats or innings-pitched, didn't know who was hitting and who wasn't, didn't know if any pitchers were running over the legal limit of innings pitched, didn't even give a damn who was winning the pennant. . . . He tried to reach them . . . tried to find out what was the matter, but it was strangely as though they were running from him, afraid of his plan, seeing it for what it was: the stupid mania of a sentimental old fool.   (P. 176)

Like the quantum physicist, whose visual observations interfere with the delicate operations of an atomic field, Henry's interventions destroy the Association's original system of order.[21] When Lou Engel comes over, Henry gets out his game and they begin to play. As is typical of Henry's recent luck, Lou proceeds to do infuriatingly well against all logic. Eventually Henry's team stages a mild rally—a triple-6 scores a couple of runs for Henry's team and moves the game to the "Special Stress Chart." This perks up Henry who knows that one more roll of 6-6-6 will bring the Extraordinary Occurrences Chart into play, and then just about anything could happen. Anxiously, Henry rolls the retributive dice and sees "2-6-6, a lot less than he'd hoped for" (p. 198). Suddenly Henry's fragile universe is upset, completely "inundated" when Lou spills a can of beer all over the game. Lou is banished by Henry, his footsteps heard "descending the stairs," and after a little cleaning up, Henry "stared at the mess that was his Association" (p. 199). This scene is another good example of the way Coover telescopes a variety of mythic and literary allusions. Lou, of course, is Lucifer (Lou Engel = "Fallen Angel"), and their game parallels the deadly struggle between Jahweh and his arch enemy. In a similar fashion we can also find parodic echoes of the flood and the banishment of Lucifer.

After Lou has left, Henry once more considers his alternatives. Just as Jahweh is said to have considered destroying the world after it had hurt him (in Genesis 5.5–7), so too does Waugh now contemplate turning his back on the Association by physically moving the game to another part of his apartment or destroying it altogether. Henry has considered these alternatives before and rejected them, in part because "the urge to annihilate . . . seemed somehow alien to him" (p. 104). Now, however, Henry sees that an annihilation, a sacrifice, may be the only way his Association can be saved. If retribution could be dealt out to Jock Casey, who was pitching for Lou when the beer was spilled, then perhaps order could be reestablished. Henry thus reaches down and tips the 2 of his last roll of 2-6-6 to another 6. This brings into play the Extraordinary Occurrences Chart, and Henry can now murder Jock Casey with another roll of 6-6-6.

As Henry seems vaguely to realize, he is now at the crossroads, for this is his last chance to recommit himself to reality. To kill Casey would involve the sort of total commitment to his fiction which Henry has all along shied away from. As Jackson Cope says, this type of total, illegal control would substitute "sacrifice for chance, commitment for causality, predestination for percentages."[22] Henry cautions himself about what he is considering: "Do you really *want* to

save it? . . . Yes, if you killed that boy out there, then you *couldn't*
quit, could you. No, that's a real commitment, you'd be hung up for
good, they wouldn't *let* you go" (p. 201). According to the New Testament, God must have been placed in a similar sort of position in trying to decide whether to turn his back on the "mess" the world had
become or to commit himself more fully to it by offering his son to
be sacrificed.

Just as he does in many of his fictions, Coover is here deliberately
shifting the allegorical patterns and elements in the middle of his
book. In this case the confusion arises because until this moment,
when Henry decides to sacrifice Casey, Damon has all along seemed
to be the redemptive Christ figure. Now we must reorient our thinking to see Damon's killer, Casey (whose initials perhaps should have
tipped us off), as being the "real" Christ. This moment of decision is
the climax of the book: as Henry peers down at Casey waiting alone
on the mound, the scene at the ball park silently reverberates, like a
palimpsest sheet's imperfect erasures, with echoes of Golgotha:

Casey, waiting there on the mound. . . . Lean, serious, melancholy even. And
alone. Yes, above all, alone. Stands packed with people, but faceless, just
multi-colored shirts. Just a scene, sandy diamond, green grass, ballplayers under the sun, stadium of fans, umpires, and Casey in the middle. Sometimes
Casey glanced up at him — only a glance: come on, get it over, only way. . . .
A terrible silence. And Casey looked up.   (Pp. 201–02)

Finally Henry whispers, "I'm sorry boy" and sets the dice down one
by one to the fatal 6–6–6, the number of the beast of Revelation:
"Pitcher struck fatally with line drive through the box; batter safe on
first, runners advance one." The finger of God has now touched history, and Jock Casey's sacrificial death has saved the Association. As
a sign of the new covenant, Henry arcs a "red and golden rainbow
. . . of half-curdled pizza over his Association" and retires into a
"deep, deep sleep" (p. 202).

Chapter 8, the complex and puzzling last chapter of *The UBA*,
should probably be viewed as an apocalyptic epilogue to the rest of
the novel.[23] Here there is no narrative interaction between the players and Henry whatsoever; in fact, the whole chapter is seen only

through the eyes of the players, and Henry himself never once appears. God, in other words, has either died, has withdrawn for places unknown, or now pantheistically *is* his Association. Henry does, however, seem vaguely to permeate this chapter, and although we can't be certain, he may still "literally" be present (thus when one player says, "Look up, good man. Cast your eye on the Ineffable Name and give praise. . . . What does it say?" he receives the answer, "100 Watt" [p. 232]). The players are obviously still Henry's creatures: they maintain the narrative voices he gave them and have absorbed his conscious and unconscious concerns, passions, and conclusions. One hundred baseball seasons, however, have passed since we last saw Henry and his Association; considering Henry's state of mind when we last saw him, it isn't surprising that things have developed in a pretty strange manner during this intervening period. The result is that a variety of Henry's tendencies in the direction of confused philosophical, religious, and ontological speculations have blossomed—or wildly mutated in some cases—into integral parts of the players' lives. Because they have no real choice in the matter, the players go along with the game even though it seems to many of them to be pointless and possibly even insane. As is typical of so many Coover characters, the players have found that their efforts to uncover the meanings and patterns behind their activities are constantly thwarted by the complicated, ambiguous nature of the signs that lie all around them. Consequently, philosophical and religious skepticism seems to be running rampant. Privately, several of the ballplayers have concluded that any search for meaning in their Association is bound to fail because, as one player puts it, "God exists and he is a nut" (p. 233).

This last chapter centers around "Damonsday," a yearly ritual similar to a passion play in which the players reenact a combination of the games in which Damon and Jock Casey were killed. The parts in the Damonsday drama are played by rookies who are assigned to play the roles of each of the original players as a sort of initiation rite. The chapter gradually focuses on Hardy Ingram and Paul Trench, who have been designated to play the roles of Damon and his batterymate Royce Ingram. In the meantime, we observe the other ballplayers standing around, speculating about the Association, trying to disengage myth from history, and engaging in all sorts of mock-scholarly discussions about theology and philosophy. As in *The Brunists*, the parallels that Coover draws between the players' speculations and those of "legitimate" religious and philosophical thinkers are not only humorous but effectively satiric. Typical of the controversies which rage among the Association's intelligentsia are arguments about what "really happened" in the fateful year LVI. As we learn from Hardy (Damon) Ingram, a number of books have come out recently which bear considerable resemblance to our own New Critical approaches to the Bible:

Book he's been reading lately. *The Doubter.* One of the flood of centennial Bancroft biographies out this year. Author tries to show that Barney Bancroft [Damon's manager], not Rutherford or Casey or Hardy's own progenitor Royce Ingram, was actually the central figure, the real heart and point of the Parable of the Duel, as they call it now. Rutherford and Casey seem to be giants, this guy claims, but really are only subhuman masks, predesigned roles, while Bancroft is the only one wholly rounded and thus truly human participant in that incredible drama. Maybe the only *real* one.   (P. 223)

The meaning of history itself has become another favorite topic among the players, and several of them have devised theories about this subject which sound remarkably similar to those put forward by Coover in *The Origin of the Brunists*. Some claim, for example, that the history they are familiar with is simply a fiction, an invention of someone else's overproductive imagination. From our perspective, of course, it is easy to see that their history *is a fiction* on at least two levels: it is the creation of Henry's confused, inconsistent imagination which itself is the product of Coover's own powers of invention. A small number of the players have developed a Berkeleyan view of their own nature which comes remarkably close to being accurate. One player, for instance, has suggested that, "We have no mothers, Gringo. The ripening of their wombs is nothing more than a ceremonious parable. *We are mere ideas hatched whole and hapless, here to enact old rituals of resistance and rot.* And for whom, I ask, for whom? (p. 230, emphasis added). As we have already seen, the players literally are "mere ideas, hatched whole and hapless" and thus their relationship to Henry closely parallels the relationship between characters in a book and their author. Actually, we should always remember in *The UBA* that whenever we view the Association we are one step removed from the normal fictional situation. Like "The Murder of Gonzago" in *Hamlet,* the Association is a fictional creation of a character in a fiction. As Richard Gilman notes, the players of Henry's Association are in effect "characters for whom Waugh is the novelist in the same way that Coover is his."[24] Here the structure of Coover's novel helps reinforce his point about the ramifications of such fiction making: we watch the players speculate about their own natures and laugh at their inability to arrive at anything other than subjective stabs in the dark; this naturally suggests a parallel with our own tendency to populate the world with fictions and myths; but we recognize that the players are only ideas created by Henry; but then Henry is only an invention of Coover; and Coover and ourselves . . . ? The potential agitation which this kind of device produces in us has been explained by J. L. Borges — the modern master of this sort of labyrinthine, circular tale — as follows: "Those inversions suggest that if the characters in a story can be readers or spectators, then we, their readers or spectators, can be fictitious."[25]

Just as he did in *The Brunists,* Coover also uses his last chapter (self-consciously) to undercut many of the patterns and mythic devices which he has been developing. Because *The UBA,* like his earlier novel, deals primarily with the relationship between man and his fictions, Coover insures that no single truth emerges and that no allegory or historical parallel is developed too consistently. Thus Coover creates his last chapter out of a confused welter of myths, religious allusions, bits of folklore, allegories of the Old and New Testaments, metaphysical speculations, and so on. The following are typical of the parallels and allusions set in motion by Coover: mention is made of the "sun god slain by the monster darkness" (a reference to Damon), of the mythical "blind beast" (Casey), and of Hardy Ingram's connection to "the avenging giant of the bloody past" (Royce Ingram); we hear of "the Parable of the Duel," "the Great Atonement Legend" and of the powers which "cut Rutherford in pieces, that didst deck that daemon"; these latter Orphic references are extended when Hardy Ingram is swarmed over by a crowd of women who tear and pull at him. In the midst of these veiled allusions and obscure parallels, it seems impossible to distinguish between human invention and fact. For us, as for the players, there are too many signs and too many transformations that impede even as they guide our search for pat answers.

Facing an absurd universe and knowing that any order to be found is arbitrary, the ballplayers are tempted to adopt a position of radical skepticism and despair. But Coover is also anxious to demonstrate that fictions are the only way we have of organizing and dealing with the world—and that these fictions should be appreciated for their utility, beauty, and ability to generate new possibilities. Ideas such as "meaning," "beauty," and "God" may well be only human invention, mere fictions, but they are useful and perhaps even necessary concepts. Coover's epigraph to *The UBA* from Kant's *Critique of Judgment* helps illuminate this position and confirms that this is one of the book's central issues: "It is here not at all requisite to prove that such an *intellectus archetypus* is possible, but only that we are led to the idea of it."[26] Kant is here discussing the idea of God (the "intellectus archetypus") and claims that the notion of God is natural and "completely satisfactory from every *human* point of view for both the speculative and practical use of our reason."[27] As Kant had demonstrated in *The Critique of Pure Reason,* man can never objectively prove that God exists. But even though God may be a fictional assumption, our belief in him may be a *necessary* assumption for the guidance of such things as scientific investigation and the practical needs of morals. Coover's epigraph indicates that it isn't really so important to prove that such a being exists, or even could exist, as it is to show that man is "led to the idea of it"—that we have to contemplate objects and events *as if* they are the products of design, even though they may not be so in reality. As the last chapter gradually focuses on the moral crisis experienced by Paul Trench, Coover develops the same Kantian implications.

Paul Trench, the rookie assigned to play the role of "Ingram the Avenger," is a composite man of faith who has been led to a philosophical outlook which has much in common with modern existentialism. He too seeks meaning in the face of absurdity, for a reason to continue playing life's senseless "game"; he too feels the dread, the sense of shame and regret: "Beyond each game, he sees another, and yet another in endless and hopeless succession. He hits a ground ball to third, is thrown out. Or he beats the throw. What difference, in the terror of eternity, does it make? He wants to quit—but what does he mean 'quit'? The 'game'? Life? Could you separate them?" (p. 238). In following the same path as many modern religious skeptics, Trench has come to question the traditions in which he has been raised. Of his reaction to these traditions, we are told, "Discovering their fallibility, he encountered the pathos of life, then reasoned that the Age of Glory was perhaps no different than this, his own inglorious times" (p. 238). Having initially rejected an identity based on a tragic conception of himself ("He became suspicious when he realized the idea gave him a certain grim pleasure"), Trench adopted and then discarded a self-concept based on hate ("There was something he was enjoying that seemed wrong, a creature of false pride"); recently Paul has been led to "the final emptiness" in wondering, like Camus, whether or not going on in life with no apparent reason is not "a kind of cowardice" (p. 238). In the midst of these self-doubts, he has tried on many occasions to rekindle his faith. He has listened to Raspberry Schultz who preaches a kind of Association version of Pascal's "Great Wager" argument: "I don't know if there's really a record keeper up there or not. . . . But even if there weren't, I think we'd have to play the game as though there were." To this Paul wonders, "Would we? Is that reason enough? Continuance for its own inscrutable sake?" (p. 239).

Paul's doubts seem to have reached a crisis stage as the moment of the ritualized game approaches. Like many modern existential heroes, Paul feels himself "en-Trenched" in a dreary, deterministic routine and wants to break out of this pattern, even if it means self-destruction or the annihilation of the conventions which give meaning to his existence. Before the first batter can step in, however, Paul impulsively walks out to the mound to talk with his batterymate, now ritualistically transformed into Damon Rutherford. This transformation helps us understand what is always occurring within the structures of all games and fictions: meaning is being arbitrarily assigned to something (everyone agrees that "player X" *is* Damon Rutherford) which is then expected to conform to the conventional pattern. The problem for Damon is similar to that of Tiger Miller: both encounter a group of people who ignore the fictional nature of the "game" before them. All during this final chapter of *The UBA*, we receive hints that "the whores of whores, Dame Society, in all her enmassed immortal fervor" (p. 229) is intent on seeing *real* bloodletting and vengeance. As Arlen Hansen suggests, "The horror lies in the confirmed recognition that Dame Society is imposing in a literal way the ritualized structure upon them [Paul and Hardy], *insisting* that they conform themselves to it."[28] The meeting on the mound between Trench (Royce) and Hardy (Damon) is a moment of epiphany; not only has a supernatural being manifested itself—Damon, now once again in his original role as savior—but also Paul, now himself magically transformed into Royce Ingram, is given a sudden, transcendental insight into the nature of his universe and, consequently, into the nature of games and rituals:

And then suddenly Damon sees, *must* see, because astonishingly he says: "Hey, wait, buddy! You *love* this game, don't you?"

"Sure, but . . ."

Damon grins. Lights up the whole goddam world. "Then don't be afraid, Royce," he says.

And the black clouds break up, and dew springs again to the green grass, and the stands hang on, and his own oppressed heart leaps alive to give it one last try; . . . it doesn't even matter that he's going to die, all that counts is that he is *here* and here's The Man and here's the boys and there's the crowd, the sun, the noise.

"It's not a trial," says Damon, glove tucked in his armpit, hands working the new ball. Behind him, he knows, Scat Batkin, the batter, is moving toward the plate. "It's not even a lesson. It's just what is." Damon holds the baseball up between them. It is hard and white and alive in the sun.

He laughs. It's beautiful that ball. He punches Damon lightly in the ribs with his mitt. "Hang loose," he says, and pulling down his mask, trots back behind home plate.   (P. 242)

This final scene vividly demonstrates what so much of Coover's fiction suggests. As Damon says, "the game" is not a "trial" or a "lesson"—it simply *is*. All their futile arguments and questions are finally irrelevant to the wonder and excitement of the present moment, which has plenty of room for developing new patterns within the shifting confines of the game.[29] The mysterious baseball that Damon holds up also helps make the point that Arlen Hansen has summarized:

A baseball, when employed in a baseball *game,* is a conventional agent for creating pattern and meaning. It affords a means for bringing into being certain human abilities and qualities that might otherwise go unexpressed. . . . It is the *conventionalized structure* of the baseball game that makes such manifestations of grace possible. Outside the context of this structure, the baseball—as a thing in itself—has no special meaning or function.[30]

In a universe such as ours, in other words, a baseball is like every other element we encounter: outside of the special context of the game or fictional system, it is meaningless, "It's just what it is." Rather than trying to sort out the "real meaning" of these systems (an effort which, as Kant suggests, is ultimately futile), we should only consider whether or not we understand the meanings within the context of the game itself. If we love the game, as Paul/Royce does, then we should "play ball" and enjoy the game for the ongoing structure of order and beauty that it can provide. The danger faced by all of Coover's characters is that they become so enraptured by their own designs and inventions that they begin to feel that the circuit is closed, that no other interpretations are possible. Indeed, many of the stories in *Pricksongs and Descants* are designed to counter any such dogmatic approaches and to demonstrate the freedom with which the artist (the exemplary fiction maker) operates within the patterns.

Pricksongs and Descants

In "The Hat Act," the last of the twenty-one fictions collected by Coover in *Pricksongs and Descants,* a magician appears on stage and performs a variety of feats of wizardry. As he performs, we are given the reactions of an impatient, highly critical audience. Although they applaud vigorously and laugh at especially spectacular successes, they are also easily bored; if they are not constantly provided with new feats, their cheers and whistles soon turn to silence and then to loud boos.

"The Hat Act" tells us much about Coover's short fiction because, like the magician, Coover continually presents the fabulous and improbable to surprise us and jar us out of our expectations. Like the magician's audience, we are forced to view the ordinary perpetually transformed into new shapes and patterns. Indeed, the magician in "The Hat Act" is representative of all the fiction-makers in Coover's work from the religious fanatics in *The Origin of the Brunists* to J. Henry Waugh to Richard Nixon in *The Public Burning*. All these characters are actively engaged in the magical transformation of daily reality into their own systems. The magician is an especially appropriate symbol of Coover's fiction-maker, for anthropologists suggest that creative art may well have sprung initially from magic and magical representations.[31]

Whereas Coover's longer works tend to examine the broad base of fictional systems through which we perceive the universe, his short fictions usually deal much more directly with *literary* fictions, the sources of their appeal, the problems which face those who want to create them, and the way in which they affect our relationship to reality. In addition, Coover wholly abandons the quasi-realistic framework employed in his novels and relies instead on either prenovelistic formal strategies (such as are found in fairy tales, romances, and fables) or on wholly nontraditional, experimental techniques. The effect of both these approaches is to emphasize through form the invented, purely fictive nature of the story before us; rather than trying to give the illusion of having reflected empirical reality (the goal of the realistic novelist), Coover hopes to magically transform reality — which, in his terms, has already been fictionalized by the time it reaches human consciousness — into fresher, more useful fictions. Or, to use Coover's own words, "The world itself being a construct of fictions, I believe the fiction maker's function is to furnish better fictions with which we can reform our notions of things."[32] Meanwhile by flaunting his artifice and fictional design, Coover establishes a distance between reader and text; as with the works of Rabelais, Sterne, and many modern metafictionists, his stories offer the reader a dialogue instead of identification—a dialogue which is directed at the story we are reading. Coover's stories always present their characters, events, symbols, and other literary devices as literary elements drawn from a much larger set of possible relationships. Thus the reader is continually made aware that the pattern set before him is arbitrary and can be broken, that other perspectives are possible, and that the reader and Coover are engaged in a game of choices. A character in the introductory piece to *Pricksongs* makes this clear when he says that what will follow is "an elaborate game, embellished with masks and poetry, a marshalling of legendary doves and herbs" (p. 18). Like Lévi-Strauss's handling of mythic material, Coover's approach emphasizes the transformational possibilities of elements and directs our attention to pattern and structure rather than to content. By accepting the transformational possibilities within language and fabulation, Coover suggests, we observe the exemplary process of the artist countering the effects of both death (stasis) and randomness (chaos)—a process which also helps demonstrate his central point about the dangers of allowing our fictions to rigidify.

In order to insure that his readers respond to his stories as fictional arrangements, Coover often uses plots, characters, imagery, and other aspects of design which are drawn from a variety of well-established sources: from fairy tales, biblical stories, tall tales, folk legends, cultural stereotypes, and other familiar literary motifs. Like other contemporary manipulators of myth (John Barth, John Fowles, Iris Murdock, Ishmael Reed, Barthelme), Coover relies on this sort of material precisely because our responses to it are pre-set; since the material is familiar and our responses predictable, Coover can manipulate these expectations by rearranging the familiar patterns into unfamiliar—but frequently wondrous or liberating—shapes. Coover hopes that his strategies will create in their formal manipulations a sort of freedom from mythic imperatives which Robbe-Grillet has recently described: "As his imagination manipulates the mythological material, the novelist establishes his freedom which exists only in language."[33]

Coover's use of prenovelistic forms suggests one of the reasons why his stories, paradoxically, may seem modern or experimental.

Because these forms are ancient and have been largely ignored since the rise of the novel (at least until recently), they may today seem fresh and innovative. Coover's intentions can also be compared to musical structures, an analogy hinted at by the title of his collected stories, *Pricksongs, and Descants*. The puns in the title— the "death-cunt-and-prick songs" mentioned by Granny in "The Door" (p. 16)—suggest the primary motifs of many of the stories: sex, death, violence, and the grotesque. But "descant" and "pricksong" are also basically synonymous musical terms. Coover has defined "descant" as follows: "'Descant' refers to the form of music in which there is a *cantus firmus,* a basic line, and variations that the other voices play against it. The early descant, being improvisations, were unwritten; when they began writing them, the idea of counterpoint, of a full, beautiful harmony emerged."[34] One useful way to view many of Coover's short fictions is as variations of or "counterpoints" to the basic line of the familiar mythic or literary "melody." His comment about the "full, beautiful harmony" which emerged from the descant emphasizes the positive aspect of his intention. Not merely wanting to debunk myth and pattern, Coover hopes to use them to design new, harmonious forms.

One of the ways Coover attempts to create new perspectives on familiar material is simply by telling the familiar story from an unfamiliar point of view. Coover's biblical tales, for example, rely on this method (these stories include "The Brother," "J's Marriage," and "The Reunion").[35] In "J's Marriage" we are told of Joseph's surprised response to Mary's mysterious impregnation and of their subsequent marriage. Joseph's bewildered and annoyed reaction to the pattern of his life gives us a new outlook on this story. Coover invents many details which weren't important to the myth, but which are crucial to his manipulation of it: what, for example, was their sex life like after they were married? (nonexistent, except for one instance which may have been only a dream). What sort of relationship did Jesus have with Joseph? (they ignored each other). How did Joseph die? (of consumption at a tavern, his face resting in a glass of wine). Joseph, who is referred to only by a Kafkaesque "J," is a slightly parodic forerunner of the modern existential man; like the townsfolk of West Condon, he strains to find meaning and significance in the seemingly irrational events of his life. Joseph differs from Coover's other major characters, however, because he is unable to create a workable system whereby to put the pieces of his life together. Mary's explanation of her pregnancy is difficult for Joseph to accept because he is unable to reconcile it with any rational conception of God:

She explained to him simply that her pregnancy was an act of God, and he had to admit against all mandates of his reason that it must be so, but couldn't imagine whatever had brought a God to do such a useless and, well, yes, in a way, almost vulgar thing. . . . No power of mental effort provided a meaningful answer for him; it was simply unimaginable to him that any God would so involve himself in the tedious personal affairs of this or any other human animal, so inutterably unimportant were they to each other.   (P. 117)

Unable to find a framework in which to organize such events, Joseph at last "simply gave in to it, dumped it in with the rest of life's inscrutable absurdities" (p. 117). Without the inclination to accept even the "tragic fiction" (in this he resembles Paul Trench), Joseph dies ignobly, thinking of his life that "in spite of everything, there was nothing tragic about it, no, nothing there to get wrought up about, on the contrary" (p. 119). Thus Joseph provides a gloomy example of a man unable to accept the aid of fictional systems.

In "The Brother" Coover again retells a familiar biblical story— Noah, the ark, the flood—from a new and revealing perspective. The story centers not on Noah and the other survivors of God's wrath, but on Noah's unnamed brother—one of the victims. From this angle Coover capitalizes on many dramatic ironies by presenting the frightened "other side's" point of view. Told in an unpunctuated Joycean monologue which uses an incongruously modern-sounding idiom, the story quickly wins our affection for Noah's brother. This brother even helps Noah build the ark, mostly to humor "him who couldn't never do nothin in a normal way just a huge oversize fuzzy-face boy" (p. 93). As the brother reports it, Noah before the flood is a pretty ludicrous figure; we see, for example, the bemused attitude of the brother and Noah's neighbors as they watch the building of the huge ark on the top of a hill ("How the hell you gonna get it down to the water?" someone asks, p. 92), the reactions of Noah's not-so-amused wife ("She's over there hollerin at him how he's getting senile and where does he think he's sailin to and how if he ain't afraid of runnin into a octypuss on the way he oughta get back home," p. 95), and so on. Because we know what will follow, our reaction to even the humorously reported scenes is strained; certainly the fact that there is no biblical logic provided to help justify what is happening emphasizes the human aspects of the scene and makes Noah's refusal of aid to his brother seem cruel and cold.

The three stories grouped under the heading of "The Sentient Lens" are complicated metafictional examinations of the hold which fictional patterns and designs have over us. On one level, they may even be viewed as replies to a specific literary approach: the "new realism" of Robbe-Grillet with its "camera-like" objectivity. A truly realistic narrative, according to Robbe-Grillet, requires such an objective method, for only in eliminating all tendencies in the direction of anthropomorphism, including the elimination of all metaphors and analogies, can a writer allow objects their own identity and free man from a constricting humanism. Rather than appropriating the humanistic lie that "man is everywhere," the writer must acknowledge the inevitable, final gulf between himself and all things which are "other." The eyes of man must "rest on things without indulgence, insistently: he sees them but he refuses to appropriate them, he refuses to maintain any suspect understanding with them, any complicity; he asks nothing of them; toward them he feels neither agreement nor dissent of any kind."[36] A writer who wishes to capture this true state of man's relationship to the world must attempt to furnish some sense of this total "otherness" of things outside himself. According to Robbe-Grillet, this can best be achieved in fiction by relying on neutral descriptions of objects and events, descriptions which are "cleansed" and "uninfected" by analogy and metaphor and which are therefore "camera-like" in their objectivity. As he explains:

To describe things, as a matter of fact, is deliberately to place oneself outside them, to confront them. It is no longer a matter of appropriating them to oneself, of projecting anything onto them. Posited, from the start, as *not being man*, they remain constantly out of reach and are, ultimately, neither comprehended in a natural alliance nor recovered by suffering. To limit oneself to description is obviously to reject all the other modes of approaching the object: sympathy as unrealisitic, tragedy as alienating, comprehension as answerable to the realm of science exclusively.[37]

It would be difficult to imagine a literary or philosophical viewpoint which would more directly oppose that of Coover than the views just summarized. Given Coover's definition of man as metaphor maker, any such claim to objectivity or realism would naturally be viewed with distrust; Robbe-Grillet's strategies would, therefore, be seen as futile efforts to ignore the fact that man is forever trapped within his own fiction-making machinery. For Coover the very notion that a writer can duplicate the supposedly neutral, objective vision of a camera would be ridiculous. As we have already seen, Coover fully accepts the Kantian suggestion that man's relation to the "objective world" is always mediated by categories of the mind; these categories insure that when man deals with the world, his perceptions from the outset are symbolic; they are, in effect, "contaminated" by man *by definition*. In the "Sentient Lens" stories, Coover parodies some of Robbe-Grillet's ideas by making the *camera itself* an involved, humanistic narrator.

The scenes of each of the "Sentient Lens" stories are reported to us as if seen through the lens of a camera. But in keeping with Coover's intentions, the lens which narrates the action is a "sentient" lens, not neutral at all but very responsive to the scene it is observing. In the following passage from "Scene for Winter," for example, Coover allows the lens to relate the scene in images which are obviously anthropomorphic in nature:

The snow has folded itself into drifts, or perhaps the earth itself is ribbed beneath, cast into furrows by fallen trees and humps of dying leaves—we cannot know, we can only be sure of the surface we see now, a gently bending surface that warps and cracks the black shadows of the trees into a fretwork of complex patterns, complex yet tranquil, placid, reflective; the interlaced shadows and polygons of brightly daylit snow suggest the quavering stability of light, the imperceptible violence and motion of shadow.   (Pp. 168–69)

Not only are the images presented here in "humanized" language, but also the lens is responding actively to what is happening. Thus, when an unexpected noise occurs, the lens is obviously excited with anticipation:

> Brief sharp crackling sound! . . . Again! Next to us, up close: the columnar trunk of a great pine. Crack! In the wood. Yes, again! The subtle biting voice of wood freezing. We hesitate, expectant, straining to hear it again—but our attention is suddenly shaken, captured by a new sound, an irregular crumpling smashing noise that repeats itself four or five times, stops, then sounds again.   (P. 169)

The second of the "Sentient Lens" stories, "The Milkmaid of Samaniego," is one of Coover's most interesting examinations of the way fictional patterns dominate our perceptions of reality. The scene, again reported through the restrictive eye of a lens, is anticipated for us long before it actually begins; we are told that a milkmaid is approaching, though "we've nothing present to let us suppose it" (p. 174). Instead of focusing on the milkmaid, however, at first we see only a man with yellow teeth chewing vacantly on a hunk of bread. Although our field of vision centers on this man, something seems to suggest that a milkmaid is approaching. Thus we become "aware" of her, despite the fact that we cannot yet actually see her:

> We are, then, aware of her undeniable approach, aware somehow of the slim, graceful pitcher, the red kerchief knotted about her neck, her starched white blouse and brightly flowered skirt, her firm yet jubilant stride down the dusty road, this dusty road leading to the arched bridge, past the oaks and cypresses, twisted wooden fences, the haphazard system of sheep and cattle alongside the occasional cottage and frequent fields, fields of clover, cabbage, and timothy, past chickens scratching in the gravel by the road, and under the untempered ardor of the summer sun.   (P. 175)

This unseen but somehow perceived landscape with the milkmaid approaching owes more to painting than to literature for its specific, almost inevitable details. We can "see" the milkmaid in much the same way that we can anticipate the events in Coover's biblical stories or fairy tales; the basic pattern or design has yielded these details to us so often that we can "create" the scene even before it physically appears in front of us. The lens/narrator explains this sense as being "almost as though there has been some sort of unspoken but well understood prologue, no mere epigraph of random design, but a precise structure of predetermined images, both basic and prior in us, that describes her to us before our senses have located her in the present combination of shapes and colors" (p. 175).

This scene, then, is created out of the same sort of "mythic residues" that were the materials of many of Coover's other stories; and because of the power of these residues to rigidify our responses, it is difficult for us to respond to this scene in any way other than conventionally. Like the cowpokes in Coover's play, *The Kid,* the lens is suspicious of elements which threaten to disrupt these familiar conventions and patterns. Of the man who has mysteriously intruded into the scene, for example, the lens comments unapprovingly that "even had the ambiguity of our expectations allowed a space for him . . . we probably would not have had him just at the bridge, just where our attention might at the wrong moment, be distracted from the maid" (p. 175). Noticing other unexpected elements about the man—his "tattered black hat," his "torn yellow shirt," his "fixed and swollen right eye"—the lens adds that "these are all surprises, too, and of a sort that might encourage us to look for another bridge and another milkmaid, were such a happy option available" (p. 175).

Fortunately the "real" milkmaid appears, exactly matching our expectations except in some trivial details (her kerchief is daffodil yellow instead of red, for instance). The process of her approach is described in careful detail until the lens is again distracted by some actions of the man: "As she walks her skirt flutters and twists as though caught by some breeze, though there is none. Here—but the man, this one with the tattered hat and bulging eye, he stands and— no, no! the maid, *the maid!*" (p. 176). Fully content to rest in the groves of convention, the lens wants only to present the familiar scene without interruption. But when the scene dissolves into a conventional, idyllic farmyard, another gratuitous element—a young boy—appears. The lens begins to describe the boy, emphasizing his sexual qualities, and then attempts to return to the pre-set material: "Not more than a dozen paces away, a tall lad, dark and fine boned with flashing brown eyes and bold mouth, curries a thickchested coal-black bull, his sturdy tanned—but no more of that! for, in short, he looks up, they exchange charged glances." (p. 178). As is typical of Coover, *the established pattern* here is shattered, the narrator having lost control of his material. Despite the pleas of the lens ("No! not—!"), the young boy, whom we have probably expected to be *defending* the maid from the attack of the old man, is soon attacking the milkmaid himself, tearing at her dress, knocking the pitcher of milk from her head.

When the dissolve is concluded and we see the original scene again, the familiar elements can no longer create the proper picture; with the aid of the unkempt, yellow-toothed man, the milkmaid tearfully sets her stoneware jug aright. Initially frightened by his appearance, the maid soon accepts the intruder and his friendly intentions. Silently they contemplate the pattern which has led them to this moment: the sun, the road, the now empty pitcher. The man indicates that other sources can compensate her for her loss; withdrawing some coins from his pockets, he shows them to the maid: "They are few, but of gold and silver. They look, to tell the truth, like nothing less than a whole private universe of midsummer suns in the man's strong dark hand" (p. 179). This moment recalls the epiphany at the close of *The UBA,* and it serves a similar function. These mysterious coins are similar to the gleaming white baseball which Damon held up for Paul Trench; both images represent objects *whose significance must be recreated* by man each time he comes in contact with them. The story concludes with the empty pitcher—now discarded and unneeded in the presence of the new alternatives, although originally a central element in the design—shattering into fragments:

The pitcher, thought at first to be stable in the grass at the foot of the bridge, is actually, as we can now see, on a small spiny ridge: it weaves, leans, then finally rolls over in a gently curving arc, bursting down its rust-colored veins into a thousand tiny fragments not unlike the broken shells of white eggs. Many of these fragments remain in the grass at the foot of the bridge, while others tumble silently down the hill into the eddying stream below.   (P. 179)

The Spanish epigraph to this story (*mira que ni el presente esta seguro*) has already suggested that the elements of the present secure scene will not always remain certain.[38]

The "Sentient Lens" stories are typical of the way Coover constantly places shifting alternatives before us—a process that will reach new proportions with Richard Nixon's fumbling efforts to make sense of the Rosenberg case in *The Public Burning*. In all of Coover's work the suggestion seems to be that fixed perspectives are false perspectives and that attributing "meaning" to events may be useful but should always be done with the awareness of alternative possibilities. Like Donald Barthelme, Coover often mockingly thrusts significance in the reader's face, even in situations where interpretation seems unlikely. This "game" of interpreting symbols is openly played in "Panel Game," the earliest and most significant of the "Exemplary Fictions" which were collected in *Pricksongs*. Set up as a kind of closet drama (a favorite form for Coover), "Panel Game" presents an "Unwilling Participant" who is chosen to sit on a television game show panel in the midst of several mysterious, possibly allegorical figures (an "Aged Clown," a "Lovely Lady," and "Mr. America"). Soon the "Merry Moderator" is introduced and the Unwilling Participant is plunged into a complex, incomprehensible game whose rules he does not understand. Urged on by the moderator ("But what does it mean? *What does it mean?*"), he senses that the game has something to do with deciphering language but no useful rules or connections seem to emerge; like all of Coover's major characters, the poor participant finds meaning everywhere and cannot separate his own fancy from the intentions of the game. He also resembles many of Coover's later characters, such as the West Condonites in *The Brunists* and Nixon in *The Public Burning,* in demonstrating a fundamental distrust of transformation and process as he frantically tries to assign fixed meanings, to shape patterns, and to create order from the mass of ambiguous, confusing signs that lie all around him.

In "Klee Dead," another metafictional tale which deals with the perils of interpretation, a self-conscious narrator finds it impossible to play his role as an all-knowing storyteller who is supposed to explain why one Wilbur Klee has committed suicide. This narrator knows very well that the reasons behind a suicide are usually much too complicated to be presented neatly in a story of this sort. He does manage to point out several potentially revealing signs (Klee's dentures, a scrap of paper which may be a suicide note), but he also confesses that these may well be only "lifelike forgeries." He demonstrates at several points that he *can* present realistic stories with all the expected details and soothing illusions about cause and effect, but these stories have nothing to do with Klee (except in some vague, anagrammatic way) and are, in fact, simply parodies of the realistic method. In the end we are left with "virtually nothing. . . . And a good fifteen, twenty minutes shot to hell" (p. 111).

Perhaps Coover's most surreal story, "The Marker," presents another allegorical quest for vital artistic forms in today's world. In it we find a young man named Jason preparing to go to bed with his wife. After putting a marker in his book, he turns out the light and begins to search the room unsuccessfully for his wife. Totally disoriented and confused, Jason—the artist/quester—wanders around the room, trying to use the familiar reference points to guide him, until, at one point, he arrives back where he had started; eventually, with the aid of his wife's laughter, he finds his bed and begins to make love to his wife. While thus engaged, Jason momentarily wonders with alarm "if this is really his wife" (p. 90), but he rejects these thoughts "since there is no alternative possibility." Most of Coover's characters who deny the possibility of other views meet unhappy ends, and the case is no different with Jason: soon his lovemaking is interrupted by a police officer and four assistants who burst into the bedroom unannounced. Horrified, Jason discovers that although it is his wife who lies beneath him she is now a rotting corpse, which "follows him punishingly in movement for a moment, as a sheet of paper will follow a comb" (p. 91). Throwing off the past, then, even a hideously disfigured corpse, is evidently not an easy task; and, as Jason discovers, the consequences of paying so much loving attention to something which is dead are serious indeed. The police officer makes sure that Jason will no longer create anything when he "pulls out Jason's genitals flat on the tabletop and pounds them to a pulp with the butt of his gun" (p. 91). Just before leaving, the officer delivers a speech which unmasks the metafictional intent of the story:

"You understand, of course," he says, "that I am not, in the strictest sense, a traditionalist. I mean to say that I do not recognize tradition *qua* tradition as sanctified in its own sake. On the other hand, I do not join hands with those who find inherent in tradition some malignant evil, and who therefore deem it of terrible necessity that all customs be rooted out at all costs. I am person-ally convinced, if you will permit me, that there is a middle road, whereon we recognize that innovations find their best soil in traditions, which are justified in their own turn by the innovations which created them. I believe, then, that law and custom are essential, but that it is one's task to review and revise them. In spite of that, however, *some things still make me puke! . . . Now get rid of that fucking corpse!"* (P. 91)

This speech neatly summarizes Coover's own fictional approach which denies that tradition is "some malignant evil" to be "rooted out at all cost"; Coover instead suggests that a "middle ground" should be established that recognizes that "innovations find their best soil in traditions." The officer's pretentious, scholarly-sounding explanation is, of course, totally incongruous to the grotesqueness of the situation and resembles similar insertions that are found in Barthelme's works. The speech is also typical of the way in which metafictional self-reflections arise in Coover's stories in places we least expect them. The implications of the officer's speech really cut two ways: it is about time, it is suggested, that the "lights be turned on" for many writers who have been making love to something long dead—like, say, the realistic novel; on the other hand, the officer's "middle road" also hints that if writing nowadays must involve any-thing disgusting or ugly then, liberal though he is, it too should be rejected—or, as the narrator of "The Magic Poker" says, "There's nothing to be gained by burdening our fabrications with impieties. Enough that the skin of the world is littered with our contentious artifice . . . without suffering our songs to be flattened by savagery" (p. 30).

Pricksongs and Descants also contains a series of structurally re-lated stories that are Coover's most radical departures from realistic norms to date. In these stories, as with the best fictions of Borges and Nabokov, the structure itself is used to serve his central thesis about the dangers involved in dogmatic perspectives on our fic-tional systems. These stories—which I have elsewhere labeled Coover's "cubist stories"[39]—can be usefully approached by compar-ing Coover's intentions with those which generated the cubist revolution in painting earlier in this century. Making analogies between different art forms should always begin by respecting their differences, but in this case the cubist analogy seems to me to be especially helpful in identifying a context in which we can respond to these experimental stories.

Even a cursory glance at Coover's cubist stories ("The Magic Poker," "The Gingerbread House," "The Elevator," "Quenby and Ola, Swede and Carl," and "The Babysitter") reveals that they share with the cubists' works a general reaction against mimetic methods of presentation and emphasize instead the formal manipulation of the artist's elements. More significant for my analogy with cubist painting, however, is the fact that, like the cubists, Coover forces his audience to deal with the elements of his works as mere artifacts or conventions and creates a deliberate ambiguity of event which directly parallels the cubists' spatial ambiguity and which confounds his audience's desire for outer referents. Picasso's rejection of realism and his developing spatial ambiguity was partially a response to his own interest in primitive art (which ignored mimetic principles in terms of perspective and proportion in favor of a subjective interpretation) and in the somewhat earlier experiments of Paul Cézanne.[40] These interests influenced Picasso to move far beyond Matisse and the Fauvists, who were using color with an unprecedented freedom and arbitrariness in the period just before Picasso produced what is generally regarded as the first cubist masterpiece, *Les Demoiselles d'Avignon*. In creating *Les Demoiselles* Picasso broke away from perhaps the two most important characteristics of European painting since the Renaissance: the classical norm for the human figure and the spatial illusionism of one-point perspective. By running together planes otherwise separated in space and by combining multiple viewpoints into a single form, Picasso boldly created a precedent of great significance for the later cubist paintings. As we will see, Coover's cubist stories are developed via structuring devices that are closely related to these two key methods of departure from representational norms.

As should be evident from our discussion of his other works, Coover shares with the cubists the relativistic view that the role of the artist is not to render reality unambiguously but to create realities whose ambiguities suggest something of our own relationship to the world. Robert Rosenblum's discussion of the larger implications underlying the cubist method also helps define Coover's intentions:

For a century that questioned the very concept of absolute truth or value, cubism created an artistic language of intentional ambiguity. In front of the cubist work of art, the spectator was to realize that no single interpretation . . . could be complete in itself. And in expressing this awareness of the paradoxical nature of reality and the need for describing it in multiple and even contradictory ways, Cubism offered a visual equivalent of a fundamental aspect of twentieth century experience.[41]

Coover's cubist stories create exactly this vision of "multiple and even contradictory" views of reality; like cubist paintings, they are consistently structured to force the viewer to consider competing realities as equally "real" or true. Their method of presentation is fairly easy to describe; in many ways the process is similar to watching film rushes of the same scene shot several times from different angles, the action moving slowly forward in spurts and sputters because of so many retakes. Basically, Coover assembles all the elements of a familiar, often even banal situation—characters, setting, symbols, imagery—and then starts the story on its way. But as soon as any sort of clear pattern begins to establish itself, he stops the action, retraces his steps, and allows other plot lines to develop. The later plots sometimes complement the earlier ones and at other times directly contradict them; but all variations are allowed to exist as possibilities and none is insisted upon as the "real" one. After all, the stories seem to suggest, because *any* of the possible actions is purely an invention, why should our view of the situation be limited to any one perspective of it? Coover's method, it should be emphasized, is a more radical departure from realistic norms than the multiple presentations of other works which might be labeled cubistic (Durrell's *Quartet,* Faulkner's *The Sound and the Fury, As I Lay Dying,* or *Absalom, Absalom!* Gide's *The Counterfeiters*). In reading these earlier works, the reader cannot accept any *one* perspective as leading to the truth; but there is still the sense in these works that a locus of truth is present, not within the text itself but within the *reader,* who assembles the different elements simultaneously and then decides on the proper interpretation. But with Coover's stories it is a fruitless task to attempt to separate fantasy from reality, the "real" perspective from imaginary or distorted ones, just as similar inquiries into cubist paintings or a "cubist movie" like *Last Year at Marienbad* lead only to dead ends.

In presenting all the forks of the road, Coover abandons one of realistic fiction's strongest conventions—that the author should choose one specific narrative "path" and then follow it to a conclusion. Writers have relied on this convention for an obvious reason: they believe this is the way the objective world operates. Coover abandons this principle, just as the cubists abandoned one-point perspective, because the assurance of the existence of the objective nature of reality has faded. As we discussed in chapter 1, many modern artists have rejected realistic conventions because, to quote John Weightman, "Any realism of social context is out of the question, because reality is infinite and multifarious and can only be rendered by partial and mutually exclusive grids. There are no plots in nature, so that to tell a story in terms of cause and effect is to accept a naive linear fiction."[42]

Probably the simplest of the cubist pieces is "The Elevator," a story which Coover has said generated most of the others.[43] The story clearly shows Coover's approach and opens as follows:

Every morning without exception and without so much as reflecting upon it, Martin takes the self-service elevator to the fourteenth floor, where he works. He will do so today. When he arrives, however, he finds the lobby empty, the old building still possessed of its feinting shadows and silences, desolate though mutely expectant, and he wonders if today it might not turn out differently.   (P. 125)

What follows this opening section are fourteen different short sequences, each numbered and each describing different elevator trips for Martin. The total number of sequences, fifteen, corresponds to the fourteen floors of the building plus the basement, but the sections do not follow each other in any apparent temporal or causal order. We learn, for example, that Martin has an uneventful ride, fights or doesn't fight an office bully, takes the elevator to a non-existent fifteenth floor, makes love to or is repulsed by the elevator operator as they plunge to their death, and so on. Coover has commented that this story "is based purely on number and musical analogues,"[44] a cryptic remark which does, however, suggest some useful ways of considering these cubist stories. The musical analogy has already been suggested: one way to view the different sections in "The Elevator" is as variations or counterpoints (the "pricksong" or "descant" idea) to the familiar plot line (an ordinary ride in an elevator). The concept of number is also important. For example, the magical number seven figures prominently in the story's development, as it does in many of Coover's works: it has been seven years since Martin began working in this building; there are usually seven people in the elevator; what is probably the most important scene takes place in the seventh section. More importantly, mathematics provides a key analogy with what Coover is doing here, an analogy suggested by the epigraph Coover chose for *Pricksongs* taken from Valéry's "Variations on the Eclogues": "Therefore they set me this problem of the equality of appearance and number." Like a mathematician toying with the different possible permutations of a set of given elements, Coover constructs "The Elevator" (and his other cubist pieces) so that each section can be seen as a permutation or transformation of the set of original elements (the main characters, the plot possibilities, the symbols employed, and so on).

Although at the end of "The Elevator" Martin decides not to take the elevator trip at all, we should not assume that the other sequences were all fantasies, daydreamed by Martin as he actually stands before the elevator. Readers who try to recreate the "real events" of any of the cubist stories will be frustrated and will have misunderstood their nature. As with Duchamp's *Nude Descending a Staircase,* what we are given here is not a static picture of reality but the presentation of a process, a way of looking at things. The fact that different sequences contradict one another should not disturb us any more than the fact that the same curved and rectilinear shapes are used to confound the anatomy of the human form and guitar in Braque's *Man with a Guitar* or Picasso's *Ma Jolie [Woman with Guitar].* In "The Elevator" all the events, including the contradictory ones, are allowed to freely intermingle. Each of the events within the story's "set" is equally real—or fictional—for every sequence creates its own reality as it is presented.

As is true of all the cubist stories, "The Elevator" is clearly linked to Coover's more conventional fiction. Death and sexual violation dominate the action here, just as they do in nearly all the stories in *Pricksongs*. Also typical is the way Coover creates his characters and situations in a flat, nonrealistic manner. But as presented by Coover, seemingly infinite possibilities are held within this small set of elements. Martin himself senses this as he considers the nature of the Kantian categories: "This small room, so commonplace and so compressed, he observes with a certain melancholic satisfaction, this elevator contains them all: space, time, cause, motion, magnitude, class. Left to our own devices, we would probably discover them" (p. 129). Yes, the possibilities of an elevator used as a literary or metaphysical symbol are indeed almost limitless; and perhaps if left to ourselves, we would figure them all out eventually. But meanwhile Coover starts us on our way. If we look at the elevator as a literary symbol, for instance, we find that many of the obvious possibilities have been anticipated: the elevator as a social microcosm; the elevator as a phallic symbol; the elevator as a coffin; the elevator as a jail—"He steps inside: this tight cell! he thinks with a kind of unsettling shock"; "Martin imagines suddenly he is descending into hell. *Tra la perduta gente,* yes!" Critics of practically any persuasion should be able to find something of interest here.

The elevator also allows Coover to exhibit his delight in verbal forms, his ability to control a dizzying variety of styles—a quality which he demonstrates in all his work. Thus the style in the individual sections switches rapidly from the apocalyptic ("I, Martin, proclaim my omnipotence! In the end, doom touch all! MY doom! I impose it! TREMBLE!"), to pornographic parody ("His gaze coolly courses her belly, her pinched and belted waist, past her taut breasts, meets her excited stare"), to a bawdy, colloquial joke ("But hey! theres this guy see he gets on the goddamn elevator and its famous how hes got him a doodang about five feet long"). The story thus implies that you aren't taking advantage of the possibilities which are open to you.

Perhaps Coover's most successful cubist story is "The Babysitter." In his prologue to *Pricksongs,* Coover speaks admiringly of the "synthesis between . . . reality and illusion, sanity and madness, the erotic and the ludicrous, the visionary and the scatalogical" (p. 77), and in this story he makes this synthesis vital. The tale is composed of over one hundred short sections which weave a variety of alternative possibilities. The elements of this story are drawn from familiar territory: a teenage babysitter arrives, middle-class parents depart for a party, the babysitter settles down for an evening of television, diaper changing, and perhaps some making out with her boyfriend Jack if he should stop by. These elements, despite their fragmentation, make up a plot line we are all familiar with, but other combinations are possible; relying on material drawn mainly from cultural stereotypes and myths, television shows, and pornographic clichés, Coover conjures up a variety of our society's stock fears and wishes, fantasies and dangers.

"The Babysitter" is therefore composed of the same sort of shifting, contradictory possibilities as "The Elevator." Here, too, the many switches in voice and style provide Coover with the chance to parody a variety of literary conventions and styles and to keep the borderline between fantasy and reality fluid at all times. Most readers—especially upon their first reading of the story—are probably tempted to figure out which of the sections are "real" and which are merely the converging, overlapping "fantasies" experienced by the principal characters of the story. Coover allows us to do this kind of sorting throughout the first part of the story, but gradually he begins to allow the various "fantasies" to intermingle *with each other*—an obvious impossibility in terms of realistic norms. Thus one of the scenes begins with Jack, the babysitter's boyfriend, fantasizing about seducing the babysitter with the assistance of his friend Mark: "Mark is kissing her. Jack is under the blanket easing her panties down over her squirming hips" (p. 222). But this scene is suddenly interrupted by the entrance of Mr. Tucker—an appearance seemingly imagined by Mr. Tucker earlier in the narration. At this point the reader must ask himself how Mr. Tucker's fantasy was able to intrude upon the fantasy being experienced by Jack. The answer, of course, is that Coover is not interested in the fantasy/reality distinction we are trying to impose; that these two plot elements are here fused should not bother readers any more than the fact that the cubists often run together planes otherwise separated in space or use a single line to suggest two different subjects or features.

Although it soon becomes obvious that it is impossible to untangle the different levels of reality in "The Babysitter," beneath the shifting plot lines there are certain social implications. Coover uses the television programs which the babysitter watches (spy stories, westerns, convoluted love stories) to mirror the sexual aggressiveness and more covert hints of violence in the Tucker household and at the party; appropriately enough, during several of the rape scenes, images from the television set are reflected over the bodies of the participants. Coover is careful, however, to leave the idea that the television is *causally related* to the social context of violence completely up to our own discretion. Other parallels are less subtle: before the two boys decide to visit the babysitter at the Tuckers', we see them playing a pinball game which is described in parodically sexual and sadistic terms: "He pushes a plunger with his thumbs and one ball pops in place, hard and glittering with promise. . . . He heaves his weight gently against the machine as the ball bounds off a rubber bumper. He can feel her warming up under his hands" (pp. 208–10). Later in one of the rape scenes, this metaphor is repeated: "The television lights flicker and flash over her glossy flesh. 1000 WHEN LIT. Whack! Slap! Bumper to bumper. He leans into her, feeling her come alive" (p. 235). That people are confused enough to direct their sexual feelings toward machines in this story is not really surprising, for every character (including the children) seems driven by sexual obsessions of one sort or another. This sexual obsessiveness is as evident at the drunken cocktail party attended by the Tuckers as it is back at their house; gossip and lewd jokes make up the main topic of conversation, and the central event of the evening is the game of "Get Dolly Tucker Back in Her Girdle Again," played to the delight of all on the living room floor. Coover's story thus demonstrates the way in which sex and violence are peculiarly intermixed in our society's public and private fantasies, its various forms of entertainment, even in its most mundane activities. Obviously, however, the social message of this story is slight and presented heavy-handedly. Actually Coover seems to use the cliché implica-

tions he draws much like Donald Barthelme in many of his stories—
simply as further literary elements which can be manipulated for
ironic or parodic purposes.

The two other interesting cubist stories in *Pricksongs,* "The Magic
Poker" and "The Gingerbread House," are both based on fairy tales.
In "The Gingerbread House" Coover presents forty-two short sections to create a variety of possible outcomes to the familiar Hansel
and Gretel fairy tale. The tale is notable in part for its development
of the overtones of sex and violence contained in the original story, a
development created by the innuendoes of language rather than by
overt action. "The Gingerbread House" is also a good example of the
way in which Coover deliberately undercuts, reverses, or obscures
the familiar associations we may have brought to the story. Rather
than simply altering the pattern, he allows parts of the original story
to engage other possibilities openly. For example, he draws in materials or characters extraneous or contradictory to the original story
(such as the dove or the man with white hair). At other times he suddenly switches the symbolic or allegoric implications we are familiar
with. For instance, rather than having the black witch (evil, experience) kill the dove (purity, grace), Coover has the young boy (innocence, goodness) brutally do the job. Indeed, the basic opposition
between the two innocent children and the evil witch is undermined
by a variety of hints pointing to a willing sexual connection between
them. In addition to such basic reversals, Coover plants an over-
abundance of familiar images and symbols (doves, butterflies, flowers, colors, etc.), but he does not allow them to grow and establish
their familiar pattern (or *any* pattern, for that matter). Thus we probably notice that some sort of color imagery is being employed in this
story, because specific colors recur in section after section. But
when we try to establish a consistent "meaning" in this color imagery, we find that our analysis is mocked; the final meaning of colors,
like whiteness in *Moby Dick* or *The Narrative of Arthur Gordon Pym,*
remains ambiguous. As the reader/critic, we are placed in exactly the
same position as many of Coover's characters: in trying to sort out
the ambiguities before us, we are inundated with meaning, surrounded by what Neil Schmitz has termed "iconic words, ostensible
keys to ostensible meanings."[45]

"The Magic Poker," the most complicated of Coover's cubist

stories, is composed of various fragments of fairy tales, legends, myths, and speculative histories. It opens with a godlike narrator busily setting the stage for some expected visitors:

I wander the island, inventing it. I make a sun for it and trees—pine and birch and dogwood and firs—and cause the water to lap the pebbles of its abandoned shores. . . . I impose a hot midday silence, a profound and heavy stillness. But anything can happen. (P. 20)

As was the case in "Klee Dead," the narrator occupies the center of the stage; as other scenes and characters are introduced, he never allows us to forget that they are *his* scenes and creatures, the products solely of his imagination. When the central symbol of the story—the magic poker—is introduced, he proudly reminds us that he alone is responsible for its being there: "It is long and slender with an intricate worked handle, and it is orange with rust. It lies shadowed, not by trees, but by the grass that has grown around it. I put it there" (p. 21). From the beginning we see the narrator's obsessive control over the fiction he is building, his fumbling efforts to keep us entertained, his ambivalence about what he is doing. He resembles many of Coover's victims of artifice, struggling to understand the nature of what he is creating and often confusing his inventions with reality. He is another of Coover's magicians, a self-conscious Prospero who represents Coover himself; as he manipulates the different elements of his story, he is hopeful of entertaining us but also constantly reminds us that it is he who pulls the doves from the hat. The story therefore has the dual focus which we find so often in Coover's work: on the one level, we watch the highly artificial characters struggling to work out their fictional destinies on a magical island; at the same time, we observe the narrator trying to assemble the story, self-consciously considering *his* destiny as a creator of stories.

As the narrator begins to sketch in the details and characters of his story, he also becomes increasingly aware of his constructions *as objects.* Indeed, in much the same fashion as Waugh's Universal Baseball Association or Nixon's fantasies about the Rosenbergs in *The Public Burning,* the story itself gradually becomes a fiction which slowly assumes a reality of its own and begins to envelop its creator.

At one point, the narrator admits that his metaphors seem to be developing a stubborn sense of "reality" and "hardness" of their own:

At times, I forget that this arrangement is my own invention. I begin to think of the island as somehow real, its objects solid and intractable, its condition of ruin not so much an aesthetic design as an historical denouement. I find myself peering into blue teakettles, batting at spiderwebs, and contemplating a greenish gray growth on the side of a stone parapet. I wonder if others might wander here without my knowing it; I wonder if I might die and the teakettle remain.   (P. 33)

Clearly, the problems facing this narrator lie at the heart of all of Coover's work. The process we observe in "The Magic Poker" is that of a fiction gradually assuming its place in the world, with its creator often mistaking his "aesthetic design" for the design of the universe. Eventually, "by some no doubt calculable formula of event and pagination" (p. 40), the narrator disappears entirely into his creation, with only the island remaining behind: "The lake is calm. Here a few shadows lengthen, a frog dies, a strange creature lies slain, a tanager sings" (p. 45).

The narrator not only succumbs to his own invention but also faces the same sorts of problems that all modern writers do. As Neil Schmitz summarizes, "Throughout 'The Magic Poker' the narrator is . . . bemused, at once the systematizing writer and a witness to the fecundating power of words. Traditional fiction, like the mansion in which nineteenth century novel-lives might well have been lived, is wreckage; Coover himself a vandal writing on its deserted walls."[46] As the narrator examines the wreckage of language and symbols that lie strewn around him, he occasionally strains too hard and gives in to excesses. In the cottage where he has been imagined, the caretaker's son squats over a teakettle and produces a "love letter." But the narrator intervenes, aware that his absolute power of invention has allowed him to go too far; in the process of analyzing what he is doing, he provides a good example of how Coover undercuts his use of symbolism by alluding to its presence:

A love letter! Wait a minute, this is getting out of hand! What happened to that poker, I was doing much better with that poker, I had something going

there, archetypal and even maybe beautiful, a blend of eros and wisdom, sex
and sensibility, music and myth. But what am I going to do with shit in a rusty
teakettle?   (P. 30)

The magic poker which the narrator manipulates with such evident delight resembles the literary elements in all of Coover's stories
in that it can be transformed into whatever is needed. Thus the
poker appears at one point as the familiar archetype of fairy tales
which, when kissed by a beautiful girl, changes magically into a
handsome enchanted prince. It also can usefully serve the narrator
as a phallic symbol or, more generally, as a symbol of creativity
(much like the writer's equally phallic pen). It is later employed,
however, as a *parody* of these symbols, as when one of the girls
"kisses the rusted iron poker, kisses its ornate handle, its long rusted
shaft, kisses the tip. Nothing happens. Only a rotten taste in her
mouth" (p. 26). In another variation, the poker repulses any magical
suggestions at all: when the girl discovers it, she finds it "not so rusty
on the underside—but bugs! *millions* of them!" (p. 25). Less con-
spicuously, but more practically, the poker is also put to use as a
substitute for the missing leg of a piano, as a magic can, as a
weapon, as a kettle stirrer, and even as a convenient simile for the
narrator himself: "Yes, and perhaps tomorrow I will invent Chicago
and Jesus Christ and the history of the moon. Just as I have invented
you, dear reader, while lying here in the afternoon sun, bedded
deeply in the bluegrass like an old iron poker" (p. 40). Here the narrator literally becomes the cumulative symbol of the story, and he
withdraws permanently into his language. As Neil Schmitz explains
this withdrawal:

"The Magic Poker" thus turns sinuously in upon itself. Figurative language,
Coover's enchanted poker, remains that instrument that . . . releases the
writer from his metafictional anality, his obsessive control over the fiction he
is creating. . . . Coover envisions an escape into language, the writer's essence.
. . . Language grows on this "invented island" and finally reclaims the artifice
of Coover's narrator.[47]

"The Magic Poker" effectively draws together many of the concerns we have seen operating in much of Coover's short fiction. Us-

ing a familiar form, he restructures the elements of this form into new shapes which deny the adequacy of our previous perspectives. At the same time, the central problem of all of Coover's work emerges: how does man maintain his precarious balance between using and appreciating his inventions, and becoming lost within them? Like many of his stories, "The Magic Poker" deals with fictions in a literary sense and metafictionally examines the relationship between a writer and his inventions. But the implications of this story extend to the other categories of fiction making, the more general categories of myth, religion, history, and art which Coover deals with more directly in his novels.

The Public Burning

With the publication of his long-awaited novel, *The Public Burning* (1977), Robert Coover was for the first time recognized as a major literary talent. Conceiving the work as "just a simple theater idea"[48] in 1966, Coover worked on the novel for almost a decade and suffered through a variety of personal setbacks in trying to get his controversial manuscript accepted by a publisher. Even a cursory glance at the novel's panoramic contents—narrated in part by Richard Nixon and having to do with the volatile Rosenberg case—explains some of the reluctance of the publishing industry to touch it. After being accepted and then rejected by at least two publishers, *The Public Burning* finally found a champion in editor Richard Seaver and was published by Viking Press in the summer of 1977. Even before the book was published, it had attracted considerable attention: the *Washington Post* anticipated its arrival by hailing the book as "a great work of art . . . the kind of book you come across once in a lifetime," and Viking editor Theodore Solotaroff proudly announced that it was "not just the novel of the year—it may be the novel of the decade."[49] Although critical reaction to Coover's massive (534-page), highly experimental work was mixed, even most critics who felt that it did not fully succeed were willing to admit its importance. Thus Thomas R. Edwards concluded his mixed review in the *New York Times Book Review* by saying, "This book is an extraordinary act of moral passion, a destructive device that will not easily be defused."[50] In the first extended examination of the work, Geoffrey Wolff was even more emphatic about the book's enduring importance: "I would guess that since World War II, only *Lolita, Invisible Man,* and *Catch-22* are in its class for durability. But for the risks it runs, for its capacity and reach, for its literary and probable social consequences, nothing I know of written in our language since the war can touch it."[51]

In certain fundamental ways, *The Public Burning* extends the vision of a chaotic, disruptive universe and the enormously complex operations of history that Coover presents in all his fiction. Likewise, the metafictional intent behind this work is again very evident as Coover examines the relationship between man's fictional systems and the reality they seek to explore. But although Coover continues to deal with man's need for order and the incredible variety of ways he has developed to cope with flux, *The Public Burning* is in almost every way a broader and more ambitious work than anything he had previously published. Beyond these major thematic concerns, *The Public Burning,* at its most accessible level, does a brilliant job of re-creating the apocalyptic mood and paranoiac spirit of the early 1950s; even more remarkably, its portrait of Richard Nixon proves to be a subtle, credible, and strangely compassionate characterization.

The complexity and breadth of Coover's vision here results in part from his intricate interweaving of an enormous amount of factual data into his fictional narrative. Indeed, in a very important sense this book is a tribute to language's ability to create coherence, and it literally embodies Coover's central point about man's talent in manipulating the elements of his existence into new, exciting plots and patterns. As Coover commented, the role of the artist—the exemplary fiction-maker who represents us all—is to become "the mythologizer, to be the creative spark in this process of renewal: he's the one who tears apart the old story, speaks the unspeakable, makes the ground shake, then shuffles the bits back together into a new story."[52] Much like Joyce in *Ulysses* (probably the best analogue of Coover's attempt), Coover meticulously builds his mythic framework out of a welter of facts, figures, dates, public testimony, and other real data. Everything that might possibly have a bearing on the

Rosenberg case—from the cold war crisis (including the Korean War background) and political intrigues in Washington right up through a wide range of cultural and pop-culture events in America—is included here. As a result the book seems to operate on what we might term a deliberate strategy of excess, with the reader's difficulties in approaching the text mirroring Richard Nixon's own dilemma in unraveling the complexities of the Rosenberg case. Like Nixon, we are confronted with a bewildering assortment of facts, figures, lists, quotes, pseudo-quotes, song lyrics, trial testimony, movie plots, and dozens of other potential clues. It seems as if everything that was going on in America and around the world during this period had some sort of direct bearing on the Rosenberg case—even the significance of such films as *High Noon* and *House of Wax* which are repeatedly referred to and which provide meaningful cultural analogues to the larger dramas that are unfolding. All this material is transformed by Coover's hand to create a vivid sense of exactly what was occurring in the public consciousness on June 19, 1953 when the Rosenbergs were executed. The central magic of this work is therefore similar to Joyce's achievement in *Ulysses* or Pynchon's in *Gravity's Rainbow* and *V.* in that Coover succeeds in making his encyclopedic details seem aesthetically appropriate: all the details *seem* to be meaningful, seem to be forming themselves into the shapes and patterns that Coover wishes to establish. And it is precisely the nature of these shapes that is the focus of Coover's metafictional concern here, for these shapes represent the fictions that we all generate to create a bulwark against chaos: the shape of history, the shape of paranoia, the shape of simplistic oppositions (us versus them, communism versus democracy, God versus the devil, good versus evil), the shape of art, the shape of literary narratives.

The story of *The Public Burning* is told in twenty-eight sections which are narrated alternately by Richard Nixon and, in various voices, by Coover. Although a prologue and epilogue extend the action somewhat, the book focuses on the two days and nights that precede the execution of the Rosenbergs. Coover stages this execution at Times Square—the "luminous navel" of the United States (p. 164), a "place of feasts, spectacle, and magic . . . the ritual center of the Western World" (p. 166). The actual execution itself, which is highly reminiscent of the climactic ending of *The Origin of the Brunists,* is presented as a powerful, circus-like finale that serves as a public exorcism and ceremonial return to what Coover has called "dreamtime." As he explains, "dreamtime" involves "the inner truths, legends, mythos of the race, the origins, the mysterious beginnings of the tribe. . . . The point of a ceremonial return to dreamtime is basically regenerative: to recover belief in the tribe and get things moving again."[53] It is crucial to understanding Coover's intentions in *The Public Burning* to see that the Rosenbergs are supposed to represent something much more than mere pawns of the cold war strategy or cogs destroyed when our judicial machinery runs amuck. Instead, Coover presents the Rosenbergs as archetypal victims, the central participants in a celebratory ritual which Uncle Sam hopes will enable America to recapture a sense of community and momentum which it has lost in its battle with the Phantom. That their execution takes place in the spring at Times Square—"an American holy place long associated with festivals of rebirth" (p. 4)—helps underscore this fundamental association. At one point Uncle Sam bluntly explains to Nixon the specific purpose of the extravagantly staged execution: "Oh, I don't reckon we could live like this all year round . . . we'd only expunctify ourselves. But we do need an occasional peak of disorder and danger to keep things from just peterin' out, don't we" (p. 95). The execution is a blatantly theatrical spectacle designed to combine ritualistically elements of entertainment (Cecil B. DeMille chairs an entertainment committee and is assisted by Busby Berkeley, Betty Crocker, Walt Disney, Ed Sullivan, and the Mormon Tabernacle Choir—among others), religious archetypes celebrating rebirth and regeneration, and various anarchical and sexual impulses which will presumably free the populace for renewal once they have torn everything apart.

Although Coover fills nearly all the sections of the book with a sense of bitterness, irony, and outrage, he also manages to suggest a sympathetic understanding of how communities are led to such destructive results. The chief danger to which all of the major participants in the novel succumb—except, curiously, Richard Nixon—is the familiar mistake made by so many Coover characters: the danger of dogmatizing beliefs, the danger of taking self-generated fictions too literally, the danger of relying too completely on fragile, oversimplified systems (such as historical or political perspectives) and of not seeing how utterly inadequate they are to deal with the enormously complex, constantly shifting nature of reality. Thus all the major characters—the Rosenbergs, Uncle Sam, Nixon, the Phantom—react to the prospect of randomness in the same way: they storify it, creating soothing possible fictions that they can feel comfortable with. Like *The Brunists* and *The UBA*, *The Public Burning* exhibits Coover's obvious fascination with the power of history to subjugate events to pattern—to create connections, causal relationships, and stories when most observers can find no meaning at all. As a result, one of the central preoccupations in the novel is with "the mosaic of history" (p. 226), how man is able, through language, to arrange and rearrange the random elements of existence into historically significant events. In trying to uncover all the relevant facts in the labyrinthine Rosenberg case, Richard Nixon is soon led to ponder the nature of man's efforts to organize his experience and to analyze the crucial role which language has in creating this system:

What was fact, what intent, what was framework, what was essence? Strange, the impact of History, the grip it had on us, yet it was nothing but words. Accidental accretions for the most part, leaving most of the story out. We have not yet begun to explore the true power of the Word, I thought. What if we broke all the rules, played games with the evidence, manipulated language itself, made History a partisan ally? Of course, the Phantom was already onto this, wasn't he? Ahead of us again. What were his dialectical machinations if not the dissolution of the natural limits of language, the conscious invention of a space, a spooky artificial no-man's land, between logical alternatives?
(P. 136)

Nixon here voices a view of history-as-artifice that we have seen being developed in much of Coover's earlier fiction,[54] and he is also perceptive about the ability of the Phantom to organize the random elements of history into fictions useful to his cause. But what Nixon fails to realize at this stage is that Uncle Sam is also involved in such deceptive manipulations. While making a complete fool of himself in a hilarious game of golf with Uncle Sam, Nixon listens as his boss presents his own cynical view of history:

Hell, *all* courtroom testimony about the past is ipso facto and teetotaciously a baldface lie, ain't that so? Moonshine! Chicanery! The old gum game! Like history itself—all more or less bunk . . . the fatal slantindicular futility of Fact! Appearances, my boy, appearances. Practical politics consists in ignorin' facts! *Opinion* ultimately governs the world. . . . And so a trial in the midst of all this flux and a slippery past is just one set of bolloxeratin' sophistries agin another—or call 'em mettyfours if you like, approximations, all the same desputt humbuggery.   (P. 86)

Nixon at this point is still too desperate for Uncle Sam's favor to see the deeper relevance of this message ("I still hadn't figured out what Uncle Sam was up to," he admits). Uncle Sam, relying on the American public's bewilderment and rage over their loss of world power, has constructed a simple fiction which conveniently reduces the complex political and historical realities of the world into a neatly organized black-and-white scenario: the Phantom (communism) is after us (the "Free World") and is willing to do anything to destroy us, including the adoption of any number of insidious disguises; anything connected with us is good and must be protected at all costs, while anything connected with the Phantom is evil and must be destroyed.

This simplistic good-versus-evil world view is subtly assisted by news media anxious to present their own picture of a tidy universe reducible to the "5 W's." Coover is careful to establish that the role of supposedly neutral news disseminators such as *Time* or even the more reputable *New York Times* is to grab onto details and organize them into coherent patterns. Like the role of historians, then, the function of journalists exactly parallels the role of Coover in this book, or the role of any artist. But journalists also falsify this experience for the public by pretending that the circuit is closed, that interpretation and ingenious organization is actual fact. Like the West Condonites in *The Brunists* and Dame Society in *The UBA,* the American public in *The Public Burning* is shown to be desperate for assurances and frighteningly susceptible to effective manipulators who wish to establish their own rules. Certainly it is not an accident that the actual deaths of the Rosenbergs and the near-deaths of Tiger Miller and the Association's ballplayers all derive from the public's inability to accept the arbitrary nature of fictional systems.

Although Coover is once again mocking our tendency to be un-critical in accepting the literal veracity of our inventions, he is also well aware of man's basic fear of paradox and transformation. Here, as in all of Coover's fiction, the desire for coherence is presented as intimately related to the artistic impulse itself which seeks to orga-nize a selective number of elements drawn from life's overabun-dance into an aesthetically pleasing and significant whole. As we read *The Public Burning,* we are constantly aware of Coover's efforts to transform the events of history into the system of language called the novel. Richard Nixon informs us that language is used "to tran-scend the confusions, restore the spirit, recreate the society!" (p. 234). In a crucial sense, then, Coover's efforts in this novel become an exemplary achievement of the imagination to cope with confu-sion via language; Nixon's own struggles to solve the Rosenberg puz-zle become a metafictional representation of Coover's efforts to create a truthful presentation of an enormously complex set of ele-ments. In one of the most important theoretical passages in all of his work, Coover summarizes his view of how man tries to deal with dis-order and randomness with the fiction-making process:

Raw data is paralyzing, a nightmare, there's too much of it and man's mind is quickly engulfed by it. Poetry is the art of subordinating facts to the imagina-tion, of giving them shape and visibility, keeping them *personal.* It is, as Mother Luce has said, "fakery in allegiance to the truth," a kind of interpre-tive re-enactment of the overabundant flow of events, "an effective mosaic" assembled from "the fragmentary documents" of life, quickened with auda-cious imagery and a distinct and original prosody: "noses for news lie betwixt ears for music." Some would say that such deep personal involvement, such metaphoric compressions and reliance on inner vision and imaginary "sources," must make objectivity impossible, and TIME would agree with them, but he would find simply illiterate anyone who concluded from this that he was not serving Truth. More: he would argue that objectivity is an im-possible illusion, a "fantastic claim" ("gnostic" is the word on his tongue these days), and as an ideal perhaps even immoral, that *only* through the frankly biased and distorting lens of art is any real grasp of the facts — not to mention Ultimate Truth — even remotely possible.   (P. 320)

This passage, with its acknowledgment of the "frankly biased and distorting lens of art" and its insistence on "subordinating facts to the imagination" could well stand as Coover's assessment of his own attempts in *The Public Burning* to present "an effective mosaic" of the age. It also demonstrates the combination of irony, sympathy, and honesty which typifies Coover's presentation of man's efforts to discover reliable and objective systems.

The Uncle Sam of *The Public Burning* embodies a peculiar mixture of wild energy, folksiness, meanness, and opportunism—a mixture which has helped shape the United States. In the novel's shocking epilogue, however, all of his folksiness disappears and the ugly realities behind his cruel, power-seeking nature are unmasked. When Nixon accuses him of being "a butcher," "a beast," and "no better than the Phantom!", Uncle Sam defends himself by saying that death and destruction are part of what we must accept if the "game" is to be kept running smoothly: "It ain't easy holdin' a community together, order ain't what comes natural, you know that, boy, and a lotta people gotta get killt tryin' to pretend it is, that's how the game is played" (p. 531). Moments later as he prepares to sodomize Nixon—thereby investing him with the "Incarnation of Power" that will manifest itself publicly fifteen years later—Uncle Sam brutally announces that if he is to be loved, he should be loved for the powerful, lusty figure that he has always been:

You wanta make it with me . . . you gotta love me like I really am: Sam Slick, the Yankee Peddler, gun-totin' hustler and tooth-n'-claw tamer of the heathen wilderness, lusty and in everything a screamin' meddler, novus ball-bustin' ordo seclorum, that's me, boy—and goodnight Mrs. Calabash to any damfool what gets in my way! . . . You said it yourself: they's a political axiom that wheresomever a vacuum exists, it will be filled by the nearest or strongest power! Well, you're lookin' at it, mister: an example and fit instrument, big as they come in this world and gittin' bigger by the minute! Towerin' genius disdains a beaten path—it seeks regions hitherto unexplored—so clutch aholt on somethin' an say your prayers, cuz I propose to move immeejitly upon your works!"   (Pp. 531–32)

This frightening revelation, which seems uncomfortably accurate even as a caricature, suggests that the real source of evil in America grows precisely out of its strength and power and its willingness to use these assets to dominate others.

Caught in the midst of these titanic struggles, the Rosenbergs are presented as tragic, largely sympathetic pawns who are perhaps too eager to accept their roles as exemplary victims. Part of their trouble, as Nixon sees it, is their "self-destructive suspicion that they were being watched by some superhuman presence" (p. 104), a suspicion which dehumanizes them by suggesting that they are acting out predetermined roles in a drama controlled by exterior forces. At one point Nixon wonders if the whole Rosenberg case might be simply a complete fabrication, a story which the main characters have duped themselves into believing: "And then what if, I wondered, there were no spy ring at all? What if all these characters *believed* there was and acted out their parts on this assumption, a whole courtroom full of fantasists . . . the Rosenbergs, thinking everybody was crazy, nevertheless fell for it, moving ineluctably into the martyr roles they'd been waiting for all along, eager to be admired and pitied" (p. 135). The Rosenbergs are destroyed, in part, because of their foolish trust in the operations of such arbitrary systems as history and justice. Even Nixon, who is at once both naive and cynical about the operations of history, is quick to realize that "they've been seduced by this. If they could say to hell with History, they'd be home free" (p. 305). Julius especially seems to have been too quick to place his trust in the judicial process, and thus he becomes an easy victim for men like J. Edgar Hoover who know the rules of the game and are able to manipulate all the angles to their own benefit. Unaware that the opposition has changed the rules and rigged the outcome with the umpire, Julius continues to believe until it is too late that justice will somehow prevail. Ethel, on the other hand, is a less passive and more passionate victim; because she is more cynical and self-conscious about the struggle she is engaged in, she is less gullible than Julius and ultimately her death is therefore more heroic. Certainly their willingness to accept their tragic roles is nurtured by their involvement with communism with its own dogmatic insistence that there exist objective systems (historical patterns, economic forces) which are inevitable but which man can decipher to his advantage. Consequently the Rosenbergs not only are victimized but even emphasize their "stage roles" as abstract pawns.

Remarkably, Richard Nixon emerges as the novel's most perceptive and sympathetic character as he lurches, clownlike, toward his destiny "at the center" of apocalypse in Times Square. Coover obviously did extensive research into Nixon's background, from his youth right up through his early political career. All the familiar Nixon qualities are here: the smug self-righteousness, the obvious malice and insecurity masked by a phony affability, the self-pity combined with an appetite for power and success. But Coover's portrayal is no mere caricature, for Nixon emerges as a resilient figure who manages to get up after every pratfall, whose intentions are often misunderstood and misrepresented, and whose paranoia and other peculiar personality traits are convincingly portrayed. We are probably expected to laugh at Nixon's constant comparisons between himself and various other American heroes like Lincoln, Teddy Roosevelt, Horatio Alger; but one of the most telling aspects of the way Coover uses Nixon is the fact that Nixon's career really *does* seem to embrace a lot of the American Dream. In his own bungling but energetic manner, Nixon's desire to be near the sacred "center" represents a fundamental faith in the American way. As he explains, "I have faith: I believe in the American dream, I believe in it because I have seen it come true in my own life. TIME has said that I've had 'a Horatio Alger-like career,' but not even Horatio Alger could have dreamed up a life so American—in the best sense—as mine" (p. 295). From our perspective today—a perspective that is crucial to the many oppositions and juxtapositions that Coover wishes to establish—our awareness of the many abuses and deceits that would follow Nixon's eventual "incarnation" allows us to realize that his career does indeed teach us a great deal about what has gone wrong with the American Dream.

Nixon's role in *The Public Burning* is really twofold: he is both clown and middleman. First of all, he plays the important role of clown who assists the ringmaster—Coover—by creating laughter which will release tension and allow the audience to refocus its attention on the main entertainment at hand. As Coover explains in an interview, this first role helps explain why Nixon was created as a basically sympathetic character: "My interest in Nixon—or my story about him—grew out of my concept of the book as a sequence of circus acts. That immediately brought to mind the notion of clown acts, bringing the show back down to the ground. You have to have a thrilling high-wire number, and then the clown comes on, shoots off a cannon, takes a pratfall, drops his pants, and exits. And then you can throw another high-wire act at them. So naturally I looked for the clownish aspects of my narrator, and you can't have an unsympathetic clown."[55] Obviously the clownish aspect of Nixon's role is very evident: we watch him smear himself with dog excrement, make a fool of himself in front of his family, unwittingly hand Uncle Sam an exploding cigar, and — as a capper — become magically transported from a sexual encounter with Ethel Rosenberg onto the stage in Times Square with his pants down.

Nixon's second role is more complex and difficult to define, but it is equally significant: it is the role of middleman caught between his desire to be loyal to Uncle Sam (and perhaps move himself closer to the day he can be transformed into Sam's incarnation) and his sympathetic identification with the Rosenbergs. As Nixon himself explains his role, "Dwight Eisenhower and Julius Rosenberg would never understand each other, but I could understand — and contain — both" (p. 373). A bit earlier, Nixon had elaborated on his "middle" position by saying, "As the villain, I was also the hero, the bridging took place in me, and I had ever since been the healer of rifts, the party unifier, the fundamentalist who could perceive the Flux" (p. 362). What Nixon wants desperately is what all of Coover's major characters want: some sort of balance, a center point which will provide relief from paradox and the freedom to operate within the extremes of chaos and rigidly fixed patterns. "Paradox was the one thing I hated more than psychiatrists and lady journalists" (p. 136), he admits, and much later in the novel he complains, "Ah, why did nothing in America keep its shape, I wondered? Everything was so fluid, nothing stayed the same, not even Uncle Sam" (p. 334). Nixon yearns for assurances and stability, but as he begins to involve himself in the incredible maze of clues and false scents of the Rosenberg case, he finds himself — like the Unwilling Participant in "Panel Game" — drowning in a sea of undecipherable signs and ambiguous messages. Ironically, Nixon's "drive to center," to which all the events in the book serve to propel him, can only serve to defeat his quest for final answers, for Times Square "is the most paradoxical place in all America" (p. 164). Nixon's role as a sort of super sleuth offers some interesting parallels (and contrasts) to the attempts of the American public at large to uncover meaning. Despite his vested interest in the case, Nixon actually shows more sensitivity and perceptiveness in the Rosenberg proceedings than does the general public. Realizing that the easy explanations of the prosecution and news media are false and oversimplified, Nixon is the only major character other than Justice Douglas who seriously doubts the Rosenbergs' guilt and is willing to do something about it. There is a lot of J. Henry Waugh in Coover's Richard Nixon: his numerological speculations, his mythic concept of names, his corny dramatic daydreams into which he is constantly projecting himself. Above all, Nixon shares with Waugh a terrifically active imagination which he uses to link up details into theories, to constantly invent false scents, and strained, improbable connections. For poor Nixon, everything seems to reverberate with a mysterious significance; thus finding a story he can believe in becomes an almost impossibly heroic effort. "I felt like I'd fallen into a river and was getting swept helplessly along," he whines during the middle of his investigations (p. 334). In his humorous and occasionally poignant efforts to make sense of a shifting, ambiguous universe, Nixon represents us all.

One of the most fascinating results of Nixon's overactive imagination is his tendency to discover—or invent—identifications between himself and the Rosenbergs. As he gradually begins to sort through the details of the case, Nixon soon decides that he and the Rosenbergs are at once both psychic doubles and mirror opposites of one another. In thinking of Julius Rosenberg, for example, Nixon gets right to the heart of the matter when he suggests that their "mirror images" of each other also reflect an intimate bond: "We were more like mirror images of each other, familiar opposites. Left-right, believer-nonbeliever, city-country, accused-accuser, maker-unmaker. I built bridges, he bombed them. . . . He moved to the fringe as I moved to the center" (p. 137). Nixon's sympathetic identification with the Rosenbergs results in part from his finding in their shattered lives a distorted echo of his own Horatio Alger career. Like him, for example, the Rosenbergs were always anxious to uncover the secrets of political and historical events and to participate in the destiny of America. In considering their radical days as college students, Nixon concludes that the Rosenbergs wanted to "get out of the overt activities of college days and withdraw to the very center of the heresy that excited them: why not? After all, I'd become Vice-President of the United States of America by a chain of circumstances not all that different, one thing drifting into the next, carried along by a desire, much like theirs, to reach the heart of things, to participate deeply in life" (p. 128). More fundamental to understanding his obsession with the Rosenbergs, however, is the fact that the Rosenbergs represent to Nixon a secret side of himself that he has always longed to explore but which he has never been allowed to acknowledge publicly. Extremely self-conscious about his own personal inadequacies, Nixon is especially drawn to Ethel Rosenberg, for he finds in her the warmth, idealism, and passion that have been absent in his own life. In his vivid daydreams of the courtship of Ethel and Julius, Nixon, like Henry Waugh, constantly projects himself into the scenes. Significantly, one of his most striking conjurings involves the moment when Ethel said to Julius concerning his political involvements, "I'll help you." To this, Nixon—who has felt rejected and victimized since childhood—comments with a sense of bitterness and longing, "No one had ever said anything like that to me."[56]

Nixon's desire to be at the center of things, to be a part of Uncle Sam's vision, is clearly a yearning for power, but just as importantly, it is a yearning for love. Certainly these desires help illuminate the book's final scene in which Nixon is first of all raped by Uncle Sam and then responds to Sam's conciliatory remarks—"You're my everything, sunshine—*you're my boy!*"—by thinking, "Of course, he was an incorrigible huckster, a sweet-talking con artist, you couldn't trust him, I knew that—but what did it matter? Whatever else he was, he was beautiful (how had I ever thought him ugly?), the most beautiful thing in all the world." Nixon is now "ready at last to do what [he] had never done before," and confesses, "I . . . I *love you, Uncle Sam!*" (p. 534). These same impulses had led Nixon to various sexual fantasies about Ethel Rosenberg earlier in the novel and eventually to a dramatic confrontation with her at Sing Sing in which, for the first time, he is able to act out the role of impassioned lover that he always imagined he could play. Spouting all sorts of melodramatic corn—"Admit it, Ethel! You've dreamed of love all your life! You dream of it now! I know, because I dream of it too! . . . You're an artist, Ethel, a poet! You know what love is, what it might be! All the rest is just lies!" (p. 435)—Nixon finally grabs Ethel and urges her to reject all the "lies of purpose" that have led her to the gas chamber:

> "We've both been victims of the same lie, Ethel! There *is* no purpose, there *are* no causes, all that's just stuff we make up to hold the goddam world together—all we've really got is what we have right here and now: being alive! *Don't throw it away, Ethel!*" (P. 436)

This comic but occasionally moving love scene between Nixon and Ethel is Nixon's finest moment in the novel, for it is the one time that he is able to overcome his role as clown and victim and become his "own man at last!" (p. 442).

In his efforts to sort out meanings and create for himself a freedom in which to maneuver, Nixon should remind us of the UBA's ballplayers. This analogy works on several levels. Like them, Nixon is trying to unravel myth and separate fact from invention; unknown to Nixon, just as it was unknown to the players, everything within his sphere of action *has* been laid out in advance, in part by Coover (the shaper of elements within the novel) and in part by history itself. Just as Paul Trench struggled in the last chapter of *The UBA* with his tragic role, Nixon is constantly bothered with the sensation that he is an actor in a play that has already been written: "Applause, director, actor, script: yes, it was like—and this thought hit me now like a revelation—it was like a little morality play for our generation!" (p. 120). What distresses Nixon about this realization is what lies behind the classic existentialist argument against the existence of God: to admit a higher order is to deny one's own freedom to operate. Yet to deny this higher authority and confront the "lie of purpose" is also difficult for Nixon, as is indicated by his desire to discover final answers and assign everything to predetermined categories. Thus part of his attraction to Uncle Sam is that he views Sam as "our Superchief in an age of Flux" (p. 341). In one of the book's most important scenes, Nixon takes a harrowing ride with the disguised Phantom, whose later designation as "The Creator of Ambiguities" (p. 336) helps crystallize the opposition, and is given a lecture which should sound familiar to readers acquainted with Coover's previous work:

"Look," he said, his voice mellowing, losing its hard twang, "can't we get past all these worn-out rituals, these stupid fuckin' reflexes?" It wouldn't do any good to grab him, I knew. The ungraspable Phantom. He was made of nothing solid, your hand would just slip right through, probably turn leprous forever. "They got nothin' to do with life, you know that, life's always new and changing, so why fuck it up with all this shit about scapegoats, sacrifices, initiations, saturnalias—? . . . life's too big, you can't wrap it up like that!"

(P. 273)

At this stage, Nixon is too frightened to grasp the importance of this message; later, however, he begins making discoveries of his own that confirm the Phantom's basic premise. Realizing that what has been bothering him all along was "that sense that everything was somehow inevitable, as though it had all been scripted out in advance," Nixon goes on to provide a neat summary of what much of Coover's work suggests:

But bullshit! There were no scripts, no necessary patterns, no final scenes, there was just *action,* and then *more action!* Maybe in Russia History had a plot because one was being laid on, but not here—*that was what freedom was all about!* It was what Uncle Sam had been trying to tell me: *Act—act in the living present!* . . . This, then, was my crisis: to accept what I already knew. That there was no author, no director, and the audience had no memories— they got reinvented every day! . . . It served to confirm an old belief of mine: that all men contain all views, right and left, theistic and atheistic, legalistic and anarchical, monadic and pluralistic; and only an artificial—call it political—commitment to consistency makes them hold steadfast to singular positions.   (Pp. 362–63)

It is because of his recognition that "nothing is predictable, anything can happen" that Nixon decides to work out his own script: to go to the Rosenbergs and try to extract a confession, even though he rightly senses that "in a sense [he] was no more free than the Rosenbergs were, [they had] both been drawn into dramas above and beyond those of ordinary mortals" (p. 367). Nixon's few moments with Ethel Rosenberg represent the culmination of his efforts to extract a kind of freedom within the rigid confines of history; the portrayal of these struggles, which blend comedy, pathos, and tragedy in near equal proportions, is *The Public Burning*'s major triumph.

DONALD BARTHELME: 3
THE AESTHETICS OF TRASH

The final possibility is to turn ultimacy, exhaustion, paralyzing self-consciousness and the adjective weight of accumulating history . . . to make something new and valid, the essence whereof would be the impossibility of making something new.

John Barth, "Title"

After a life rich in emotional defeats, I have looked around for other modes of misery, other roads to destruction. Now I limit myself to listening to what people say, and thinking what pamby it is, what they say. My nourishment is refined from the ongoing circus of the mind in motion. Give me the odd linguistic trip, stutter and fall, and I will be content.

Donald Barthelme, *Snow White*

On August 31, 1963 the *New Yorker* carried a story entitled "Player Piano," which was written by an almost totally unknown thirty-year-old writer named Donald Barthelme. Athough few readers or critics could have anticipated it at the time, the appearance of this brief, surreal story in a magazine as rich in literary heritage as the *New Yorker* must today be regarded as one of the most significant events in recent literary history. Ever since that date, the steady stream of Barthelme's fictions that have appeared in the pages of that magazine has undoubtedly served as a constant source of inspiration to other young experimental writers. Indeed, especially during the late 1960s and early 1970s, Barthelme's work probably had more impact on American innovative fiction than that of any other writer.

Even today, more than fifteen years since his *New Yorker* debut, much of Barthelme's work—particularly his output up through his collection *Sadness*—still seems enormously fresh and vital. Because of his stories' resistance to paraphrasable interpretations, their surreal landscapes, unusual characters, and fragmented, seemingly **99** chaotic style, Barthelme's fictional methods have often been compared to those of surrealist or minimalist painters, pop artists, and such writers as Kafka, Beckett, Ionesco, and Borges. More important to this study, however, is the inward, metafictional quality of his writing, the way he uses his fiction to explore the nature of storytelling and the resources left to language and the fiction-maker. As was true with Coover, Barthelme's metafictional concerns are intimately related to his other thematic interests: the difficulties of expressing a total vision of oneself in a fragmenting universe, the failure of most of our social and linguistic systems, the difficulties of making contact or sustaining relationships with others. But above all, Barthelme has been our society's most consistently brilliant critic of the language process itself and of the symbol-making activity of modern man. And like the work of Coover and William Gass, Barthelme's metafictional examinations of how our symbols and fiction systems operate—or fail to operate—offer direct and revealing insights into the sadness, anxieties, terrors, and boredom of the modern world.

Rather than attempting to examine each of Barthelme's novels and collections of fiction—a repetitious process, as it turns out—this study will first of all make some general observations about his thematic and stylistic approaches and will then examine more closely two representative early works: Come Back, Dr. Caligari (1964) and Snow White (1967). This approach will emphasize the metafictional continuity of Barthelme's work and will not analyze the relatively unimportant ways his work has evolved during his career. Barthelme's literary methods and major thematic concerns have remained relatively stable over the years and, in fact, his recent works—with the exception of Great Days (1979)—seem to be suffering from too much of this very "sameness." For a period in the late 1960s, especially in City Life (1970), Barthelme seemed very interested in exploring the possibility of using visual and typographic elements to reinforce certain moods or themes. And, as several critics have suggested, there seems to be a greater sense of acceptance or resignation in Barthelme's recent work, a less rebellious or despairing attitude than we find in the early works.[1] But for the most part Barthelme's metafictional interests have remained remarkably consistent throughout his career.

An Overview of Barthelme's Fictions

The title of one of Barthelme's best short stories, "Critique de la Vie Quotidienne," offers a good summary of what has always been the principal focus of his fiction: the attractions and frustrations offered by ordinary modern life. As Alan Wilde suggests in his perceptive examination of Barthelme's work, it is this scaled-down range of interests which may be what is most distinctive about his work: "The articulation [is] not of the larger, more dramatic emotions to which modernist fiction is keyed but of an extraordinary range of minor, banal dissatisfactions . . . not anomie or accidie or dread but a muted series of irritations, frustrations, and bafflements."[2] Certainly the reaction of Barthelme's characters to "la vie quotidienne" is easy to summarize, as a few of their remarks pointedly indicate:[3]

"I was happier before."

"Like Pascal said: 'The natural misfortune of our mortal and feeble condition is so wretched that when we consider it closely, nothing can console us.'"

"I've been sorry all my life."

"I spoke to Sylvia. 'Do you think this is a good life?' The table held apples, books, long-playing records. She looked up. 'No.'"

"The paradigmatic artistic experience is that of failure. . . . The word *is* unsatisfactory; only a fool would deny it."

Nearly all of Barthelme's work to date has been permeated by this overwhelming sense that life is not as good as we expected it to be—"The world in the evening seems fraught with the absence of promise," says the disgruntled narrator of "La Critique." This lack of satisfaction on the part of Barthelme's characters is produced by a series of closely connected personal anxieties which are neatly balanced by Barthelme's own evident artistic anxieties and the anxieties presumably experienced by Barthelme's readers. Indeed, there is a significant relationship in Barthelme's fiction between his *characters'* struggles to stay alive, to make sense of their lives, and to establish meaningful connections with others, and *Barthelme's own* struggle with the disintegration of fictional forms and the deterioration of language. Often Barthelme's self-conscious, metafictional approach allows these struggles to operate concurrently within the stories (many of his main characters even being surrogate artist figures), the two serving to reinforce or symbolize each other. Meanwhile, *we ourselves* provide a third aspect of this relationship: as we grapple with the elements to organize and make sense of them, we provide an additional sort of analogue or reflection of this struggle with disintegration. The relationship between these personal and metafictional concerns can be seen more clearly in the following schematic listing:

PERSONAL	METAFICTIONAL
Ennui with life's familiarities (both animate and inanimate); ongoing personal fight against the "cocoon of habituation which covers everything if we let it" (S, p. 179)	Anticipation of the reader's sense of boredom; need to invent new revitalized literary forms
Sense of personal, political, and social fragmentation	Impulse toward collage, verbal fragmentation, free association, and other methods of juxtaposition to break down familiar sense of order
Inability to sustain relationships with others (especially women)	Inability to rely on literary conventions (linear plots, notions of cause and effect, realistic character development, etc.) which tie things together into a pleasing whole
Sexual frustration and anxiety; sense of impotence and powerlessness in comparison with others	Artistic frustration and anxiety; belief that art is useless and can never effect significant change
Inability to know; impulse to certainty blocked (and mocked) by lies, disguises, simplistic formulas, and the irreducible mystery of life	Refusal to explain or clarify, denial of hidden or "deep meanings" with tendency instead to "stay on the surface"

Inability to communicate with others; frustrating sense that language blocks or betrays the feelings one wishes to express	Suspicion that language has become "drek," so full of "stuffing" and clichés that meaningful communication with an audience is impossible
Inability to create change in one's condition, a condition made more difficult by one's self-consciousness which serves to paralyze one from spontaneous, possibly liberating, activities	Sense that one must accept language's limits and its trashy condition (hence the "recycling tendency," with clichés and drek being transformed into new objects); self-consciousness making the telling of traditional stories impossible

In Barthelme's fiction, then, the sources of dissatisfaction as well as the means of coping with it are intimately connected for both the artist and the ordinary person. Although the specific manifestations are varied, these parallel struggles often have to do with the attempt to maintain a fresh, vital relationship with either words or women—an obsession which is evident in the works of many other contemporary male metafictionists such as Gass, Coover, Barth, Sukenick, and Federman. Moreover, Barthelme's characters are typically shown not only to be painfully aware of their own personal and sexual inadequacies but, more generally, to be disgruntled or bored with the systems they rely on to deal with their fragmented, meaningless lives. Simply stated, their fundamental problem is twofold: on the one hand, they are bored with their humdrum lives and humdrum relationships with others and are therefore constantly seeking a means of overcoming their rigidly patterned but ultimately inconsequential lives; on the other hand, Barthelme's characters fear any loss of security and are unable fully to open themselves to experience because they find it so confusing, ambiguous, and unstable and because they don't trust the systems at their disposal for coping with it. Paradoxically, then, their very awareness of the dismal realities around them makes it all the more difficult for them to face up to the frightening moment when they must go forth and confront "the new." The narrator of "Subpoena," after being forced to dismantle his "monster-friend" Charles, offers a good summary of these mixed feelings: "Without Charles, without his example, his exemplary quietude, I run the risk of acting, the risk of risk. I must participate, I must leave the house and walk about" (*S*, p. 116). Even more pointed are the remarks of the narrator of "The Dolt" (possibly Barthelme himself) regarding a would-be writer's inability to think of anything to say: "I myself have these problems. Endings are elusive, middles are nowhere to be found, but worst of all is to begin, to begin, to begin" (*UP*, p. 65).

Thus, the question for Barthelme's characters remains: given a reality which is chaotic, and given the fact that the system of signs developed by man to help him deal with reality is inadequate—"Signs are signs and some of them lie," says the narrator of "Me and Miss Mandible"—how does one generate enough humanly significant, exciting moments to insure that one is alive? Certainly one cannot rely on any exterior systems to help find assurances and solutions. As Alan Wilde suggests, "In a general way, what Barthelme takes his stand against are pretentions to certainty and the insistence on perfection; large demands and great expectations; dogmatisms and theories of all kinds."[4] Like Coover's characters, then, Barthelme's characters find themselves constantly confronting worn-out systems which fail to operate successfully—systems such as the government, the church, the military, the news media, and a changing series of intellectual systems. (Psychiatry, existentialism, literary criticism, and Freudian psychology are among Barthelme's favorite targets.) Indeed, Barthelme often seems to suggest, perhaps playfully, that the acceptance of any final claims to truth and certainty may result in a deadening of our ability to respond naturally to experience. In "The Photograph" Barthelme suggests precisely this point when he has one scientist suggest to another that they should burn the photographs they have discovered of the human soul:

"It seems to me to boil down to this: Are we better off *with* souls, or just possibly *without* them?"

"Yes. I see what you mean. You prefer the uncertainty."

"Exactly. It's more creative. Take for example my, ah, arrangement with your wife, Dorothea. Stippled with uncertainty. At moments, we are absolutely *quaking* with nonspecific anxiety. I enjoy it. *Dorothea* enjoys it. The humdrum is defeated. Momentarily, of course." (*GP*, pp. 158–59)

As Barthelme well knows, any solution to casting off this "cocoon of habituation"—which deadens our responses to art, to other human beings, and to ordinary reality—can only be provisional in nature. But the key for Barthelme, just as it was for Coover, lies in our "keeping the circuits open," in our remaining open to experience sufficiently so that new responses and new systems can be produced to generate the freshness and vitality we all seek. This is the overt subject matter of a number of Barthelme's best fictions, such as "The Balloon" and "Daumier," in which Barthelme examines how art can rescue man from the ordinary.

Barthelme's much-analyzed metafiction, "The Balloon," presents a wonderfully deft and amusing allegory about the status of an art object's relationship to both its creator and its public.[5] As with Coover's "The Magic Poker," the narrator of "The Balloon" opens his story by describing his creation and then reminding us of his control over it: "The Balloon, beginning at a point on Fourteenth Street, the exact location of which I cannot reveal, expanded northward all one night, while people were sleeping, until it reached the Park. There I stopped it" (*UP,* p. 15). Although we discover in the very last paragraph of the story that this balloon had a specific meaning and served a specific purpose for the narrator—(it is revealed to be "a spontaneous autobiographical disclosure, having to do with the unease I felt at your absence, and with sexual deprivation" (*UP,* p. 21), the narrator apparently does not intend for this private meaning to be apprehended by his audience. Indeed, his main interest seems to be simply to add another interesting object to the landscape of Manhattan. As he explains:

But it is wrong to speak of "situations," implying sets of circumstances leading to some resolution, some escape of tension; there were no situations, simply the balloon hanging there . . . at that moment there was only *this balloon,* concrete particular, hanging there.   (*UP,* pp. 15–16)

Not surprisingly, the public experiences some initial difficulties in its attempts to analyze the balloon; but eventually the fundamental epistemological uncertainty of the times forces people to take a more practical approach to the balloon's presence:

There was a certain amount of initial argumentation about the "meaning" of the balloon; this subsided, because we have learned not to insist on meanings, and they are rarely even looked for now, except in cases involving the simplest, safest phenomena.   (*UP,* p. 16)

Rather than seeking external "meanings," the public soon contents itself with using the balloon for its own private uses: "It was agreed that since the meaning of the balloon could never be known absolutely, extended discussion was pointless, or at least less purposeful than the activities of those who, for example, hung green and blue paper lanterns from the warm gray underside, in certain streets, or seized the occasion to write messages on the surface" (*UP,* p. 16). Soon the balloon is also being used much like any other arbitrary coordinate system to assist people in orienting themselves: "People began, in a curious way, to locate themselves in relation to aspects of the balloon: 'I'll be at the place where it dips down into Forty-seventh Street almost to the sidewalk, near the Alamo Chile House'" (*UP,* p. 20).

The balloon also serves another function that reveals much about the role that Barthelme believes that art can play for a regimented, easily bored public. As the narrator suggests, the balloon offers an archetypal representation of the limitless freedom of the imagination itself:

It was suggested that what was admired about the balloon was finally this: that it was not limited or defined. . . . This ability of the balloon to shift in shape, to change, was very pleasing, especially to people whose lives were rather rigidly patterned, persons to whom change, although desired, was not available. The balloon . . . offered the possibility, in its randomness, of mislocation of the self, in contradistinction to the grid of precise, rectangular pathways under our feet. The amount of specialized training currently needed, and the consequent desirability of long-term commitments, has been occasioned by the steadily growing importance of complex machinery, in virtually all kinds of operations; as this tendency increases, more and more people will turn, in bewildered inadequacy, to solutions for which the balloon may stand as a prototype, or "rough draft."   (*UP,* pp. 20–21)

Like all good art objects, then, the balloon effectively provides a sense of freedom and a moment of distraction from the mundane, stifling effects of reality. Because its shifting, ambiguous surface allows it to be played with and freely interpreted, the balloon also serves as a reminder of the freedom we all have in confronting experience itself.

In "Daumier," Barthelme explores how the fictional "construction of surrogates" allows a writer to accommodate himself to his unsatisfactory "real" life. The story—which in its labyrinthine structure resembles a miniaturized *Universal Baseball Association*—opens with the writer/narrator Daumier explaining to his wife the nature of the "great dirty villain," the self: "Now, here is the point about the self: it is insatiable. It is always, always hankering. It is what you might call rapacious to a fault. The great flaming mouth to the thing is never going to be stuffed full" (*S*, pp. 163–64). In response to this view of the self, Daumier has decided that the construction of surrogate selves in his fiction will help ease his plight. As he suggests, "The false selves in their clatter and boister and youthful brio will slay and bother and push out and put to all types of trouble the original, authentic self" (*S*, p. 163). In fact, Daumier has already succeeded in creating a fictional Daumier who "is doing very well" because he "knows his limits. He doesn't overstep. Desire has been reduced in him to a minimum" (*S*, p. 164). During parts of the story we observe this second Daumier operating in his own fictional setting, transporting a number of lovely young women across the "plains and pampas of consciousness" (*S*, p. 164). After a while the fictional Daumier becomes especially enamored of one particularly attractive woman, a long-legged, kindly lady named Celeste; and, as in *The UBA* and "The Magic Poker," we begin to observe a "real" character becoming obsessed with his own creation. Thus the real Daumier notes at one point, "I then noticed that I had become rather fond—fond to a fault—of a person in the life of my surrogate. It was of course the girl Celeste. My surrogate found her attractive and no less did I; this was a worry. I began to wonder how I could get her out of his life and into my own" (*S*, p. 177).

Sensing that his one fictional construction is not really enough to sate his rapacious self, Daumier next decides to invent another surrogate, "a quiet, thoughtful chap who leads a contemplative life" (*S*,

p. 178). This second person provides us with one of the most direct statements available of what Barthelme feels must be done to accommodate oneself to the world. After a lengthy period of self-analysis, he says, "It is easy to be satisfied if you get out of things what inheres in them, but you must look closely, take nothing for granted, let nothing become routine. You must fight against the cocoon of habituation which covers everything if you let it. There are always openings, if you can find them. There is always something to do" (S, p. 179). This solution sounds remarkably similar to the advice Henry Waugh gives himself just after he sacrificed Jock Casey: "The circuit wasn't closed, his or any other: there were patterns, but they were shifting and ambiguous and you had a lot of room inside them" (UBA, p. 143). At the story's end, the fictional Celeste has entered into the "real" Daumier's life, while he has temporarily packed away his other surrogates until he feels he will need them. Daumier seems well aware that this solution is but a momentary relief from the demands of the self, but nevertheless this projection has provided exactly the sort of imaginative "opening" that frees the ordinary from its tediousness and allows us to go on. The story concludes with Daumier himself rephrasing his surrogate's advice: "The self cannot be escaped, but it can be, with ingenuity and hard work, distracted. There are always openings, if you can find them, there is always something to do" (S, p. 183).

Barthelme also knows, however, that the ability of the artist to create a new, vital form of distraction is a self-generating problem, for what is new and fresh today is destined to soon lose these qualities. Often, as in "The Glass Mountain," Barthelme depicts man striving to unlock the new only to discover that what he has produced is merely another cliché. In this story, the artist/narrator seeks to escape from his ugly, hostile surroundings to the magical realm of art; but what he finds is merely more conventions, more clichés: when he finally reaches the end of the search he tells us, "I approached the symbol, with its layer of meaning, but when I touched it, it changed into only a beautiful princess" (CL, p. 71). "The Flight of the Pigeons" deals with the difficulties of sustaining the new even more directly, as when its narrator says, "Some things appear to be wonders in the beginning, but when you have become familiar with them, are not wonderful at all. . . . Some of us have even thought of folding the show—closing it down" (S, p. 139). Clearly this struggle with the new has wide implications for the ordinary man as well as for the artist; indeed, as many other metafictionists have observed (see, for example, John Barth's "Title" in *Lost in the Funhouse*), people's tendency to become tired of the familiar is just as damaging to personal relationships as it is to the artist. Thus we should realize that the narrator's remarks in "The Party" apply to us equally as well as they do to the writer: "When one has spoken a lot one has already used up all of the ideas one has. You must change the people you are speaking to so that you appear, to yourself, to be still alive" (S, p. 61).

Compounding the difficulties of both the artist and the ordinary individual is the decay of the communication process itself at a time when modern man is becoming increasingly inundated with supposedly meaningful symbols. "You can't even eat breakfast any more without eating symbols as much as anything else," said William Gass in a recent interview,[6] and Barthelme's fiction constantly examines the various ways that man is betrayed by these very symbols. The main problem facing us all, of course, is the trashy, brutalized condition of language itself which makes our communication process almost completely bog down—hence the "sludge quality" of our language—how it is filled with "stuffing"—which is described more thoroughly in *Snow White*. As a result of his views about language, Barthelme often suggests that language itself may be responsible for the isolation of his characters, their inability to put the pieces of their lives together, and their inability to sustain personal relations. Consequently, ambiguity constantly stalks their lives. They are, quite literally, unable to make sense of their lives or of what is going on around them—though, as the earlier quotation from "The Party" suggests, there does seem to be the Beckett-like hope that if they go on, if their *words* go on, things may finally come together. One indication of this self-reflexive interest in the linguistic process is the way these characters so often question each other about the meaning and implication of words, though they are almost never able to come up with any definite conclusions. The failures and dissatisfactions created by these linguistic investigations serve to reflect the larger pattern of failure and dissatisfaction in their lives. Information can be gathered, of course—for example, about Robert Kennedy in "Robert Kennedy Saved from Drowning" or about one's father in "Views of My Father Weeping"—but final answers or insights are beyond them. This epistemological skepticism, evident in many Barthelme stories, tends to keep our attention focused on the surface of the events. When his characters—or we ourselves—try to gain "deeper" insights or teleological explanations about what has happened, the search inevitably ends futilely with our efforts often being anticipated and directly mocked.

Both "Robert Kennedy Saved from Drowning" and "Views of My Father Weeping" offer formal critiques of the whole information-gathering process. Each of these stories, which Jerome Klinkowitz has termed "experiments in epistemology," is composed of brief, seemingly unrelated bits of prose which will supposedly provide enough information to clear up the basic mystery of their subjects.[7] "Views" opens with a casual introduction of violence: "An aristocrat was riding down the street in his carriage. He ran over my father" (CL, p. 3). The rest of the story describes the narrator's frustrating efforts to uncover the meaning of this murder and of his father's character. As Coover does in his cubist stories, Barthelme here takes all the elements of a familiar literary framework—in this case, the stock characters and language of a cheap nineteenth-century melodrama or detective thriller—and manipulates our conventional expectations for his own purposes. Much of the enjoyment of the piece comes from Barthelme's uncanny ability to mimic worn-out style and conventions while totally undermining or trivializing the easy assumptions they make. This mimicry also tends to keep our attention focused on the process of the story unfolding while distancing us from its human reality.

Not surprisingly, the story's narrator finds it difficult to relate the bits of contradictory evidence he uncovers. In fact, he finds even the simplest of statements difficult to make without qualification—he is not even sure that he can identify his father. As he tells us, "Yes, it is possible that it is not my father who sits there in the center of the bed weeping. It may be someone else, the mailman, the man who delivers the groceries, an insurance salesman or tax collector, who knows. However, I must say, it resembles my father" (CL, pp. 3–4).

While trying to maintain a straightforward method of investigation, the narrator soon discovers that anything he is told is qualified by later considerations. For example, when he questions a witness, he is told that the man in the carriage "looked 'like an aristocrat'"; but this just leads him to consider the fact this description might simply refer to the carriage itself because "any man sitting in a handsome carriage with a driver on the box . . . tends to look like an aristocrat" (*CL,* p. 4). Certainly the old signposts and clichés no longer seem useful to his investigation. When he discovers that the driver's livery was blue and green, for instance, this seems like a substantial clue. But even this proves to be useless because, as he explains, "In these days one often finds a servant aping the more exquisite color combinations affected by his masters. I have even seen them in red trousers although red trousers used to be reserved, by unspoken agreement, for the aristocracy" (*CL,* p. 8).

Finally, when the denouement arrives, the narrator is able to talk with Lars Bang, the driver of the carriage, who explains the death away as a mere accident caused by the father himself. But within one sentence of this "final resolution," contradictory data is added by a dark-haired girl who defiantly announces that "Bang is an absolute bloody liar" (*CL,* p. 17). The story ends with the word "Etc.," an ending which, as Jerome Klinkowitz suggests, "cheats us of the supposedly false satisfaction fiction supplies"[8] and which also suggests that we are familiar enough with the material at hand to continue the story ourselves if we should desire.

Like "Views of My Father Weeping," the "Robert Kennedy" story also mocks our traditional epistemological assumptions. Ostensibly the story aims at illuminating the nature of an ambiguous referent— the life of Robert Kennedy—by the usual method of gathering bits of factual and interpretive information. These descriptions are assembled for us, but because the reports are so contradictory and banal, we never gain any real insight into the subject. Once more, much of the information we receive is immediately qualified or contradicted.[9] The story opens with the news that Kennedy "is neither abrupt with nor excessively kind to associates. Or he is both abrupt and kind" (*UP,* p. 33). When Kennedy himself talks, his words are inevitably created out of political clichés—"Obsolete facilities and growing demands have created seemingly insoluble difficulties and present methods of dealing with these difficulties offer little prospect of relief" — pure blague — "It's an expedient in terms of how not to destroy a situation which has been a long time gestating, or, again, how *to* break it up if it appears that the situation . . ." — or useless redundancies — "I spend my time sending and receiving messages. Some of these messages are important. Others are not" (*UP,* pp. 36, 41, 33). As Klinkowitz has pointed out, the main thrust of the story is basically that "the conventional epistemology fails,"[10] and this failure is underlined in the last section in which Kennedy is saved by the narrator from drowning. Because of the story's title and because of the dramatic nature of the events, we surely expect a revelation into Kennedy's character at last. But even here Kennedy "retains his mask" and when he emerges from the water, he offers a noncommittal and very *un*revealing cliché: "Thank you" (*UP,* p. 44).

Because of their skepticism and self-consciousness, most of Barthelme's characters react very differently from Coover's inveterate fiction makers to the prospect of a random, absurd universe. In "See the Moon," one of Barthelme's most famous stories, the narrator provides a striking metaphor for the epistemological dilemmas faced by so many Barthelme characters. The story opens with the narrator explaining that he is conducting certain "very important lunar hostility studies"; he goes on to explain that "at night the moon [is] graphed by the screen wire, if you squint. The Sea of Tranquility occupying squares 47 through 108" (*UP,* pp. 151–52). If we consider the relationship that exists between the narrator, the moon, and the porch screen he uses as a personal grid system, we find a nicely defined metaphor for the way Barthelme seems to view man, reality, and the fragile, artificial systems man has devised to help him organize his experience. Like the equally arbitrary grid system developed by Descartes for analytic geometry, the screen is a neatly patterned but artificial system which doesn't give us any clues about the real nature of the moon (Kant's *ding an sich*). Yet the screen is *useful* to the narrator in that it creates a certain temporary order and meaning; like the balloon in "The Balloon," the screen itself remains ambiguous even though it can be used to help us locate ourselves in relation to other objects. As we have discussed in chapter 1, from the postmodern perspective we can view *all* of our fictional grid systems—including science, mathematics, history, and art—to be, epistemologically speaking, really no different from this porch screen.

The narrator in "See the Moon" is therefore representative of most Barthelme characters in that he perceives the world, in Alan Wilde's words, "as a kind of haphazard, endlessly organizable and reorganized playground."[11] Unlike Coover's typical characters, who tend to invent systems and then rely on them too absolutely, Barthelme's characters are often all too aware of the way reality seems determined to resist our efforts to categorize and control it. "See the moon," says the narrator after explaining how his screen porch functions. "It hates us" (*UP*, p. 152). Because of his desire to discover some underlying sense of coherency in the elements of existence, the narrator has pinned objects from his past onto his wall. These objects are "souvenirs" which he hopes "will someday merge, blur—cohere is the word, maybe—into something meaningful. A grand word meaningful" (*UP*, p. 152). Within the story itself, these souvenirs are transformed into the text of words which the narrator produces for us with the same hope of generating some sort of meaning. Before us pass fragments of his past life, anecdotes about his family, his friends, his own experiences, none of which he is able to organize into the neat patterns, supported by explanatory cause-effect relationships, that were available to previous literary generations. Acutely aware of how his self-consciousness about the limitations of our systems hinders his ability to create pleasing, well-rounded wholes, the narrator jealously comments about contemporary painters:

I wanted to be a painter. . . . You don't know how I envy them. They can pick up a Baby Ruth wrapper on the street, glue it to the canvas (in the right place, of course, there's that), and lo! people crowd about and cry "A real Baby Ruth wrapper, by God, what could be realer than that!" Fantastic metaphysical advantage. You hate them, if you're ambitious.   (*UP*, p. 152)

Unable to connect the pieces together—hence the famous statement, "Fragments are the only form I trust"[12]—this narrator can only wistfully hope that the fragments of his existence will someday mysteriously come together. In the meantime, what frightens him the most is the prospect of initiating his as yet unborn child into this whole process:

> You see, Gog of mine, Gog o' my heart, I'm just trying to give you a little briefing here. I don't want you unpleasantly surprised. I can't stand a startled look. Regard me as a sort of Distant Early Warning System. Here is the world and here are the knowledgeable knowers knowing. What can I tell you? What has been pieced together from the reports of travelers. . . . What can I do for him? I can get him into A.A., I have influence. And make sure no harsh moonlight falls on his new soft head.   (*UP,* pp. 164–65)

What we have been examining thus far has been the "first level" of Barthelme's fiction—the personal struggles of his characters with disintegration and fragmentation. On the second level, however, the reader is usually aware that Barthelme himself is engaged in the same epistemological struggles that plague his characters—struggles that are intimately related to the disintegration of fictional forms and the decay of language itself. Self-conscious about the inadequacies of such fictional conventions as linear sequence, causal explanations, and well-rounded characters, Barthelme finds himself in a difficult position as a writer. As we have already seen in our discussion of "Robert Kennedy" and "Views of My Father," Barthelme feels that he cannot offer his readers the easy assurances which lie at the center of most realistic narratives, and he is equally suspicious about the ability of language to probe beneath the surfaces of things. In "Paraguay," for example, Barthelme suggests that the modern experience presents special difficulties to the writer simply because of the sheer quantity of *things* that we are bombarded with:

> The softening of language usually lamented as a falling off from former practice is in fact a clear response to the proliferation of surfaces and stimuli. Imprecise sentences lessen the strain of close tolerances. Silence is also available in the form of white noise.   (*CL,* p. 27).

Faced with both the "proliferation of surfaces and stimuli" and the loss of confidence in our systems' ability to explain and define reality, Barthelme's work is characterized by his refusal to present well-rounded characters, supply easy explanations, or make causal connections. As a result his characters never develop into psychologically convincing people so much as mere linguistic consciousnesses or collections of odd words. Realistic characters and events, suggests Barthelme, are patently false because the elements out of which they are created—words, plot conventions, arbitrary connections— have proven unable to depict faithfully how human beings operate in the world. So, instead, Barthelme contents himself with creating literary fragments, anecdotes, and sketches which he skillfully builds out of the clichés and verbal drek of our contemporary idiom. Barthelme's emphasis on "surface" and on process is further heightened by his manipulation of style and the technological aspects of print on the page which serve to keep the reader aware of the writing itself and to discourage the reader's search for "depth." Wilde summarizes this tendency as follows:

The use of collage, of fragments, of pictures and black spaces; the sudden irruption of large, capitalized remarks, which may or may not comment on the surrounding text; . . . the constant experimentation with styles, ranging from the severely paratactic to the most involutedly subordinative: all function, of course, to call attention to the fact of writing (or *ecriture,* as we are learning to say), to the medium in which Barthelme and his perceptual field intersect.[13]

Thus like Coover, Gass, and other metafictionists, Barthelme often creates fictions which reflexively examine their own status as artifacts even as they proceed. The point which seems to unify the intentions of all the metafictionists is that there is a close analogy between the author's difficulties in composing and organizing a work of fiction and our own attempts to build the fiction we call our life. It is at this point that the second, reflexive level of Barthelme's fiction intersects with the first and third levels: the point at which personal and literary disintegration serve to mirror and reinforce each other.

As has already been mentioned, this third level in Barthelme's fiction is the role that we ourselves play as we confront the often absurd, seemingly random and meaningless elements in his fictions. Typically these fictions present us with a surreal mixture of the mundane and the peculiar; often the structure employed is fragmentary, with bits of words and visual elements threatening to disassemble completely into noncontiguous puzzles or, as with Kafka, mysteriously appearing to present themselves as ambiguous allegories. Like the "protagonists" of the first two levels—i.e., Barthelme's characters and Barthelme himself—we as readers probably sense that it is up to us to hold the pieces together, to find hidden clues in the elements before us, to create some sense of order and meaning without our responses being too rigidly determined. Like Barthelme's characters, we find ourselves trying to unmask the meaning of symbols and to uncover patterns—and, similarly, our efforts are usually mocked. We may even begin to share their suspicions that any order or meaning to be found is the product primarily of our own fiction-making ability, that Barthelme's stories are "merely" what they first appear to be: wonderfully deft and amusing verbal constructions that show us something of the nature of contemporary living, but which don't really "mean" anything in the way we would expect. Although I do not wish to push the "nonmeaning" aspect of Barthelme's fiction too far,[14] the possibility that many of his fictions can be analyzed as constructions to be encountered as we encounter other objects in the world brings up several crucial points about contemporary innovative fiction.

Like Beckett, Joyce, and Flaubert, Barthelme often seems primarily interested in assembling all possible combinations of words, and in the process he exposes the condition of the current status of our language. Thus like many modern painters—and again like Beckett—his art is reductionary in that he throws away ideas and concentrates instead on the effect of words themselves. Given Barthelme's pessimistic attitudes about the condition of contemporary language, probably the best phrase to describe his fiction is one which he coined himself in *Snow White*: "the leading edge of the trash phenomenon." In the much-quoted passage which produced this phrase, a manufacturer of plastic buffalo humps gives the following speech which reveals what Barthelme's "aesthetics of trash" is all about:

Now you're probably familiar with the fact that the per-capita production of trash in this country is up from 2.75 pounds per day in 1920 to 4.5 pounds per day in 1965, the last year for which we have figures, and is increasing at the rate of about four percent a year. Now that rate will probably go up, because it's *been* going up, and I hazard that we may very well soon reach a point where it's 100 percent. Now at such a point, you will agree, the question turns from a question of disposing of this 'trash' to a question of appreciating its qualities, because, after all, it's 100 percent, right? And there can no longer be any question of 'disposing' of it, because it's all there is, and we will simply have to learn how to 'dig' it. . . . So that's why we're in humps, right now, more really from a philosophical point of view than because we find them a great moneymaker. They are 'trash,' and what in fact could be more useless or trashlike? It's that we want to be on the leading edge of this trash phenomenon, the everted sphere of the future, and that's why we pay particular attention, too, to those aspects of language that may be seen as a model of the trash phenomenon.   (*SW*, pp. 97–98)

By building his novels and stories precisely out of "those aspects of language that may be seen as a model of the trash phenomenon," Barthelme reflects the increasing banality and vulgarization that is rapidly becoming 100 percent of our society. Barthelme shares with both Coover and Gass a deep concern for the way in which language has assumed a dead, cliché-ridden character, as is demonstrated in today's mass culture represented by television, newspapers, movies, and supermarket best-sellers. For Barthelme, however, Gass's call for a new poetry of language and Coover's for a revitalization of fictional designs is useless, for the "trash" is "already 100 percent." What is needed, then, is a means of appreciating the trash ("digging it")—an appreciation which Barthelme assists by building new artifacts out of the verbal garbage that he finds around him.

An obvious, but perhaps inexact, analogy that comes immediately to mind would be one between Barthelme's fictions and a painter's collage, which is similarly built out of "found" elements. And, indeed, the analogy with painting in general and with the collage in particular is very useful in understanding the relationship between many of Barthelme's fictions and their "meaning." Up until now, we have been considering Barthelme's fictions primarily as "meaning systems" which indicate, however indirectly, something about current conditions in the world. As our examination of Barthelme's metafictional impulses has already indicated, his fictions can be analyzed as "saying something" about related personal and literary dissatisfactions with the modern world. Barthelme's work also mirrors other specific aspects of the world in much the same way that a painting by El Greco or Rembrandt might indicate something about a particular country's mode of dress, its architecture, or even its system of values. On the other hand, like some of Coover's fictions, Barthelme's works often seem to function mainly as ways of looking at things; in this respect, his fictions are like the paintings by the cubists or the Italian Futurists: they aren't nearly as interesting for what they themselves have to tell us about the world as for presenting different methods of viewing or thinking about it.

Obviously these analogies with painting are inexact and are open to objection. Yet it is interesting that we have come to accept this idea of the art object *as object* in painting—and we have always accepted it in music—but the idea has never really caught on in fiction writing. This probably has to do with the nature of the writer's medium: words seem to always be "pointing" somewhere, to have a referential quality about them that lines and colors or sounds and rhythms do not necessarily possess (William Gass discusses this idea at several points in *Fiction and the Figures of Life*). Many contemporary writers, however, are seeking new means and strategies with which to focus the reader's attention on the book as object. In an important early essay entitled "After Joyce," Barthelme discussed this idea of the work of fiction as a new reality or object in the world, rather than as a comment upon a previously existing reality. Referring to what he terms "the mysterious shift that takes place as soon as one says that art is not about something but *is* something," Barthelme says:

With Joyce, and to a lesser degree Gertrude Stein, fiction altered its placement in the world in a movement so radical that its consequences have yet to be assimilated. Satisfied with neither the existing world nor the existing literature, Joyce and Stein modify the world by adding to its store of objects the literary object—which is then encountered in the same way as other objects in the world. The question becomes: what is the nature of the new object? Here one can see an immediate result of the shift. Interrogating older works, the question is: what do they say about the world and being in the world? But the literary object is itself "world" and the theoretical advantage is that in asking it questions you are asking questions of the world itself.[15]

Barthelme acknowledges that the point he makes here is hardly new, although it was not usually emphasized by the theme-conscious writers who largely dominated American fiction in the 1930s, 1940s, and 1950s. But this idea lies at the center of innovative fiction of the past ten years, with its emphasis on the writer's obligation not to mirror reality or express something (be they private or social realities), but to *add new objects to the world.*

Let's imagine Barthelme sitting in his Manhattan apartment—his "studio," we'll call it—about to begin building one of these "literary objects." All around him are *words.* Words issue from his radio and television, which drone on tirelessly. Newspapers cover his floor, along with all sorts of popular magazines and obscure, scholarly journals. The bookshelves which line his walls are filled with the works of his favorite authors (Kleist, Kafka, Kierkegaard, William Gass, Walker Percy). Through his open window he can hear people walking down the street exchanging banalities and gossip; words even seem to linger in the air from the incredibly boring, pretentious party he went to the night before. Obviously, he has plenty of material at hand, but how to put it down, how to organize it? As a postmodern metafictionist, Barthelme sees no reason to limit what he can build to what resembles everyday life, a model which will mimic an exterior order. Besides, what with cameras, recording devices, xerox machines, and assembly lines, reality is being reproduced often enough as it is. He is not even sure that there *is* an exterior order; maybe cause and effect, beginnings and endings, and character motivation are just conventions developed by fiction writers. Like many other modern artists, Barthelme is also interested in getting his audience more actively involved in the artistic process; he wants to force their participation, break down the old creator/consumer barriers. So he won't order his stories in a linear way or give them the sort of "finish" his readers expect; he'll even add random elements which the reader may or may not attempt to assimilate, along with other elements ostensibly untransformed from the real world. One of his intentions is to make the reader create his/her own connections and associations in order to link them up—let them do some of the work. He is finally ready to begin writing:

> We defended the city as best as we could. The arrows of the Comanches came in clouds. The war clubs of the Comanches clattered on the soft, yellow pavements. There were earthworks along the Boulevard Mark Clark and the hedges had been laced with sparkling wire. People were trying to understand. I spoke to Sylvia. "Do you think this is a good life?" The table held apples, books, long-playing records. She looked up. "No." Patrols of paras and volunteers with armbands guarded the tall, flat buildings. We interrogated the captured Comanche. Two of us forced his head back while another poured water into his nostrils. His body jerked, he choked and wept. . . . And I sat there getting drunker and drunker and more in love and more in love. We talked.
> "Do you know Fauré's 'Dolly'?"
> "Would that be Gabriel Fauré?"
> "Then I know it," she said. "May I say that I play it at certain times, when I am sad, or happy, although it requires four hands." *(UP,* p. 3)

This passage, taken from the opening to "The Indian Uprising," was chosen because it contains much of what is characteristic of Barthelme's fiction: the surrealism, the sense of chaos and fragmentation, the unexpected combination of words, the casual overtones of violence, the sexual despair, the sadness, the banality, the clichés. We might say, "Excellent! Barthelme has created a brilliant symbol of the modern wasteland." But it can also be argued that although we can apply Barthelme's story to the world in this manner—just as we can apply Euclid's geometry to the everyday world—this is not to say that Barthelme's intention is really to make a statement "about the world" (just as Euclid's geometry, so it turns out, is not really "about the world" either). Indeed, the characteristics listed above may be viewed as deriving not from the nature of the world but from the nature of modern language.

To see what this means, we might imagine a sculptor who is building an object which he covers with strips of print from his morning newspaper. Someone who sees this object might say, "Oh, I see—this artist is trying to comment on the United States' involvement in Angola, along with something about dissention on this year's Yankees." But because newsprint is the medium of this artist, it might be argued that although his object does "say" these things, it really shouldn't be analyzed as being "about" them; actually, such an object could probably best be viewed, in the self-referential sense we have been discussing, as being "about" newsprint as a medium. In short, considering the nature of the society from which Barthelme draws his materials (and his "materials" are words, concepts, systems of thought), it shouldn't be surprising that his stories frequently exhibit violence, confusion, utter banality, and cliché, hackneyed thinking. The fact that words are "trashy" and that the rational systems built out of them are full of holes can, in some respects, be seen as being beside the point for Barthelme — though not necessarily for his characters — just as painters have not been kept from using straight lines in their work despite Einstein's discoveries about the curved nature of space. Thus the process involved here can be likened to a "recycling approach" in which the drek of familiar, banal language is charged with a renewed freshness via the mysterious sea-change of art.

At the end of a remarkable piece of metafiction entitled "Sentence," Barthelme observes that both writers and philosophers have had to face the fact that because language is a human system, it therefore has its limitations. This discovery has been "a disappointment, to be sure, but it reminds us that the sentence itself is a man-made object, not the one we wanted of course, but still a construction of man, a structure to be treasured for its weaknesses, as opposed to the strengths of stones" (*CL,* p. 121). This passage, which might serve as a gloss on Wittgenstein, also emphasizes what Barthelme, Coover, and Gass all use as a starting point in their fiction: that stories made of words and sentences can never escape their purely constructed, fictive nature, and that the awareness of this condition, far from being a source of despair for the author, can actually free the writer to take full advantages of the treasures of language — even bankrupt language. We can now turn to a more detailed examination of two early representative works, *Come Back, Dr. Caligari* (1964) and *Snow White* (1967), — which exhibit most of Barthelme's characteristic formal and thematic preoccupations and also illustrate how his metafictional interests were developed.

Come Back, Dr. Caligari

Although *Come Back, Dr. Caligari* was Barthelme's first collection of fiction, it immediately established most of the major issues that he would deal with during the next fifteen years of his career. Like nearly all of his later fiction, the stories in *Caligari* examine such things as failed relationships, sexual and artistic frustrations, the role of the artist, and the gap which exists between the phenomenal world and the system of signs we have devised to help us cope with a disjointed, unfathomable universe. Frequently, as in "Florence Green is 81," "The Big Broadcast of 1938," "Me and Miss Mandible," and "For I'm the Boy Whose Only Joy Is Loving You," these themes are subtly intertwined, with the main characters' related personal and epistemological difficulties suggesting some of Barthelme's problems in presenting a series of meaningfully connected events. While Barthelme's metafictional concerns with the deterioration of language and with the inadequacies of conventional literary forms are often direct and self-conscious (as, for example, in "Florence Green" and "For I'm the Boy"), these interests are also exhibited indirectly in less obviously metafictional stories in his characters' obsessive questioning of the nature of words, symbols, and the communication process—and their feeling that they have been betrayed by them. In his more stylistically experimental stories—"The Joker's Greatest Triumph," "The Piano Player," "The Viennese Opera Ball," "To London and Rome," "Up Aloft in the Air"—Barthelme's choice of certain nontraditional conventions, such as the pop-art recycling of clichés in "The Viennese Opera Ball," "Florence Green" and "The Joker's Greatest Triumph," the collage approach and surrealist features of most of the stories, the marginal commentary in "To London and Rome," speak to us directly about the bankruptcy of previous literary forms. Such stylistic devices thereby call our attention to his own choice of arrangements and to the status of these stories as fictional constructions.

In the first story of the collection, "Florence Green is 81," we find a perfect example of how Barthelme joins together his metafictional and personal themes. As with "The Viennese Opera Ball," the story at first seems to demonstrate Barthelme's "collage method," with various bits of verbal garbage juxtaposed to create a vivid sense of the absurdities and banalities of contemporary thought. The setting is a dinner party being given by Florence Green who opens the story with a mysterious remark—"I want to go to some other country" (p. 3)—and then falls asleep.[16] Meanwhile the narrator, a Protean would-be writer who creates a series of disguises with which to hide his true identity, offers us a miscellaneous assortment of descriptions of the other guests at the party, conflicting versions of his past life, speculations about our reactions to his story, plus tidbits of seemingly unrelated factual data. Because much of the informational content of this story is presented in a jumbled, unstructured way—"I am free associating, brilliantly, brilliantly, to put you into the problem," is how the narrator, Baskerville, puts it—the reader may initially experience some difficulties in deciding what the story is about or how the narrative fragments relate to one another. But this associational collage method actually helps to reinforce one of his central points: that for the artist as well as for the ordinary individual, an openness to process at the expense of finished products should lie at the center of our experience; that the permanence and final answers we hoped to discover (in art, in the sciences, in our personal relationships) were naive pipedreams. By breaking up the syntax and the usual associations that most readers are familiar with, Barthelme, in Tony Tanner's words, "seeks to simulate the strange confluence of words and things which is our actual experience, so that the commonest objects from kitchen, bathroom or street are mixed up with the commonest clichés of intellectual talk."[17]

   The narrator is well aware of the problems that the reader is likely to be having in trying to respond to the story; in fact, Baskerville constantly offers us self-conscious asides about what he is doing, his motives and literary strategies, and, above all, his fears that he will be unable to fulfill his role as author and will bore us: he is, in his words, "a young man but very brilliant, very ingratiating, I adopt this ingratiating tone because I can't help myself (for fear of boring you)" (*CB*, p. 4). A bit later he suggests that his relationship to us as readers is that of a patient to a doctor: "Reader . . . we have roles to play, thou and I; you are the doctor (washing your hands between hours) and I, I am, I think, the nervous dreary patient."[18] Apprehensive about his ability to keep us interested—we are, no doubt, sophisticated, suspicious, and impatient with tired literary archetypes and conventions—Baskerville repeatedly seeks ways of livening things up, of colorfully explaining away complications or ambiguities. He also often pauses in his narrative to question his motives, anticipate our reactions, and analyze his performance so far. "Did I explain that?" he asks us, after reintroducing some autobiographical material. "And you *accepted* my explanation?"—a mocking gesture that undermines all that he has told us about himself. Despite such occasional bravado, Baskerville is obviously extremely insecure about his role as a writer. Admitting that he is a "simple preliterate" (CB, p. 11) and that he doesn't even like his only novel, Baskerville also acknowledges midway through his narrative that, despite his frantic efforts, "I am boring you, I sense it" (CB, p. 12). He is, in short, an early representative of many of Barthelme's self-conscious artist-figures (as in "The Dolt," "See the Moon," "Daumier," and many others) who are laboring to find viable ways of organizing the jagged elements of their experience into a pleasing, artistic whole.

Baskerville's artistic problems, however, also reflect more fundamental insecurities in his personal life. "Where are my mother and father now? answer me that," he demands unexpectedly while discussing his education (CB, p. 10), and his various anxieties about money, the army, and his drinking all help contribute to our suspicion that this is a deeply disturbed individual indeed. Baskerville is also strongly attracted to women but apparently, at least until now, he has been unable to maintain any sort of meaningful relationship with them. His confession that he is "the father of one abortion and four miscarriages . . . and [has] no wife" (CB, p. 5) may perhaps be a lie, but it undoubtedly reveals the personal emptiness, sexual hunger, and dissatisfaction with the results of previous relationships that so often plague Barthelme's characters. Significantly, the woman that Baskerville longingly thinks of throughout the dinner party doesn't seem to notice his attempts to interest her and, in the end, rejects his advances. Part of his difficulties in communicating to us (and to the woman) the precise nature of his plight and desires is that he himself often doesn't appear to understand what is happening. As a result he feels adrift among remarks and events that he can't conveniently categorize or adequately explain. Certainly as a writer Baskerville is well aware of the arbitrary way in which we all assign meaning to phenomena through language; after calling Mrs. Green a "vastly rich vastly egocentric old woman nut," Baskerville explains his description by saying, "Six modifiers modify her into something one can think of as a nut" (*CB*, p. 14). But he quickly goes on to quote Husserl—"But you have not grasped the living reality, the essence!"— and then sadly notes, "Nor will I, ever," a remark which shows the limits he places on himself as a writer and as a man.

"Florence Green," then, offers an excellent introduction to the way Barthelme blends his metafictional approach with his other major thematic concerns. Baskerville is merely the first in a long line of Barthelme characters who are being slowly overwhelmed by a tedious, mundane existence and who is shown in the process of trying to put the pieces of his life into some sort of personal and artistic whole. Like a great majority of postmodern characters, Baskerville is haunted by his inability to *know* and to make sense of things, and he seems well aware of the tenuous validity of any systematic claims to truth. Although he yearns for sexual fulfillment, for meaningful relationships, for communication on any level, Baskerville is so self-conscious about his inadequacies as both an artist and as a man that, in the end, he is powerless to *do* anything about his situation. Most Barthelme characters, in fact, rarely question how they can change the nature of the mess they find themselves in. Lacking confidence in their artistic or personal ability to effect any significant change in the world, Barthelme's characters tend to fall back into a position of reluctant acceptance.[19] (Thus Ramona at the end of "City Life" says of her life's "invitation down many muddy roads": "I accepted. What was the alternative?" (*CL*, p. 180). In the meantime, they continue to produce a fictitious discourse which they hope will keep them going, animate the reader, and possibly produce some beauty or elegance in the process. "And eloquence is really all any of us can hope for," says Henry Mackie in "Marie, Marie, Hold on Tight" (*CB*, p. 122).

In "Hiding Man" another self-conscious, sexually frustrated Barthelme character again seeks assurances and stability in an inscrutable universe. In a surreal format that combines several aspects of spy thrillers, detective novels, and serious existentialist fiction, "Hiding Man" tells of I. A. Burlingame's visit to a movie house and his encounter there with a mysterious man named Bane-Hipkiss, a man of many disguises.[20] Burlingame is a Woody Allen-like character, a parodic, paranoid version of the suffering existentialist underground man who is determined to uncover the deeper levels of meaning which lie beneath appearances. His efforts to "decode" what is going on around him, however, are hindered by several things, not the least of which is his own paranoia and hyperawareness of the many possible meanings that he can assign to things. From the moment he enters the dark movie theater, everything he encounters seems to whisper secret messages to him; soon he finds himself, like Coover's Nixon or the Unwilling Participant in "Panel Game," swamped with ambiguous signs and alternative explanations for them.

In trying to decide who Bane-Hipkiss (initially disguised as a Negro) is and what he represents, Burlingame immediately reveals his paranoia and familiarity with the clichés of grade-B movies; after deciding that the boy in the lobby may be a "possible agent of the conspiracy, in the pay of the Organization" (CB, p. 26), Burlingame begins to sift through the clues which will reveal the identity of the black man: "Well-dressed Negroes behind dark glasses in closed theaters, the attempt to scrape acquaintances, the helpful friend with the friendly word, note of menace as in Dragstrip Riot and as in Terror from the Year 5000." After rejecting the apparent significance of these ostensible clues ("child's play, amateur night, with whom do they think they have to deal?"), he decides that possibly his antagonist "is purely, simply what he pretends to be: well-dressed Negro with dark glasses in closed theater." Burlingame, however, is unwilling to allow for this, for if the Negro means nothing at all, the situation isn't very interesting: "Where then is the wienie? What happens to the twist? All life is rooted in contradiction" (CB, pp. 26–27).

As his remarks should indicate, Burlingame as a character is re-enacting, in parodic fashion, our own role as reader as he tries to pinpoint the meaning of the various elements in the story. That these efforts are mocked shouldn't surprise us, for in many of his later fictions—in Snow White, "The Balloon," and in "Views of My Father

Weeping," for example—Barthelme often enjoys making fun of any attempt to assign fixed meanings to the elements before us, the point being that art, like reality, is much too complex and mysterious to be reduced to simple formulas or literary conventions; or, as Burlingame finally admits, "In these times everything is very difficult, the lines of demarcation are not clear" (*CB*, p. 29). Burlingame, then, anticipates Paul (the "prince figure" in *Snow White*) in that both have difficulty in deciphering things because of their inability to respond naturally to any situation; like the sophisticated, New Critical reader, their decision-making process and analytical machinery have become encrusted with a thick, gummy coating of literary and cultural sludge. Although Burlingame is aware of the world's constant attempts "to deny what the eye reveals, what the mind knows to be true" (*CB*, p. 30), he is much too quick to make easy analogies between media-produced realities (like the movies) and the world around him. Thus he compares the "risk and danger" he senses in his current situation to what he saw in *Voodoo Woman* and *The Creature from the Black Lagoon*. We discover that even as a child he told his confessor when he decided to give up Catholicism that "certain aspects of the ritual [of confession] compared unfavorably with the resurrection scene in *The Bride of Frankenstein*" (*CB*, p. 31).

Burlingame has chosen to give himself over to the darkness and terrors provided by horror movies in part because he sees in them the opportunity to experience symbolically the hidden dread which lies concealed beneath the comforting surface of reality. As he explains it, "Man cannot live without placing himself naked before circumstance, as in warfare, under the sea, jet planes, women. Flight is always available, concealment is always possible" (*CB*, p. 27). As a youth, a similar desire to confront "naked circumstances" led him to reject religion because it failed to understand his sexual interests and frustrations. It was because of his confessor's refusal to sympathize with Burlingame's sexual preoccupations—which were, in his words, "wholly natural and good" (p. 30)—that Burlingame apparently developed his fascination with horror movies, for they allowed him to directly confront what most people deny: "There are things in this world that disgust, life is not all Vistavision and Thunderbirds, even Mars Bars have hidden significance, dangerous to plumb" (*CB*,

p. 33). Consequently, he has given himself over to "the possibility of other rituals, other celebrations, for instance, *Blood of Dracula, Amazing Colossal Man, It Conquered the World,*" and he wonders if his fellow movie-watcher can understand "this nice theological point, that one believes what one can, follows the vision which most brilliantly exalts and vilifies the world. Alone in the dark one surrenders to *Amazing Colossal Man* all hope, all desire" (*CB*, p. 35). When the Negro pulls off his mask and reveals that he is a white man in agency with the Church—thus confirming Burlingame's view that "cheating occurs on every level" (p. 30)—Burlingame warns him that he should observe the precious message on the screen: "Pay attention to the picture, it is trying to tell you something, revelation is not so frequent in these times that one can afford to diddle it away" (*CB*, p. 36). Burlingame finally plunges a hypodermic needle into his treacherous adversary's neck. The story concludes with his declaration that ordinary man needs to face up to the dark underside of reality and not be content meekly to accept the experiences offered by the ordinary:

Most people haven't the wit to be afraid, most view television, smoke cigars, fondle wives, have children, vote, plant gladiolus, iris, phlox, never confront *Screaming Skull, Teenage Werewolf, Beast with a Thousand Eyes,* no conception of what lies beneath the surface, no faith in any manifestation not certified by hierarchy. . . . People think these things are jokes, but they are wrong, it is dangerous to ignore a vision.   (*CB*, p. 37)

"Hiding Man" therefore offers a paradigmatic view of the perils that face those wishing to escape from the pedestrian reality in which no one is willing to have "faith in any manifestation not certified by hierarchy" (*CB*, p. 99). Burlingame is possibly more sensitive than those willing to accept the version of reality dictated by the powerful majority and, like Baskerville, he is also painfully aware of the paradoxical, contradictory nature of reality which makes assigning verbal definitions and discovering patterns so difficult. Yet Burlingame, too, is caught within the game of relying on symbols to create his meaning, and his fascination with hidden meanings and "depth" is mocked here, just as it is in most of Barthelme's work.

After all, Burlingame's gesture of "hiding" in movie theaters does not allow him to confront reality but only flickering symbolic substitutes of the "depths" and horrors he suspects exist outside. What he has overlooked, then, is the danger of accepting too completely merely another system of signs—more extraordinary and less restrictive than those accepted by most people perhaps, but still merely another artificial construction. Barthelme, like Coover, consistently ridicules our reliance on any faddish system and mocks the efforts of his characters—and his readers—to secure final answers in any form. The hope seems to be that if we are jarred out of our expectations, if we are shown the inadequacies of *any* claims to certainties, then we will finally see the necessity of opening ourselves to new forms of perception.

"Me and Miss Mandible" remains as one of Barthelme's most engaging and entertaining stories. Told in diary form, the Kafkaesque tale involves a thirty-five-year-old man named Joseph who is placed in an absurd situation which he accepts without question: after years as an insurance claims adjustor, he is sent back into the fourth grade to be reeducated. The situation is then developed logically in the rest of the story. Joseph's problems are stock Barthelme afflictions: a lack of confidence in society's values, sexual frustration (after a ruined marriage, he now continually lusts after his teacher, Miss Mandible), a general sense of isolation and alienation (exaggerated here because his "peers" are only eleven-year-olds), and an overly developed degree of self-consciousness which keeps him from responding enthusiastically to the junky, rigid realities of everyday living. Joseph's experiences in the "real world" have already created in him a healthy sense of life's absurdities ("much of what we were doing was absolutely pointless, to no purpose," he says at one point). In his attitude toward his insurance job, he is characteristic of nearly all of Barthelme's people: "My former life-role . . . compelled me to spend my time amid the debris of our civilization: rumbled fenders, roofless sheds, gutted warehouses, smashed arms and legs. After ten years of this one has a tendency to see the world as a vast junkyard, looking at man and seeing only his potentially mangled parts, entering a house only to trace the path of the inevitable fire" (*CB,* p. 99). Like Burlingame, Joseph has grown to distrust the efforts of authority to dictate solutions to the puzzling absurdities of life. Of his first trip through school, he says, "I was too much under the impression that what the authorities (who decides?) had ordained for me was right and proper." He subsequently decides that he had made a crucial mistake: "I confused authority with life itself" (CB, p. 102). Appropriately, he likens his earlier life to a "paper chase" as he eagerly attempted to hunt down the "clues" to successful living—clues which were themselves merely symbols: diplomas, membership cards, campaign buttons, insurance forms, and so on.

Although the narrator has adjusted well to his new life in most respects, his sexual maturity often places him in an awkward situation with his sexually precocious classmates. "Nowhere," he tells us, "have I encountered an atmosphere as charged with aborted sexuality as this" (CB, p. 107). Barthelme frequently reminds us that sexual contact, like every other form of human contact, is denied and perverted by a society which both titillates its members and then establishes all sorts of restrictive norms. Like the works of the brilliant South American novelist Manuel Puig,[21] Barthelme's fiction constantly demonstrates the enormous power that the media, and popular movies and books in particular, have in establishing a culture's sexual roles, stereotypes, sublimations, and even its language. Barthelme is also aware of the feelings of frustration and anxiety that are generated when the reality of sexual contact cannot meet the expectations created by these cultural stereotypes. "Me and Miss Mandible" vividly shows how society's members become "educated" into this whole destructive process. As Joseph pages through a popular, lurid magazine entitled Movie-TV Secrets, he begins to realize that his prepubescent classmates are undoubtedly using these sensationalized fantasies as models of what excitements adult life holds in store for them. "Who are these people, Debbie, Eddie, Liz, and how did they get themselves into such a terrible predicament?" Joseph wonders after he is through with the movie magazine—he is reading, of course, about the misadventures of Debbie Reynolds, Eddie Fisher, and Elizabeth Taylor—and then adds, "Sue Ann knows, I am sure; it is obvious that she is studying their history as a guide to what she may expect when she is suddenly freed from this drab, flat classroom" (CB, p. 106).

More sensitive than his classmates to the disparity between

media-produced promises and their fulfillment, Joseph also understands that the sexual anxieties produced in our culture are symptomatic of the larger pattern of dissatisfaction generated by the American Dream, a phrase which is itself a media slogan. "Everything is
promised my classmates and I, most of the time," he writes in his
journal, and then he bitterly admits, "We accept the outrageous assurances without blinking" (*CB*, p. 107). With society creating such
assurances and a public eagerly accepting them, it is no wonder that
Barthelme's main characters are so depressed over the failure of life
to meet their expectations. As with Burlingame's retreat into movie
theaters, the public's obsessive attention to movie magazines and
scandal sheets demonstrates a desire to experience life only vicari-
ously through an elaborate system of signs and symbols. As we have
already seen, Barthelme exposes our uncritical acceptance of this
phony symbology primarily through his unrelenting critique of the
most important sign-system in our culture—language itself—which
he feels is directly tied to our sense of isolation and to the failure of
most of our society's key systems. In "Me and Miss Mandible" Barthelme scorns these linguistic extensions of our systems by having
Joseph frequently refer to his classmates' jargon, to popular magazine headlines, and to institutional mottoes—all of which are made
to seem silly or irrelevant. Thus after years of mistaking his insurance company's motto, "Here to Help in Time of Need", as an actual
description of his duties, Joseph now at last realizes that he has been
"drastically mislocating the company's deepest concerns" (*CB*, p.
109). And just as Baskerville in "Florence Green" understood that assigning arbitrary symbols to an object through language does not
really get us any closer to the "living essence" of its being, so too Joseph here suggests that the American public is too willing to accept
"signs as promises":

I believed that because I had obtained a wife who was made up of wife-signs
(beauty, charm, softness, perfume, cookery) I had found love. Brenda, reading the same signs that have now misled Miss Mandible and Sue Ann
Brownly, felt she had been promised that she would never be bored again. All
of us, Miss Mandible, Sue Ann, myself, Brenda, Mr. Goodykind, still believe
that the American flag betokens a kind of general righteousness. (*CB*, p. 109)

What this leads to is the great discovery of Joseph's reeducation program, a discovery which underlines the sense of betrayal, by words, by women, by society at large, that exists in all of Barthelme's work: "But I say, looking around me in this incubator of future citizens, that signs are signs, and that some of them are lies."[22]

Two other, related, stories in Come Back, Dr. Caligari, "The Big Broadcast of 1938" and "For I'm the Boy Whose Only Joy Is Loving You," provide final examples of the interconnections in Barthelme's short stories between fictional strategy, personal anxiety, and the deterioration of language. Both stories involve a character named "Bloomsbury"—an ironic Joycean reference, although the name also recalls the famous Bloomsbury Group of London who, like Barthelme's characters, were also interested in the operations of language. Bloomsbury's obsession with the properties and limits of language place him in awkward situations with his companions. In "The Big Broadcast" Bloomsbury is a radio broadcaster who occasionally singles out for special notice a particular word which he then repeats in a monotonous voice for as much as fifteen minutes—a process that parodies some of Gertrude Stein's methods. The description of what occurs when this word is presented in this fashion reveals Barthelme's own approach to uncovering the nature of modern-day language: "After this exposure to the glare of public inspection the word would frequently disclose new properties, unsuspected qualities, although that was far from Bloomsbury's intention. His intention, insofar as he may be said to have had one, was simply to get something on the air" (CB, pp. 68–69). Bloomsbury has a second, equally significant type of radio broadcast—"commercial announcements" which are actually direct public appeals to his ex-wife (ruined marriages seem to be the norm in Barthelme's work).[23] As usual, this Barthelme character is preoccupied with a sense of his own sexual inadequacies—he tells us that the subject of one of his typical quarrels with his wife was "Smallness in the Human Male"— and the conviction that his efforts to do something about his loss are useless. He admits, "He felt, although he managed to conceal it from himself for a space, somewhat futile. For there had been no response from her" (CB, p. 70).

One of Bloomsbury's chief problems in dealing with his ex-wife is that his efforts to communicate with her are constantly foiled by the banal and cliché character of his language. This problem is compounded by the fact that Bloomsbury is obsessively aware of the barrier of words that he is erecting. As a result, he is constantly calling attention to his language and apologizing for its predictable or inappropriate qualities:

On that remarkable day, that day unlike any other, that day, if you will pardon me, of days, on that old day from the old days when we were, as they say, young, we walked if you will forgive the extravagance *hand in hand* into a theater where there was a film playing. (*CB*, p. 70)

"Coo!" she said. "It doesn't sound very American to me."
"Coo," he said. "What kind of expression is that?" (*CB*, p. 76)

"Oh! how you boggled at that word *perhaps. . . .* Your chest heaved if I may say so. (*CB*, p. 75)

When Bloomsbury and his ex-wife talk to one another, their words only serve to reinforce their separateness and isolation, for as in Beckett's plays, it is only the *form* of language here, not its content, which seems to carry the conversations forward:

"You're looking at me!" she said.
"Oh, yes," he said. "Right. I certainly am."
"Why?"
"It's something I do," he said. "It's my you might say *metier.*"
"*Milieu,*" she said.
"*Metier,*" Bloomsbury said. "If you don't mind." (*CB*, p. 72)

Bloomsbury's struggles with language metafictionally reflect Barthelme's own difficulties as a writer; so too do his difficulties at understanding *anything* suggest the perils facing the modern writer, who cannot offer any opinions without qualifying them. This epistemological skepticism is often built right into the narrative structure of many of Barthelme's stories. For instance, when Bloomsbury begins to feel "disturbed," Barthelme first of all cautiously lists the probable causes for this condition—"This was attributable perhaps to the effect, on him, of his radio talks, and also perhaps to the presence of the 'fan,' or listener, in the room"—but he then quickly qualifies this explanation by admitting that "possibly it was something else entirely" (*CB*, p. 77). Like the children in "Miss Mandible," Bloomsbury's response mechanism has been deadened by a media bombardment that destroys any possibility of spontaneity. When his wife enters a bedroom with a man and locks herself inside, Blooms-bury can only run for his copy of "*Ideal Marriage* by Th. H. Van De Velde, M.D." in order "to determine whether this situation was treated therein" (*CB*, p. 78). Even when he finally decides to ravish the seductive "fan," his actions—and Barthelme's description of them—are ludicrously self-conscious: "With a single stride, such as he had often seen practiced in the films, Bloomsbury was 'at her side'" (*CB*, p. 79). When the story concludes, Bloomsbury has again lost his love and even his radio station's power has been discon-nected. But Barthelme does not allow our natural feelings of sad-ness and empathy to fully emerge here, just as he refused to allow the human dimensions to emerge in "View of My Father Weeping." Rather than providing the usual fictional illusion that we are close to the situation through language, he distances us by reminding us that his own powers of description are already infected with triteness:

He then resumed broadcasting, with perhaps a tremor but no slackening in his resolve not to flog, as the expression runs, a dead horse. However the elec-tric company, which had not been paid from the first to the last, refused at length to supply further current for the radio, in consequence of which the broadcasts, both words and music, ceased. That was the end of this period in Bloomsbury's, as they say, life.   (*CB*, p. 81)

In the other Bloomsbury story the dramatic situation is once again supplied by a broken marriage: Bloomsbury and his two insensitive friends, Huber and Whittle, are riding back from a ceremony in which Bloomsbury's ex-wife, Martha, flew away in an airplane with another man. As the story progresses, Huber and Whittle demand to know more and more about the specific circumstances surrounding the breakup. When Bloomsbury refuses to tell them, they beat him on the head with a bottle and a tire iron until they get what they want. By now we should be able to recognize that Bloomsbury's situation is a paradigm of that found in Barthelme's work: aban-

doned by his wife and betrayed by language, he is surrounded by im-
perceptive brutes who are themselves able to experience "feeling"
only as voyeurs. Partially as an escape, Bloomsbury creates a fantasy world populated by a lusty Irishwoman, Pelly, whose musical
voice he listens to as a passionate counterpoint to his current, desperate circumstances. Instead of a cold, sexually unresponsive wife
who replies to his invitation to go to bed by saying, "Hump off
blatherer I've no yet read me Mallarmé. . . . I'm dreadful bored wit'
yer silly old tool" (*CB*, p. 57), Bloomsbury's Pelly gratefully accepts
his offers of love and sex with constant reassurances of his virility:
she even calls him "yer mightiness."

When Whittle and Huber demand from Bloomsbury "the feeling"
of what it is like to be separated from his wife, the metafictional impulses of the story directly emerge. Bloomsbury resembles many recent philosophers and writers in being acutely aware of the limited
ability of language to depict accurately emotions, and he is therefore reluctant to provide his greedy listeners with descriptions of experiences of which language cannot speak. Instead he paraphrases
Wittgenstein by suggesting that he can discuss "the meaning" of
what has happened to him "but not the feeling" (*CB*, p. 62). Huber
and Whittle, anxious for fictional enchantments which can bring
some zest to their own empty, inane lives, grow increasingly irritated
at Bloomsbury's refusal to give them the story they want. "Emotion!"
complains Whittle, "when was the last time we had any?" Huber's
response—"the war"—gives a clear indication of the vacuum that
Barthelme believes is at the center of most people's emotional lives.
Whittle offers Bloomsbury "a hundred dollars for the feeling." When
Huber complains that Bloomsbury has just been using them, Barthelme carefully places his own adverbial qualifier in quotation
marks—"Huber said 'bitterly'"—to emphasize the difficulty he, the
author, has in fixing significant emotions with word tags. The story
ends with a frightening juxtaposition: Bloomsbury recalls that once
in a movie house he felt comforted by the image of Tuesday Weld
turning to him and saying, "You are a good man. You are good, good,
good" (*CB*, p. 63). These remarks caused him to leave the theater
happily, "gratification singing in his heart." This memory, which is
really only another prop created by our media to produce the illu-

sion of feeling, does not protect Bloomsbury in his current plight, for Hubert and Whittle are determined to obtain from his the substitute emotions that they believe it is the duty of art to provide. The callous violence which they use to extract from Bloomsbury the type of story they wish to hear serves as a shocking reminder of the voracity of the public's appetite for art which will satisfy their desires:

And that memory [of Tuesday Weld] memorable as it was did not prevent the friends of the family from stopping the car under a tree, and beating Bloomsbury in the face first with the brandy bottle, then with the tire iron, until at length the hidden feeling emerged, in the form of salt from his eyes and black blood from his ears, and from his mouth, all sorts of words.   (CB, p. 63)

As this discussion has shown, even in these early stories of *Come Back, Dr. Caligari* we can find most of the important aspects of Barthelme's later work already fully evident: his metafictional tendencies, his examination of the themes of alienation and sexual frustrations, his critique of sign-systems in general and of language in particular. Barthelme's vision from the very beginning has been skeptical, pessimistic, and bitterly ironic in its thematic concerns, despite his great gift for verbal wit, mimicry, and absurdist humor. If there is a sense of optimism in his work, it does not derive from the familiar modernist belief that art offers the possibility of escape from the disorders of the modern world or that art can change existing conditions; Barthelme overtly mocks these beliefs along with most other modern credos. Instead, Barthelme posits a less lofty function for art with his suggestion that it is valuable simply because it gives man a chance to create a space in which the deadening effects of ordinary living can be momentarily defied.

Snow White

What does a writer do when he thinks that language no longer communicates effectively, that words have lost their power to move or amuse us, that reality is no longer capable of sustaining mythic devices, that telling traditional stories of any kind is suspect? As though in answer to these questions, Barthelme presented us in 1967 with *Snow White,* an overtly metafictional work which seeks to exploit the decay of language and literature. Like the longer works of Coover and Gass, *Snow White*'s principal subject matter is the relationship between man and his fictions. It is not the "real world" which it seeks to represent but the status of art in general and of literature in particular. Rooted deeply in a fundamental distrust of most of the conventional principles of fiction, the book also shows an understanding of Wittgenstein's famous distinction between what can be told and what can be shown. Not a description or theory of the conditions of language and literature, *Snow White* portrays these features in its metafictional fabric.

In an essay describing the views held by many contemporary "literary pessimists," George Steiner states:

There is a widespread intimation, though as yet only vaguely defined, of a certain exhaustion of verbal resources in modern civilization, of a brutalization and devaluation of the word, in the mass cultures and mass politics of the age. . . . It is grounded in historical circumstance, in a late stage of linguistic and formal civilization in which the expressive achievements of the past seem to weigh exhaustively on the possibilities of the present, in which word and genre seem tarnished, flattened to the touch, like coin too long in circulation.[24]

Obviously, there are enormous problems for a writer who accepts the notion of the "brutalization and devaluation of the word." Essentially three courses are open to such a writer: he may, like Rimbaud, and, to an extent, like Beckett, choose what Steiner calls "the suicidal rhetoric of silence";[25] he may, like Gass, Coover, and Ishmael Reed, attempt to revitalize the word and call for strategies which can replenish the power and poetry of language — such pleas have been issued by a variety of writers in the last two centuries: by Wordsworth, by Whitman, by the French Symbolists, by the surrealists; and, finally, the writer may adopt the strategy of self-consciously incorporating the decayed, brutalized elements into his own particular idiom and make the new idiom part of his point. Such strategy is employed by Céline, by Burroughs, and as we have seen, by Barthelme.

Although 180 pages in length, *Snow White* is not so much a novel as a sustained collection of fragments, organized loosely around the Snow White fairy tale in what we have already described as Barthelme's "collage" method. Barthelme's rendition of the myth is, of course, peculiarly modern. As Richard Gilman has said:

That tale is here refracted through the prism of a contemporary sensibility so that it emerges broken up into fragments, shards of its original identity, of its historical career in our consciousness . . . and of its recorded or potential uses for sociology and psychology.[26]

Thus, as Coover does in nearly all his fiction and as Joyce does in *Ulysses,* Barthelme has turned to a familiar myth rather than to "reality" to provide a basic framework for his tale, although the "material" which he places into the framework is drawn from a wide range of literary and cultural sources.

Despite its mythic framework, *Snow White* is likely to leave an initial impression of shapelessness. As in *The Public Burning, Ulysses,* and works by other writers of encyclopedic tendencies — one thinks of Pynchon, Gaddis, McElroy, Nabokov — *Snow White* presents us with a profusion of bits and pieces drawn from books and other literary storehouses such as folktales, movies, newspapers, advertisements, and scholarly journals. Just as he does with his short fiction, Barthelme often incorporates into *Snow White* the sorts of events, names, fads, and other data which can be found in any daily newspaper. Even more often, however, these fragments are drawn from clichés of learning and literature. We find, for instance, parodies of specific literary styles and conventions, pseudo-learned digressions about history, sociology, and psychology, mock presentations of Freudian and existentialist patterns, and inane concrete poems. Barthelme's use of this heterogeneous mixture of learning and verbal trash does not contribute to any truly mimetic design but brilliantly recreates a sense of what it was like to be alive in America during the mid-1960s.

If we examine the structure of *Snow White* more closely, we find that like Coover, but unlike Joyce in *Ulysses,* Barthelme prevents his perspective from being seriously mythic to any extent. The big problem for Barthelme—as for any writer today who wishes to rely on myth in one way or another—is a self-consciousness about myth that has reached such paralyzing proportions that most myth is now employed only for comic purposes.[27] Like Coover, Barthelme obviously feels that previous mythic structures no longer can serve the writer as useful framing devices; instead the original mythic structures are mocked, parodied, and transformed (with the assistance of various elements accumulated from contemporary myths and clichés) so that in John Leland's words, "*Snow White* becomes a form of a form, absorbing the aspirations of the original structure yet surviving only as it endlessly repeats itself without resolution."[28] Indeed, in many respects *Snow White* seems to be deliberately mocking Joyce's painstaking efforts at creating mythic parallels, suggesting perhaps that the conditions of both language and reality make such devices unavailable to the modern writer.

With the example of *Ulysses* in mind, we can find parallels between the events and characters in *Snow White* and those of the established versions in Grimm's fairy tale and the Disney film. The action of the story often twists and halts unexpectedly, but eventually it fulfills the basic situation of the fairy tale. Snow White, now twenty-two years old and beautiful, has grown tired of the words she always hears and has rebelled by writing a dirty poem. She is currently living with seven men (the dwarf figures) who daily sally forth with "heigh-ho's" "to fill the vats and wash the buildings" of a Chinese food factory (*SW,* p. 8). Concerned about her promiscuity (she has sex with her roommates daily in the shower room), Snow White has rationalized that her men really only add up to two "real men"—hence their dwarfishness. Later on, the rest of the familiar cast is completed with the appearance of Jane, a young woman who is the witch figure, and Paul, the prince for whom Snow White is waiting. While Jane begins to spin her wicked web, Paul digs a bunker, sets up a dog-training program, and keeps watch over Snow White with a self-devised Distant Early Warning System—all designed to help him watch and eventually win her. Paul finally makes the fatal error of eating the "poisoned apple" himself (in this instance, the "apple" is

presented in the form of a poisoned Vodka Gibson) which the evil
Jane has intended for Snow White. As the story concludes, Snow
White is left to cast flowers on Paul's grave and, "revirginized," she
rises into the sky.

One should quickly note that any summary of this sort is extremely misleading, for Barthelme is much more intent on creating a
collage effect than on permitting a story line to develop in any
straightforward fashion. The progression of events in *Snow White* is,
for example, continually interrupted by digressions, catalogs, lists,
and seemingly gratuitous trivia. Each of the heterogeneous fragments is given its own individual section or "chapter" rarely more
than a few pages long; several are only one or two lines. Transitions
between the sections, sketchy at best, are often entirely lacking; to
establish a time scheme, for example, is quite impossible. Relying
mainly on juxtaposition rather than on the more usual novelistic
principle of transition, Barthelme creates the verbal equivalent of a
collage whose elements will, in the words of the narrator of "See the
Moon," "merge, blur—cohere is the word, maybe—into something
meaningful" (*UP,* p. 152).

Aiding this collage effect are alterations in typography between
conventional type and large black upper-case letters—much like
silent film titles. The titles seem to provide objective or authorial
perspectives on the action—a technique used, for instance, by Dos
Passos and more recently by Julio Cortazar in *Hopscotch.* This device, however, is also being used parodically, so that the authorial insights are themselves feeble imitations of the confident pronouncements of past authors. Thus the text is constantly interrupted by
such banal and inconsequential asides as:

PAUL: A FRIEND OF THE FAMILY   (*SW,* p. 47)

PAUL HAS NEVER BEFORE REALLY
SEEN SNOW WHITE AS A WOMAN   (*SW,* p. 150)

Likewise, the background sections typically turn out to be cliché,
scholarly-sounding assessments of literature, history, or psychology—
sometimes attributed to specific writers, but usually not:

THE SECOND GENERATION OF ENGLISH ROMANTICS
INHERITED THE PROBLEMS OF THE FIRST, BUT COM-
PLICATED BY THE EVILS OF INDUSTRIALISM AND
POLITICAL REPRESSION. ULTIMATELY THEY FOUND
AN ANSWER NOT IN SOCIETY BUT IN VARIOUS
FORMS OF INDEPENDENCE FROM SOCIETY:
HEROISM
ART
SPIRITUAL TRANSCENDENCE   (SW, p. 24)

THE VALUE THE MIND SETS ON EROTIC NEEDS
INSTANTLY SINKS AS SOON AS SATISFACTION
BECOMES READILY AVAILABLE, SOME OBSTA-
CLE IS NECESSARY TO SWELL THE TIDE OF THE
LIBIDO TO ITS HEIGHT, AND AT ALL PERIODS
OF HISTORY, WHENEVER NATURAL BARRIERS
HAVE NOT SUFFICED, MEN HAVE ERECTED
CONVENTIONAL ONES.   (SW, p. 76)

At other times, the passages seem to trail off into total incoherency,
as when the following neatly centered list of words appears:

EBONY
EQUANIMITY
ASTONISHMENT
TRIUMPH
VAT
DAX
BLAGUE   (SW, p. 95)

Such digressions and irrelevancies, of course, considerably impede
the narrative movement of the book and prevent Barthelme from relying on conventional novelistic devices of tension, development,
and linear plot. Indeed, even the characters in Snow White openly
conspire to refuse to cooperate with our expectations. Since for Barthelme the changes in modern society make the holding of any
mythic center impossible, we find that the mythic parallels here follow the story only up to certain points and then find appropriate alterations. As a result, the characters openly defy the traditional roles

established in the fairy tale and undercut nearly all of our expectations about them.

Like every other literary device in *Snow White,* the characters are clearly parodies of their archetypes. Because of their uniformly flat, almost comic-book nature, any sense of their actual "identities" is minimal and the whole realistic notion of developing a history for them is ignored. The book is almost devoid of the sort of details usually provided by novelists to help realize the action, such as the name of the city in which they live, physical descriptions of the characters or settings, or indications of a daily routine. Any background information that Barthelme chooses to provide is usually obscure and serves to mock and defeat our expectations. Of the dwarfs we know only that each was born in a different national forest. We are told: "Our father was a man about whom nothing was known. Nothing is known about him still. He gave us the recipes. He was not very interesting. A tree is more interesting. A suitcase is more interesting. A canned good is more interesting" (*SW,* pp. 18–19). Since we are given no physical descriptions, no backgrounds, and no idiosyncratic traits, we can "know" the characters only through the words they speak — and even here we can make only minimal distinctions. Indeed, at times even the dwarfs seem to have a difficult time identifying each other, as Kevin's remarks to Clem at one point indicate: "'That's true, Roger,' Kevin said a hundred times. Then he was covered with embarrassment. 'No, I mean that's true, Clem. Excuse me. Roger is somebody else. You're not Roger. You're Clem. That's true, Clem'" (*SW,* p. 67). Thus the dwarfs' personalities are blurred and indistinct; they are characters made up entirely of society's stock provision of jealousies, cliché opinions, psychological afflictions, and linguistic oddities. On the other hand, they are obviously grotesquely unsuited for the unselfconscious, selfless roles that the original myth asks them to play.

Even more unsuited for his role than the dwarfs is Paul, whose princely mission is to rescue Snow White from her captivity with the dwarfs and save her from the murderous intentions of the witch-like Jane. But Paul is destined to be defeated in both his attempts, apparently doomed by the conditions of contemporary life that make it impossible for him to sustain the archetype which he should embody. The type of figure Paul should be, Barthelme suggests, has been driven underground—or into parody—by the neuroses and self-consciousness facing all modern men. Paul is perhaps the most notable of a long line of Barthelme characters who are doomed to personal and sexual frustration because of their own perverse hyper-awareness. From the beginning of *Snow White,* Paul is concerned about the implications of Snow White's appearance for his own life. He seems to sense immediately that involvement with her will impose on him obligations and responsibilities he is not certain he can fulfill successfully. Thus, after he has seen Snow White suggestively hanging her black hair out of her window, Paul remarks:

It has made me terribly nervous, that hair. It was beautiful, I admit it. . . . Yet it has made me terribly nervous. Why some innocent person might come along, and see it, and conceive it his duty to climb up, and discern the reason it is being hung out of that window. There is probably some girl attached to the top, and with her responsibilities of sorts.   (*SW,* pp. 13–14)

Possibly because he is overly aware of the Rapunzel myth, Paul's response to these obligations is to flee, although he retains considerable awareness of the implications behind his actions. He realizes, for example, that conditions in today's society militate against true princeliness. In rationalizing his decision to hide in a monastery in western Nevada, Paul stops for a moment to consider the lack of opportunity for heroic action today:

If I had been born well prior to 1900, I could have ridden with Pershing against Pancho Villa. Alternatively, I could have ridden with Villa against the landowners and corrupt government officials of the time. In either case I could have had a horse. How little opportunity there is for young men to have personally owned horses in the bottom half of the 20th century! A wonder that we U.S. youth can still fork a saddle at all.   (*SW,* p. 78)

After brief sojourns in France as a music instructor and in Rome as a member of the Italian post office, Paul decides to abandon his efforts to evade his duties as a prince. As with Bloomsbury and many of modern literature's comically conceived antiheroes, Paul is totally incapable of responding naturally to any situation because his decision-making capacity has been deadened by the sludge of literary and cultural conventions. Rather than meeting his challenges directly, Paul vacillates, mediates, and filters his responses. Comically, he digs a bunker outside Snow White's house and installs an observation system which includes mirrors and dogs attached to wires. When the moment of crisis arrives, bungling Paul drinks the poisoned Vodka Gibson intended for Snow White; muttering banalities to the very end—"This drink is vaguely exciting, like a film by Leopoldo Torre Nilsson" (*SW*, p. 174)—Paul dies "with green foam coming out of his face." So much for Prince Charming.

Snow White, meanwhile, has patiently been waiting for reluctant Paul to complete his duties. As she explains to one of her anxious wooers:

> But this love must not be, because of your blood. . . . I must hold myself in reserve for a prince or a prince-figure, someone like Paul. I know that Paul has not looked terribly good up to now and in fact I despise him utterly. Yet he has the blood of kings and queens and cardinals in his veins.   (*SW*, p. 170)

As Paul soon demonstrates, Snow White is overestimating the ability of royal blood to produce a contemporary prince-figure. We may question whether such concepts as "royal blood," "princeliness," and "heroic action" were viable in any age, but literature—including history books—has conditioned us to think otherwise. We are led, like Snow White, to react to Paul through these filtered, largely literary stereotypes. As Snow White realizes, the fault may not lie so much in Paul as in our own expectations of him: "Paul is a frog. He is frog through and through. . . . So I am disappointed. Either I have overestimated Paul, or I have overestimated history" (*SW*, p. 169).

The obvious suggestion being made here is that reality can no longer sustain the values needed to create either a hero-figure or the proper ending to a fairy tale. Snow White seems to realize this when she decides to pull in her long black hair and sadly remarks:

> No one has come to climb up. That says it all. This time is the wrong time for me. I am in the wrong time. There is something wrong with all those people standing there, gaping and gawking. And with all those who did not come and

at least *try* to climb up. To fill the role. And with the very world itself, for not being able to supply a prince. For not being able to at least be civilized enough to supply the correct ending to the story.   (*SW,* p. 132)

Snow White, then, is doomed to disappointment because heroes are now created *only* in books and movies—and even there they are found less and less because reality is losing its capacity to support fictions of this kind. Consequently, we have to content ourselves with media-produced substitutes. Speaking of the dwarfs, Snow White summarized this dreary prospect:

The seven of them only add up to the equivalent of about two real men, as we know them from the films and from our childhood, when there were giants on the earth. It is possible, of course, that there are no more real men here, on this ball of half-truths, the earth, that would be a disappointment. One would have to content oneself with the subtle falsity of color films of happy love affairs, made in France, with a Mozart score.   (*SW,* pp. 41–42)

In many respects, we are expected to share Snow White's realizations as we respond to Barthelme's book: our expectations, created by previous encounters with literature, are left unsatisfied. If we are, like Snow White, disappointed with this prospect, we have overestimated language (because it can no longer communicate effectively) and reality (because it no longer produces the kinds of heroes, logical progressions, and predictable feelings which are the stuff of the traditional novel).

If we turn to the central question of the role of language in Barthelme's book, we find that, more than anything else, *Snow White* seems to be "about" the current condition of language and the possibilities which exist today for a writer for communicating something meaningful to his readers. Throughout the book a variety of very topical subjects are brought up: the Vietnam War, crowded street conditions, air pollution, political corruption. But as Gilman has observed, "The novel isn't about these things, not about their meaning or even their phenomenological appearance. It is about their status in the imagination."[29] Barthelme is, therefore, not so much interested in using such material for satiric analysis as he is in seeing how such things have affected the public consciousness, especially in how that consciousness is reflected in language. *Snow White,* then, metafictionally deals with the problems of its own composition, often analyzing itself as it moves forward—all the while mocking our interpretations and attempts at making "outer referents."

At times this anticipatory mocking has quite specific targets. As Barthelme is aware, our reaction to any work of fiction is influenced by a wide variety of literary and critical suppositions. Readers, no less than writers, have become so self-conscious about literary and critical conventions that writers have difficulty in creating anything which is not already a cliché. Having accepted this fact, Barthelme (and most of the other contemporary metafictionists) decides to have some fun with it by directly playing with these anticipations. The most obvious example is the questionnaire which Barthelme inserts in the middle of the novel. This questionnaire not only makes fun of the critical machinery we are probably using to "interpret" *Snow White* but also serves as a delightful parody of the language-form of a questionnaire itself. Like Nabokov, Barthelme also takes special delight in poking fun at Freudian psychology, as when he occasionally presents us with passages which are so teasingly Freudian that they slip over into parodic self-commentaries:

> WHAT SNOW WHITE REMEMBERS:
> THE HUNTSMAN
> THE FOREST
> THE STEAMING KNIFE   (*SW,* p. 39)

In other sections of the book the characters themselves either anticipate our interpretations of what is happening or create their own. One of the dwarfs, for instance, says of the women they watch while they are at work, "We are very much tempted to shoot our arrows into them, those targets. You know what that means" (*SW,* p. 8). And, of course, we do. Not surprisingly, Snow White is very much aware of the literary significance of letting down her hair from the window: "This motif, the long hair streaming from the high window, is a very ancient one I believe, found in many cultures, in various forms. Now I recapitulate it, for the astonishment of the vulgar and the refreshment of my venereal life" (*SW*, p. 80). Bill, the most self-conscious dwarf, is also the book's most expert symbol hunter and, at times, he even anticipates the probable sources which readers will rely on to give "meaning" to a scene. When Bill notices the long black hair hanging out of the apartment window, he asks himself whose hair it might be: "This distasteful answer is already known to me, as is the significance of the act, this hanging, as well as the sexual signifi- cance of the hair itself, on which Wurst has written. I don't mean that he has written *on* the hair, but rather about it" (*SW*, p. 92). This kind of arcane, scholarly knowledge proves to be quite useless for Bill, just as it is in assisting our own interpretations. In this instance, Bill's awareness of the variety of meanings he can attribute to Snow White's actions in no way helps him decide what to do about them, for, as he soon admits, "It is Snow White who has taken the step, the meaning of which is clear to all of us. . . . In the meantime, here is the hair, with its multiple meanings. What am I to do about it?" (*SW*, pp. 92–93).

In addition to mocking our interpretations, the novel contains various other self-referential qualities. The most important of these are the many digressions about language, including discussions of the language of *Snow White* itself. Like the fiction of Coover, Barth, Borges, and Gass, *Snow White* embodies in form as well as content the difficulties of writing in the modern age. One such "self- discussion" occurs when Dan presents a Borges-like (Klipschorn?) discussion about the nature of language:

You know, Klipschorn was right I think when he spoke of the "blanketing" ef- fect of ordinary language, referring, as I recall, to the part that sort of, you know, "fills in" between the other parts. That part, the "filling" you might say, of which the expression "you might say" is a good example, is to me the most interesting part, and of course it might also be called the "stuffing" I suppose, and there is probably also, in addition, some other word that would do as well, to describe it, or maybe a number of them. . . . The "endless" aspect of "stuffing" is that it goes on and on, and in fact, our exchanges are in large measure composed of it, in larger measure even, perhaps, than they are com- posed of that which is not "stuffing"   (*SW*, p. 96)

Barthelme, of course, is a master of creating exactly the sort of "filling" and "stuffing" that Dan is talking about—as this very passage indicates. As we have seen from our earlier discussion, Barthelme resembles Pinter, Beckett, and Ionesco in his continual interest in the linguistic idiosyncracies and banalities which people use to express themselves—and which have made the creation of literature and even communication of any sort increasingly difficult. When, as Wittgenstein says, the "language machine" begins to "run idle," not only do people become increasingly isolated from each other but also writers find that they can take nothing for granted from their readers. Thus the narration of *Snow White* is frequently interrupted so that Barthelme can explain the specific meaning of words or phrases which might be confusing or misleading. When Barthelme describes Henry's process of examining his weaknesses as "weaknesses pinched out of the soul's ecstasy one by one" (*SW*, p. 29), he becomes worried about our possible objections to his metaphor and decides to explain himself. Here, as elsewhere when he speaks with his own voice, the tone has the flat, elevated ring of a scholarly essay which is exactly suited for the mock-serious treatment he is presenting:

Of course "ecstasy" is being used here in a very special sense, as misery, something that would be in German one of three aspects of something called the *Lumpwelt* in some such sentences as "The *Inmittenness* of the Lumpwelt is a turning toward misery." So that what is meant here by ecstasy is something on the order of "fit," but a kind of slow one, perhaps a semi-arrested one that is divisible by three.   (*SW*, p. 29)

Another indication that language is not functioning properly can be found in certain passages which lose direction and slide into pure irrelevancies. The digressive method used here is not the one found, say, in *Tristram Shandy*, for it is not based on an associational logic and does not lead anywhere. A certain passage will begin with fairly ordinary novelistic intentions such as providing clarification or additional description and then uncontrollably wander off into regions of "pure blague." The following discussion of Bill by his fellow dwarfs demonstrates this method quite well. After learning that Bill is absent "tending the vats," we have an apparent digression about his clothes turn into a random selection of verbal garbage:

Bill's new brown monkscloth pajamas, made for him by Paul, should be here next month. The grade of pork ears we are using in the Baby Ding Sam Dew is not capable of meeting U.S. Government standards, or indeed, any standards. Our man in Hong Kong assures us, however, that the next shipment will be superior. Sales nationwide are brisk, brisk, brisk. The pound is weakening. The cow is calving. The cactus wants watering. The new building is abuilding with leases covering 45 percent of the rentable space already in hand. The weather tomorrow, fair and warmer.   (*SW*, pp. 119–20)

Problems with language are even more apparent in certain sections (see, for example, pp. 31, 63, 164–65) in which broken and incomplete thoughts and sentences strain to become realized but manage to appear only in incomplete, syntactically fractured fragments. The method, which has some obvious affinities with Beckett's later writing and with Burroughs's "cut-up" technique, sometimes uses ellipses to separate widely different thoughts. Like the final "Etc." in "Views of My Father Weeping," these ellipses suggest that we should assume what is being left out is not worth being printed in its entirety.

Finally, the most pervasive way in which Barthelme demonstrates the bankruptcy of language and literary traditions is the more familiar approach of parodying well-known literary styles and methods. Like the "Oxen of the Sun" section of *Ulysses, Snow White* is created out of a wide variety of narrative styles traceable to specific literary sources; in addition, allusions to these works, some direct and others veiled, are sprinkled liberally throughout the book and serve to reinforce the self-referential nature of the work. Often the short sections are created from a hodgepodge of styles, modulating rapidly between specific literary parodies (of Stendhal, Rimbaud, Shakespeare, Loren Hart, Burroughs, Henry James), current slang, academic clichés, and advertising jargon. The style, whatever its source, is usually wholly inappropriate to the subject at hand, as with an elegant sermon being delivered against "buffalo music" or a learned commentary on "The Horsewife in Modern Society."

The reversals and incongruities in Barthelme's *Snow White* and in his short fiction as well should remind us of the difficulties involved when any contemporary writer attempts to build a work of art from the words at his disposal. Certainly it is significant that Snow White's first words are: "Oh I wish there were some words in the world that were not the words I always hear!" (*SW*, p. 6). As John Leland suggests, throughout the novel "it is as if Snow White wishes to escape from 'her' fiction—the words which speak her and which she must speak—to find an existence beyond the voices articulating her existence. Snow White, however, is unable to imagine anything better; she is locked within the texts she attempts to transcend."[30] Barthelme's novel, however, proves that although fiction may not be able to transcend the limits imposed by its trashy, too-familiar materials, it can accommodate itself to this condition by metafictionally incorporating this same debased condition into its very fabric.

WILLIAM H. GASS: 4
THE WORLD
WITHIN THE WORD

POET: Yours is a species of verbal materialism.

    You can consider from on high novelists, philosophers, and all those who are subject to the word by credibility; who *must* believe that their discourse is real by its content and who *must* signify some reality. But you, you know that the reality of discourse is its words, the words only, and the forms.

Paul Valéry, "Calepin, d'un poète"

In woman's womb the word is made flesh.

James Joyce, Ulysses

DEGAS: "Yours is a hellish craft. I can't manage to say what I want, I'm full of ideas."

MALLARMÉ: "My dear Degas, one does not make poetry with ideas, but with words."

In a recent public exchange between William H. Gass, Donald Barthelme, Walker Percy, and Grace Paley, Gass introduced the idea that words and symbols may be more important and more interesting to modern man than the raw data of experience. As he put it:

Language is . . . more powerful as an experience of things than the experience of things. Signs are more potent experiences than anything else, so when one is dealing with the things that really count, then you deal with words. They have a reality far exceeding the things they name. . . . When we think about our own life, it's surrounded by symbols. That's what we experience day and night. . . . In the old days we might have supposed that the daffodil was much, much more interesting than the word daffodil, but I simply would deny that. The word daffodil is much more interesting than daffodils. There's much more to it.[1]

The point that Gass is making here—and he returns to it again and again in his essays and in his fiction—is perhaps the key to understanding his theoretical and practical approach to the creation of fiction. Indeed, more than any other living American writer, Gass constantly reminds us of the *primacy of the word* in both literature and our ordinary lives; as a critic and a writer of fiction, Gass always draws our attention to the way in which language and symbols can both enrich our experience of living in the world or separate, even destroy, this experience. Gass shares with Coover, Barthelme, and the other metafictionists a deep concern with the exhaustion and "deadendedness" of much modern literature, but his fictional methods seem at once more traditional in practice than theirs and more radical in theory. This paradox (which can be resolved, as will be shown) derives from the fact that while Gass's fiction, at first glance, appears to be realistically motivated, his theoretical approach denies fiction any mimetic validity at all.

Gass shares with Coover a fundamental optimism about the linguistic tools available to the contemporary writer that differs from Barthelme's pessimistic stance. Rather than accepting the debilitating, "fallen" condition of current language, Gass preaches a poetics of fiction which calls for "a language worthy of our world . . . experimental and expansive—venturesome enough to make the chemist envy and the physicist catch up—it will give new glasses to new eyes, and put those plots and patterns down we find our modern lot in."[2] "I have no skepticism about language," Gass recently commented in a *Paris Review* interview. "I know it can bamboozle, but I am a believer."[3] Like Wittgenstein, under whom Gass studied for a time during his graduate-school days at Cornell,[4] Gass exhibits a sophisticated understanding of the bewitching enchantments of the linguistic process; consequently, much of his fiction focuses on the same metafictional issues examined by Coover and Barthelme: the role of the artist, the relationship between man and his fictions, and the barrier of symbols that man constructs to keep the world at arm's length. By isolating his obsessive, highly imaginative characters and by pushing them deeper and deeper within themselves and their fictions, Gass frees his language from the constraints of verisimilitude and allows it to create its own design and poetic intensity. The result is a body of fiction that aims at keeping the reader sensuously imprisoned within this body. Before we turn to Gass's fiction, however, a brief look at the important opening section of Gass's first collection of essays, *Fiction and the Figures of Life*, will offer a useful introduction to his theory of fiction and to his major thematic concerns as well.

Fiction and the Figures of Life

William Gass begins his essay, "The Medium of Fiction," with a remark which illuminates all of his work to date: "It seems a country-headed thing to say, that stories and the places and people in them are merely made of words as chairs are made of smoothed sticks and sometimes of cloth or metal tubes."[5] This "country-headed" idea, of course, is not really all that simple. Indeed, as Gass often complains, fiction writers usually seem to ignore this fact; in their anxiousness to have their readers pass through their words into the magical "other world" of fiction, they are unwilling to distract them by calling attention to the building blocks of all discourse—the words themselves. Because Gass is a philosopher of language and a literary critic as well as a writer of fiction, he brings to the contemporary literary scene a unique and sophisticated combination of skills. Gass's verbal eloquence, combined with his forceful theoretical rejection of mimesis as a criterion of literary value, made the appearance of *Fiction and the Figures of Life* in 1970 an especially important literary event. Since then the book has become a kind of Bible for contemporary innovative writers, providing a convincing theoretical justification of the nonmimetic approach many of them are pursuing. Simply speaking, this view suggests that all fictions, including those of philosophy, science, mathematics, as well as literature, are primarily *meaning systems* which owe the standards of their success to internal consistency and not to the way in which they mimetically represent or correspond to the outside world. "There are no descriptions in literature, there are only constructions," says Gass in one of his most often quoted passages (*FFL*, p. 27). Thus the fiction-maker *builds* his worlds out of words, concepts, and rules of transformation and inference. The fiction-maker does not "describe" because there is literally nothing "out there" to which his words may be said properly to refer.

Gass's insistence that the worlds depicted in a work of fiction are "only imaginatively possible ones" which "need not be at all like any real one" (*FFL*, p. 9) sounds considerably like the New Critical view that works of literature are self-enclosed objects which need to be examined primarily as "internal meaning systems."[6] And, in fact, Gass's view of the literary object does resemble the New Critical position, although his opinions also seem to have been affected by the aesthetic principles of the neo-Kantians (Ernst Cassirer, Hans Vaihinger, Suzanne Langer) and the symbolist poets, especially Paul Valéry, whom Gass has referred to as "intellectually . . . the person I admire most among artists."[7] But in the assessment of Gass's aesthetic stance, the most important factor is his training as a philosopher of language and as a student of models and metaphor;[8] as a result Gass brings to fiction a disciplined understanding of how words function in sentences, in metaphors, and in fictional systems.

A few problems should be mentioned concerning Gass's aesthetic position before we begin to examine it more specifically. Readers may encounter some initial difficulties in trying to follow Gass's essays because he tends to illustrate or embody his ideas in complex, sensuously drawn analogies rather than systematically developing his ideas as a logician, philosopher, or literary critic might. These elaborate analogies may work against our categorical expectations, but this is what Gass intends: his critical essays are *themselves* illustrations of his desire to call attention to the sensuous qualities of language. Secondly, it should be remembered that Gass's emphasis on the formal properties of fiction writing and his insistence that fiction should not serve as a type of "moral barometer" are radical theories which are not popular with most literary critics, professors, or writers of fiction.[9] Finally, it would seem initially difficult to apply Gass's theories to his own fiction because it appears to be realistically motivated in the psychologically complex manner of Joyce or Faulkner. This difficulty can be overcome, however, when we begin to see Gass's characters less as realistic, psychological selves and more as *linguistic selves* whose nature is revealed to us not by their actions, dreams, or reveries but primarily by the quality of their language.[10] At this point some discussion of Gass's concept of character in fiction will introduce our analysis of his aesthetic stance.

In his essay, "The Concept of Character in Fiction," Gass asks his readers to consider carefully the question of what precisely a character in a work of fiction *is*. Although most readers and critics usually respond to characters in books as if they were simply imitations or reflections of real people in the real world, Gass suggests that a character's existence in a "verbal body" is really much more to the point. Thus Gass says that a character like Henry James's Mr. Cashmore (from *The Awkward Age*) is:

(1) a noise, (2) a proper name, (3) a complex system of ideas, (4) a controlling conception, (5) an instrument of verbal organization, (6) a pretended mode of referring, and (7) a source of verbal energy.   (*FFL,* p. 44)

In a footnote Gass elaborates on these qualities:

(1) He is always a "mister," and his name functions musically much of the time. . . . His name (2) locates him, but since he exists nowhere but on the page (6), it simply serves to draw other words toward him (3), or actualize others, as in conversation (7), when they seem to proceed from him, or remind us of all that he is an emblem of (4), and richly interact with other, similarly formed and similarly functioning verbal centers (5).   (*FFL,* p. 44)

Following this series of definitions, Gass adds a reminder that "Mr. Cashmore is not a person. He is not an object of perception, and nothing whatever that is appropriate to persons can be correctly said of him" (*FFL,* p. 44). For those used to discussing and relating to characters as if they had real bodies and real personalities, such an adamant position—"nothing whatever that is appropriate to persons can be correctly said of him"—might at first seem puzzling. Gass's basic point is that characters in books are incorporeal essences and definitions which are assigned a name and whose physical characteristics are limited to the sounds, shape, pitch, and rhythm of the words out of which they are created. Whereas we often think we can "visualize" characters and empathize with them much as we can with our next-door neighbor, Mr. Smith, Gass is quick to point out that we cannot picture characters in fiction no matter how particularly they are drawn for us in a text:

> There is no path from idea to sense (this is Descartes' argument in reverse), and no amount of careful elaboration of Mr. Cashmore's single eyeglass, his upper lip or jauntiness is going to enable us to see him. . . . Characters in fiction are mostly empty canvas. I have known many who have passed through their stories without noses, or heads to hold them; others have lacked bodies altogether, exercized no natural functions, possessed some thoughts, a few emotions, but no psychologies, and apparently made love without the necessary organs. The true principle is direct enough: Mr. Cashmore has what he's been given: he also *has* what he *hasn't*, just as strongly.   (*FFL,* pp. 44–45)

Gass's assertion that characters are "mostly empty canvas" leads to a controversial position: that our tendency as readers creatively to construct and relate to characters on the basis of our own past experiences and memories ("Why, this character Rhett Butler looks just like Clark Gable!") is actually counter to the author's intentions. As he explains, "Our visualizations interfere with Mr. Cashmore's development, for if we think of him as someone we have met, we must give him qualities his author hasn't yet, and we may stubbornly, or through simple lack of attention, retain these later, though they've been explicitly debarred. . . . These generous additions destroy the work as certainly as 'touching up' and 'painting over.' The unspoken word is often eloquent" (*FFL,* pp. 44–45). By asking readers to "follow instructions" and to refrain from "filling in the blanks," Gass goes against a lengthy tradition of reader-character relationships in fiction. Indeed, some might argue that he takes a lot of the imaginative enjoyment out of reading. Yet we would hardly find it surprising if Beethoven objected when told that an electric guitar solo had been added to fill in one of the slow spots in the *Ninth Symphony.*

Gass's explanation of why readers are so anxious to regard the people and events of fiction as being real is a familiar one: we seek escape or adventure from books through the vicarious pleasures they provide. Yet these are paltry motives, indeed, says Gass, and silly ones:

There are too many motives. We pay heed so easily. We are so pathetically eager for this other life, for the sounds of distant cities and the sea; we long, apparently, to pit ourselves against some trying wind, to follow the fortunes of a ship hard beset, to face up to murder and fornication, and the somber results of anger and love; oh, yes, to face up—*in books*—when on our own we scarcely breathe.   (*FFL*, p. 37)

Gass is equally disdainful of those who insist that fiction is valuable because of the practical information it gives us about man and the human condition:

It is not a single cowardice that drives us into fiction's fantasies. We often fear that literature is a game we can't afford to play—the product of idleness and immoral ease. In the grip of that feeling it isn't life we pursue, but the point and purpose of life—its facility, its use. So Sorel is either a man it is amusing to gossip about, to see in our friends, to puppet around in our dreams, to serve as our more able and more interesting surrogate in further fanciful adventures; or Sorel is a theoretical type, scientifically profound, representing a deep human strain, and the writing of *The Red and the Black* constitutes an advance in the science of—what would you like? sociology?   (*FFL*, p. 38)

For Gass, such efforts to see fiction as a mirror of or window into reality miss the fundamental point that characters and events in fiction are the product of *aesthetic design* and that, consequently, the "truth function" of fiction is highly questionable. As he explains in an interview:

Fiction is *not* a form of meaning, nor a means of attaining wisdom. As a philosopher, to put on the other hat, I have a very dim view of the ability of literature to give us knowledge. But fortunately, it seems to me, we can read literature without taking it seriously in that direction while seriously taking it in other directions. As long as you keep the work on the plane of making statements about the world, then the question becomes, "Are these statements wise statements, deep statements, true statements?" But in my view the integrity of the work is all that matters aesthetically. I mean, my books are made up. They're not about the world. I don't have any wisdom and I have never met a writer yet who had.[11]

These comments by Gass about the verbal status of characters and events in fiction contribute to our understanding of his own fictional approach. In both his critical essays and his fiction, Gass asks his audience to consider carefully the purely fictive, constructed nature of the work of literature and to observe how the writer takes language out of its daily operation, cuts it off from its ordinary functions, and transforms it into the artificiality of fiction. As in many of the works of Coover and Barthelme, the reader is asked to recognize a fiction as a sort of meaning system governed by a set of rules which are selected at the artist's discretion. "The esthetic aim of any fiction," Gass notes, "is the creation of a verbal world, or a significant part of such a world, alive through every order of its Being. The author may not purpose this—authors purpose many things—but the construction of some sort of object, whether too disorderly to be a world or too mechanical to be alive, cannot be avoided" (*FFL*, p. 7). Thus as a constructed artifact, the work of literature owes its primary allegiance to its *design* and its internal consistency, with the author free to manipulate his elements in any way he desires to achieve this design. Gass strongly feels that as the novel continues to grow in sophistication as an art form—it is, after all, a relative newcomer among the arts—both authors and readers will allow it a greater freedom to explore its own status *as an artifact* and will release it from the pretense that it mirrors the real world. As we noted in our discussion of Coover's "cubist stories," these freedoms have long been granted to the other arts such as music and dance and have recently been appropriated by mediums like painting and sculpture which originally were mimetically based. Indeed, Gass was among the first critics to suggest that, as the novelist begins to better understand his medium, the very real possibility of "metafiction" arises—a development made possible only after a high degree of self-consciousness has evolved. Quite rightly, Gass ties the development of metafiction directly to the analogous development of metasystems in most of the other disciplines:

There are metatheorems in mathematics and logic, ethics has its linguistic oversoul, everywhere lingos to converse about lingos are being contrived, and the case is no different in the novel. I don't mean merely those drearily predictable pieces about writers who are writing about what they are writing, but those, like some of the work of Borges, Barth, and Flann O'Brien, for example, in which the forms of fiction serve as the material upon which further forms can be imposed. Indeed, many of the so-called antinovels are really metafictions.   (*FFL*, pp. 24–25)

In his role as philosopher, literary critic, and fiction writer, Gass is also interested in exploring the different ways that words *mean* within a literary context. Again taking his inspiration from Paul Valéry, Gass often discusses the idea that words used in a fictional or poetic discourse have a wholly different ontological status than they do when they are used in ordinary reality.[12] Wittgenstein, of course, went to great lengths in *Philosophical Investigations* to demonstrate that the meanings of words are generated by the use to which they are put in various "language game" situations; thus, just as a carrot can be "transformed" into a snowman's nose under the proper circumstances, words also undergo similar transformations when they are taken out of their everyday contexts and placed within literary ones.[13] As Gass summarizes, "These words [the words of ordinary discourse] are not in any central or essential sense the same as the passionately useless rigamarole that makes up literary language, because the words in poems, to cite the signal instance, have undergone a radical, though scarcely surprising, ontological transformation."[14] Gass's claim that literary language is "passionately useless" brings to mind Valéry's famous analogy between walking/dancing and prose/poetry:

Walking, like prose, has a definite aim. It is an act directed at something we wish to reach. Actual circumstances, such as the need for some object, the impulse of my desire, the state of my body, my sight, the terrain, etc., which order the manner of walking, prescribe its direction and speed, and give it *a definite end*. . . . The dance is quite another matter. It is, of course, a system of actions; but of actions whose end is in themselves. It goes nowhere. If it pursues an object, it is only an ideal object, a state, an enchantment, the phantom of a flower, an extreme of life, a smile.[15]

Ordinarily, then, words have specific referential and utilitarian functions; in literary discourse, the utility or referential function of words disappears. Although their existence *as signs* remains, the words in literary texts are "useless" in the sense that there is nothing out there to which they refer. In "The Medium of Fiction," Gass outlines this process as follows:

Words mean things. Thus we use them every day: make love, buy bread, blow up bridges. But the use of language in fiction only mimics its use in life. A sign like GENTS, for instance, tells me where to pee. It conveys information; it produces a feeling of glad relief. I use the sign, but I dare not dawdle under it. It might have read MEN or borne a moustache. This kind of sign passes out of consciousness, is extinguished by its use. In literature, however, the sign remains; it sings; and we return to it again and again.   (*FFL*, pp. 30–31)

Thus, rather than being "extinguished" by its use, the language in an aesthetic creation remains behind for our contemplation; rather than directing us elsewhere, to the world outside the work, the words in such creations should direct us only to themselves and to other words within the text. With this in mind, Gass emphasizes *all* the qualities of words—their sound, rhythm, pace, and occasionally even their visual qualities, as well as their meanings—fully as much as a poet would. This poetic quality of Gass's prose, evident in his essays as well as in his fiction, is apparent in virtually every line that he writes and establishes the principal nonrealistic character of his fiction. Consequently, although Gass differs from Coover and Barthelme in that he doesn't rely on blatantly artificial methods such as direct authorial intrusions into the text or surreal effects, his fiction is clearly nonmimetic owing to the heightened sensory quality of his language. By "thickening" his medium, Gass reduces our tendency to "see through" language and increases the disparity between word and referent. This process exactly parallels Valéry's description of the poet's aim: "The substance of the poem must *resist* the immediate tranformation of the words into meanings. There must be similarity and correspondence of sound, rhythm, form, etc., which direct the reader's attention to the form."[16] "By the mouth, for the ear: that's the way I'd like to write,"[17] Gass has said, and even in the most seemingly realistic passages of his work, the primacy of sound and rhythm always deflects our attention away from the direction the word seems to be pointing and focuses us firmly on the verbal object in front of us.

Unlike music or painting or sculpture, however, the writer's medium seems to be intrinsically impure because words drag along behind them their accumulated meanings like so much excess baggage. A musician, for example, need not worry about the meaning of his tones or time signatures, nor do a painter's lines, shapes, and colors necessarily refer to preexisting objects (at least this is true of modern painting). But the writer works with materials that have been handled, used, and abused throughout human history. One aim of the writer, then, is to try to fuse sense (meaning) and sound so that within the context of the work the two cannot be separated. As he explains in his essay-novella, *Willie Masters' Lonesome Wife,* "And everywhere, again, he [the man of imagination] seeks out unity: in the word he unifies both sound and sense; among many meanings, he discovers similarities, and creates new and singular organizations; between words and things he further makes a bond so that symbols seem to contain their objects, as, indeed, the whale did Jonah, and for Jonah's profit in the end" (*WM,* red section). Gass is obviously well aware of the arbitrary relationship between symbol-sounds and their meanings, but he is quick to point out that "no real writer wants it that way. . . . A word is like a schoolgirl's room — a complete mess — so the great thing is to make out a way of seeing it all as ordered, as right, as inferred and following."[18] Once again, Paul Valéry provides an admirable summary of Gass's position in his essay, "Discourse on the Declamation of Verse":

Current, level language, the language that is used for a purpose, flies to its meaning, to its purely mental translation, and is lost in it like the fertilizing germ in the egg. Its form, its auditive aspect, is only a stage that mind runs past without stopping. If pitch, if rhythm are present, they are only there for the sake of the sense, they occur only for the moment as immediate necessities, as auxiliaries of the meaning they convey and which at once absorbs them without resonance, for meaning is its final aim.

But the aim of poetry is continuous delight, and it exacts, under pain of being reduced to a queerly and uselessly measured dissertation, a certain very close union between the physical reality of the sound and the virtual quickening of the sense. It demands a sort of equality between the two powers of speech.[19]

Thus, while the writer is busy building this "world within the word," his main efforts should go toward keeping his audience "kindly imprisoned in his language—there is nothing beyond" (FFL, p. 8). Just as the musician aims at capturing the consciousness of his listeners, so too the purpose of the writer is "the capture of consciousness, and the consequent creation, in you, of an imagined sensibility, so that while you read you are that patient pool or cataract of concepts which the author has constructed" (FFL, p. 33). In the perfect work of fiction, which Gass admits can never be written, the words would qualify and modify each other sufficiently so that their *final* meaning would be determined by the relationship of other words within the text: in short, a purely self-contained work.

Because this notion that a novel or short story is ideally a self-contained meaning system is Gass's most controversial and misunderstood aesthetic principle, a clarifying example is extremely useful at this point. In "The Triumph of Israbestis Tott," the opening section of *Omensetter's Luck,* a sickly old man named Israbestis Tott wanders around the streets of his home town, Gilean, Ohio, reminiscing about the past and trying to find someone who will listen to his confused stories. At one point he corners a young child, who is also anxious to tell stories of his own. The child tells Israbestis that he "lives in a tree" which "goes way up into the air and you can see clean to Columbus" (OL, p. 14). Let's examine the phrase "you can see clean to Columbus" and try to determine what these words *mean* in the context of the entire meaning system that is *Omensetter's Luck.* If such a sentence were uttered in the real world, we might analyze it something like this: the sentence literally means that from the vantage point high atop the tree, this boy can see all the way to Columbus, Ohio. However, given the geographical facts, such an interpretation is ridiculous, for Columbus is much too far away actually to be seen; therefore, what the boy *means* is simply "from up there, I can see a long way." Yet, because this "boy" is "living" within a carefully designed book, in which virtually every word fits into some overall context of meaning, we need to dig a little deeper for what this sentence means. Obviously, Gass could have chosen any number of cities to fit into this boy's hyperbolic utterance, but he chose "Columbus" because it also suggests, obliquely to be sure, that other Columbus whose name is so intimately connected with our country's history. So when the boy says he can "see clean to Columbus," this phrase also suggests being able to see back into history. This is what Israbestis, the town's unofficial historian, would like to do, but can't. The "meaning" of this boy's utterance, then, has been qualified by the meanings and relationships established throughout the novel so that the final meaning has been generated by the text itself. In the perfect work of fiction, the author would similarly choose each word, each phrase, each sentence carefully enough so that their ultimate meaning could not be separated from the entire complex of interrelated meanings which comprise the work.

Gass extends his analysis of the function of words in a literary text with his brilliant discussion of the construction of metaphors in "In Terms of the Toenail: Fiction and the Figures of Life," a discussion of Malcolm Lowry's *Under the Volcano*. The essay begins once more from the premise that a novel fundamentally differs from reality in that the details and events within its framework are aesthetically related, the product of design rather than causality. "Facts" in books never can be *verified* while the latter can be said to lack *significance* until we place them within some kind of conceptual grid-system. Thus, after noting that the everyday world "lacks significance" and that "it lacks connection," Gass offers the following examples: "If I swallow now—what of it? if I pass a cola sign—no matter; if I pet a striped cat, or tell a tiny lie, put down the tenth page of the *Times* to train my puppy—nothing's changed" (*FFL*, p. 57). But in the conceptual country of a well-made novel such as *Under the Volcano*, "there are no mere details, nothing is simple happenstance, everything has meaning, is part of a net of essential relations. Sheer coincidence is impossible. . . . Nothing like history, then, the *Volcano* ties time in knots, is utterly subjective, completely contrived, as planned and patterned as a magical rug where the figure becomes a carpet" (*FFL*, p. 58).

As we have already seen, it is crucial to Gass that the connections and relationships that exist within novels or poems are linguistic and symbolic and not related to the connections between elements of the real world. He feels that critics and readers are too anxious to find in literature mimetic "pictures" of conditions in the real world. And, as he explains, to do this is to misunderstand the nature of the artistic enterprise:

> An author may make up his own rules, like the god of the Deists, or take them from experience where he thinks he finds them ready-made; but the control which these rules exercise is little like that exercized by the laws of nature, whatever they are. The star-crossed lovers in books and plays are doomed, not because in the real world they would be, but because, far more simply, they are star-crossed. Simple slum conditions, as we know, do not so surely produce a certain sort as in novels they are bound to, and no amassing of detail is sufficient to ensure a perfectly determinate Newtonian conclusion. Authors who believe they must, to move their fictions, hunt endlessly through circumstances for plausible causes as they might hunt for them in life, have badly misunderstood the nature of their art—an enterprise where one word and one inferring principle may be enough.   (FFL, p. 20)

Even when we describe actions and events in the real world, Gass reminds us, the conclusions which we draw from these descriptions is always based on certain *linguistic assumptions,* along with the rules by which these assumptions may be applied. Thus Gass suggests, "A description can serve as a premise from which certain conclusions can be reached and this is the way ordinary argument proceeds" (FFL, p. 63). The theoretical basis of Gass's literary views is derived from the approach found in much of modern philosophy, science, and mathematics, which have come to realize the importance of carefully analyzing the relationships and definitions of the linguistic terms and assumptions of their disciplines. To understand a philosophical or mathematical problem, for example, we must understand the nature of the terms and rules of the elements which formulate them; once this process is complete we can attempt to apply this rationally ordered, formal system to the diverse contents of experience itself. In dealing with a work of fiction, the literary critic needs to follow a similar process: the critic needs to pay primary attention to the linguistic rules which the writer has relied on to create his verbal world. Because Gass believes the fictional world is always "incurably figurative" and that it functions as "a metaphorical model of our own" (*FFL*, p. 60), he is very interested in trying to explain the function of metaphors, for their method of operation directly illuminates how such fictional models operate.

Most theories of metaphor fall somewhere between two extreme positions. If we define the two basic elements of all metaphor as *tenor*—the original idea or main subject—and *vehicle*—the borrowed idea which is compared to this subject,[20]—we can summarize the range of opinions as follows: at the one end of the spectrum, as in the theory of Ogden and the early Richards, poetic metaphor is primarily of ornamental value and emotional significance; the second theory, developed by Max Black in *Models and Metaphor* and upheld by the later Richards, emphasizes the interaction between vehicle and tenor which heightens certain qualities in each other while suppressing others—a view which Gass seems to accept; finally, critics like Philip Wheelwright (*Metaphor and Reality*) and Martin Foss (*Symbol and Metaphor in Human Experience*) argue that metaphor is actually even more suited to express reality than is literal language. Thus, as Marcus Hester summarizes, the range of opinion about the theory of metaphor extends "from those which say poetic metaphor makes no assertive or truth claims to those which say poetic metaphor is more fitted to the expression of truth than even literal language. These arguments are clearly over what could variously be called the 'cognitive' status of metaphor or the 'referential' status of metaphor."[21]

Not surprisingly, Gass's theory of metaphor and model making seem to have been influenced by his dissertation director, Max Black, who claims that most metaphors are not simply substitutions of one word for another (i.e., using a word in some new sense in order to remedy a gap in the vocabulary). Rather, Black believes in the *interactive view* of metaphor in which a word or expression connotes a selection from the characteristics denoted in its literal use or sense. Usually the creator of such metaphors relies upon the stock of what Black calls "associated commonplaces"—the stock of common knowledge and misinformation which is actively involved in the public's ability to interpret one schema in terms of another. But Black also makes an important point about the ability of the literary artist to create his own series of implications and situations which will alter the meaning of the metaphor in the context of the literary work: "But in a poem, or a piece of sustained prose, the writer can establish a novel pattern of implications for the literal uses of the key expressions, prior to using them as vehicles for his metaphors. . . . Metaphors can be supported by specially constructed systems of implications, as well as by accepted commonplaces; they can be made to measure and need not be reach me downs."[22] Finally, Black's summary offers another key insight into Gass's disdain for critical paraphrase and his insistence on the ability of metaphor to make connections between differing elements:

A memorable metaphor has the power to bring two separate domains into cognitive and emotional relation by using language directly appropriate to the one as a lens for seeing the other; the implications, suggestions, and supporting values entwined with the literal use of the metaphorical expression enable us to see a new subject matter in a new way. The extended meanings that result, the relations between initially disparate realms created, can neither be antecedently predicted nor subsequently paraphrased in prose. We can comment *upon* the metaphor, but the metaphor itself neither needs nor invites explanations and paraphrase. Metaphorical thought is a distinctive mode of achieving insight, not to be construed as an ornamental substitute for plain thought.[23]

Gass's ideas about metaphor help to explain his approach to writing novels and short stories, which he has called "monumental metaphors" (*FFL,* p. 68). He thus summarizes the relationship:

The form and method of metaphor are very much like the form and method of the novel. If metaphor is a sign of genius, as Aristotle argued, it is because, by means of metaphor, the artist is able to organize whole areas of human thought and feeling, and to organize them concretely, giving to his model the quality of sensuous display. . . . The novel conceived as I suggest it should be . . . [is] a monumental metaphor, a metaphor we move at length through, the construction of a mountain with its view, a different, figured history to stretch beside our own, a brand-new ordering both of the world and our understanding.   (*FFL,* pp. 68–69)

Gass clearly agrees with Black that metaphors are far more than ornaments added for their colorful or emotional effects. In fact, metaphors have the ability to render concepts with the same sort of exactitude that other descriptive methods afford. Like Valéry, Gass often delights in comparing the inferential qualities of poetic metaphors with those used by the scientist or mathematician precisely for the shock value of the suggestion that the two methods, usually conceived to be antithetical, rely on the same basic principle. Thus Gass suggests, "In a sense yet to be fully discovered, the technique of the artist is like that of the scientist. He invariably views the transactions of life through the lens of concept" (FFL, p. 62). The latter phrase echoes Black's remark that "a memorable metaphor has the power to bring two separate domains into cognitive and emotional relation by using language directly appropriate to one as a lens for seeing the other."[24] Like scientific models, then, metaphors and works of art both provide a manner of inferring. Just as important to his position, however, is the idea that an artistic metaphor not only provides a process of inference but that it "is also a form of presentation or display" (FFL, p. 63). More than a description of a state of affairs, a metaphor *displays and demonstrates* this state rather than merely naming it or pointing to it. Paul Valéry eloquently explained this idea of metaphor in his essay on the "Philosophy of Dance" when he said, "What is metaphor if not a kind of pirouette performed by an idea, enabling us to assemble its diverse names or images? And what are all the figures we employ, all those instruments, such as rhyme, inversion, antithesis, if not an exercise of all the possibilities of language, which removes us from the practical world and shapes, for us too, a private universe, a privileged abode of the intellectual dance."[25] Such a view of metaphor helps explain Gass's famous remark that "there are no descriptions in fiction, only constructions" (FFL, p. 17), for a novel or short story creates a whole net of relationships which does not *describe* some external condition in reality but simply creates a metaphorical framework through which the artist is able to sensuously display and organize whole areas of human thought. Consequently, Gass is adamant in his reminder: "Models, however, aren't real. And metaphorical models even less so" (FFL, p. 75). Light, he reminds us, does not travel in straight lines, even though we often represent it that way, and although twice 25 is

50, 50 degrees Fahrenheit is not twice warmer than its half (*FFL*, p. 75). Finally, Gass points out that there is an important difference between a scientific model and the metaphorical model of the novel, for "although the scientific model yields testable results . . . our fictional conclusions, the inferences we draw there, remain forever in the expanding space of the novel" (*FFL*, p. 75).

Gass also agrees with Black that the terms of some metaphors interact with one another, an opinion which again emphasizes the cognitive properties of metaphors. "If a rose bleeds its petals," observes Gass, "as much strange is happening to blood as to rose" (*FFL*, p. 71). This interactive quality of metaphors allows us to see the world "in terms of the toenail" while reading, without having to make any descent to the literal. We are mistaken, suggests Gass, if we analyze a novel or a metaphor and then try to find their qualities literally embodied in the world around us; rather we should remember that the relationships suggested are only metaphorical—metaphors are "speculative instruments" (to use Richard's phrase) which create new connections and help us to notice what otherwise would be overlooked. Most importantly, metaphors sensuously display their qualities in a text which strives to achieve "the reader's ardent whole participation in what has to be a purely conceptual relation, a poetic involvement with language" (*FFL*, p. 76).

One last important aspect of Gass's literary theory is his deeply felt belief that the most significant experiences of our life are our experiences with words and symbols. Although he never develops this position at any great length, Gass returns again and again to the idea that the most interesting and important things that we encounter in life are symbols. In an interview Gass suggests that our involvement with symbols is just as significant as our direct involvement with reality. Indeed, this desire to surround ourselves with symbols is a basic human urge:

The division that is commonly made between life on one hand and literature on the other isn't tenable. Certainly literature and the language it contains is a quite different thing from things; but experience, even the most ordinary kind, contains so much symbolic content, so much language. For a great many of us in our society now, a great part of what we encounter every day is made of symbols. We are overrun with signs. Some would say that the experience provided by a book is somehow artificial, not as profound or important as some other experiences. But I think the testimony of everybody who is interested in literature—or painting or film or whathaveyou—science—is that this is not the case. Our experience of signs can often be the most profound and important of our life. In a way the point of getting control over the things of the world, nonsymbolic nature, if you like, is to begin to surround yourself with the things which man is most interested in, and those are symbols. In the broadest way, one's aim in existence is to transform everything into symbols— and many of these will be signs, as in literature.[26]

Many of Gass's characters seem to share their creator's preferences for words to the world, although their retreat into symbolic realms is obviously much less self-conscious than his. Gass's personal background provides some extremely revealing insights into the problems faced by his characters and obsessive strategies they develop to cope with them. Like all his major characters, for instance, Gass reacted to personal adversity by fleeing into a type of formalist detachment in which the manipulation of words and concepts became a substitute for engaging these problems directly. Gass reports that because of a difficult family situation ("My mother was an alcoholic and my father was crippled by arthritis and his own character")[27] he self-consciously set out to change himself. Symptomatic of this discontent with his life was his decision, made at college in a single day, to change his handwriting; this change became the starting point after which he attempted to transform everything else in his life. "That change of script," says Gass, "was a response to my family situation and in particular to my parents. I fled an emotional problem and hid myself behind a wall of arbitrary formality."[28] The creation of a similar "wall of arbitrary formality" was to be a defining characteristic of Gass's first major character, Jethro Furber in *Omensetter's Luck*, as well as of the narrators of "In the Heart of the Heart of the Country," "Mrs. Mean," and of poor Fender in "Icicles."

Although we ordinarily feel that this kind of retreat into art, abstraction, and language at the expense of direct involvement with the world is dangerous—and, indeed, this is one of Gass's great themes, just as it is for Coover and Barthelme—it is also true that such retreats offer compensations of their own. Most tend to be aesthetic rather than practical in nature, and Gass is quick to remind us that what is good for man aesthetically may often be extremely dangerous when offered as advice for daily living. Nevertheless, Gass is obviously fascinated with the idea that art may offer man a means of redemption, of recovering or transforming an ordinary, even ugly life into an artistic monument of surpassing beauty and form. Because he fully believes that a well-made sentence can contain more being than a town, that the *word* "icicle" is far more interesting than real icicles, Gass seems especially to enjoy examining in his essays those writers whose works contrast sharply with dull or miserable lives. Thus when Gass turns in his recent collection of essays, *The World Within the Word,* to examine writers such as Faulkner, Stein, Proust, Colette, Joyce, Paul Valéry, and Malcolm Lowry, the point often emerges that their fictional works constitute "a vast rescue operation," as he says of Faulkner's work (*WW,* p. 49). As a result, Gass is consistently critical of biographical or scholarly examinations which emphasize the life at the expense of the work rather than focusing on the creative results embodied in the language produced by these writers. "Faulkner's life was nothing until it found its way into Faulkner's language," writes Gass in his scathing review of Blotner's biography; "Faulkner's language was largely unintrigued by Faulkner's life" (*WW,* p. 54).

This idea that one's petty, uninteresting, or disgusting life can be "recovered" through one's literary works is a central point of departure for Gass's treatment of many of these writers. Consider, for example, his comments about the following: Of Lowry: "Redemption through art was his real creed" (*WW,* p. 26). Of Proust: "It was not to rescue time itself that he started out, but to redeem himself, to save all that life which he had let so worthlessly flow by—every moment of it—to reclaim it and then invest it with a verbal value it had never had as a human happening. . . . Proust planned to replace his life with language, to restore it to beauty as you might restore a church" (*WW,* pp. 151–53). Of Faulkner: "His fiction constitutes, in part, as Proust's does, a vast rescue operation" (*WW,* p. 49). Of Colette: "Colette turned more and more openly to autobiography, to that sort of reposeful meditation which was to make her great: the evocation of nature and the celebration of the senses, the beautiful rewording and recovery of her life" (*WW,* p. 131). Of Valéry: "For Valéry poetry had been, on principle and from inclination, an escape from the world" (*WW,* p. 159).

It is tempting to see in these remarks a sense of wistful admiration for the ability of such writers to complete a project which Gass himself, as well as many of his characters, seem only to have embarked upon. "All along," he has said, "one principal motivation behind my writing has been to be other than the person I am. To conceal the consequences of the past."[29] Certainly this notion of the artist's ability to create a self-contained world and then retreat into it is a metafictional theme uniting all of Gass's work to date. Indeed, one of his great triumphs is his ability to portray the dangers involved in such a retreat and yet still sympathetically present its sensuous, seductive appeal.

Willie Masters' Lonesome Wife

Although *Willie Masters' Lonesome Wife* (1968) was not the first of Gass's works to appear, it offers a good starting place for a discussion of his fiction. Its "essay-novella" framework allows Gass the chance to introduce his major thematic and stylistic concerns from both a theoretical and fictional standpoint. Shattering conventional expectations about how we read or how a work of fiction should be organized, *Willie Masters* is an especially clear and ambitious representation of a metafictional work—and a virtual casebook of literary experimentalism as well.

Interestingly enough, *Willie Masters* is actually only one section of a much longer work which Gass began in the early 1960s. Before he abandoned the project as being impractical—it was originally to have dealt metafictionally with almost every narrative mode known to Western literature—two other short excerpts appeared: "The Sugar Crock" and "The Clairvoyant."[30] Like *Willie Masters,* these pieces are metafictional reflections on the nature of fiction making with self-conscious narrators pondering their relationship to their creations. Although they do not provide much background for *Willie Masters,* they do introduce a few of the people who appear in the later work. Ella Bend, mentioned in passing in *Willie Masters,* is the central character in both stories; we also meet Phil Gelvin, the unresponsive lover in *Willie Masters,* as a rakish shoe salesman and "Baby Babs" Masters herself, mentioned only in an unflattering comparison with another character ("fat in the belly like a sow, thick through his thighs like Willie Masters' Lonesome Wife").[31]

Gass's basic intention in *Willie Masters* is to build a work which will literally embody the idea with which he opens his essay, "The Medium of Fiction":

> It seems a country-headed thing to say: that literature is language, that stories and the places and the people in them are merely made of words as chairs are made of smoothed sticks and sometimes of cloth or metal tubes. . . . That novels should be made of words, and merely words, is shocking really. It's as though you had discovered that your wife were made of rubber: the bliss of all those years, the fears . . . from sponge.   (*FFL,* p. 27)

Just as he does in his essays, in *Willie Masters* Gass reminds us that literature is made of words and nothing else. Here the words themselves are constantly called to our attention, and their sensuous qualities are emphasized in nearly every imaginable fashion. Indeed, the narrator of the work—the "Lonesome Wife" of the title—is lady language herself. Although the narrative has no real plot or even any fully developed characters, the book's "events" occur while Babs makes love to a particularly unresponsive lover named Gelvin; this introduces the central metaphor of the whole work: that parallels exist—or should exist—between a woman and her lover, between the work of art and the artist, between a book and its reader. The unifying metaphor is evident even before we open the book: on the front cover is a frontal photograph of a naked woman; on the back cover is a corresponding photograph of the backside of the same woman.[32] Thus Gass invites his readers to enter this work of art—a woman made of words and paper—with the same sort of excitement, participation, and creative energy that a man would ideally have in entering a woman's body in sexual intercourse.[33] The poet-narrator in Gass's "In the Heart of the Heart of the Country" explains why this metaphor is so appropriate when he says that "poetry, like love, is—in and out—a physical caress" (p. 219). Babs puts it more bluntly: "How close in the end is a cunt to a concept; we enter both with joy" (white section). As we discover from Babs, all too frequently those who enter her do so without enthusiasm, often seemingly unaware that she is there at all. Indeed, like all of Gass's major characters, Babs is an isolated, lonely individual who longs to make contact with the outside world but is unable to do so. Thus, as Tony Tanner suggests, Gass's title introduces a paradoxical notion into the work:

We may note immediately that a lonesome wife is already a potential paradox suggesting both solitude and connection, a lapsed contract, a failed union, and the text concerns itself with those things which both join and separate us—lips, sexual organs, dances, words. There is a hovering parallel between semen given and taken away (in a contraceptive) and semantics, meanings which we own and lose.[34]

As an appropriate extension of the metaphor, the central orderings of the book are loosely based on the stages of sexual intercourse. In order to embody these parallels more closely, Gass uses the color and texture of the page rather than relying on traditional chapter divisions and pagination to indicate subtle alterations in Babs's mind. Even the page itself is not ordered in the usual linear fashion; instead, typographical variations establish a different visual order for each individual page. The first eight pages are printed on blue, thin paper with very little texture; these pages suggest the rather slow beginnings of intercourse and Babs's playful, low-intensity thoughts and remembrances. The next twelve pages are thicker, more fully textured, and olive in color; this section, which is also the most varied in typography and graphics, corresponds to the rising stages of Babs's sexual excitement and her wildly divergent thoughts. Next follow eight red pages, with paper of the same texture as the first section, suggesting the climax of intercourse and the direct, intensely intellectual climax of Babs's thoughts about language. Finally, the fourth section uses a thick, high-gloss white paper like that of expensive magazines; these pages parallel Babs's empty, lonely feelings after intercourse when she realizes how inadequate the experience has been. Reinforcing the feelings produced by color and texture are the photographs of Babs's nude body interspersed throughout the book. The first section opens with a picture of her upper torso and face, with her mouth eagerly awaiting the printer's phallic S-block (not coincidentally, a similar S-block opens Joyce's *Ulysses*). As the book continues, her face becomes less prominent and her body itself is emphasized. The photo at the beginning of the white section shows Babs curled up in a fetal position, her head resting upon her knees in a position indicating her sad, lonely feelings of resignation and rejection.

But by far the most intricately developed method used by Babs to call attention to her slighted charms is the wide variety of type styles with which she constructs herself.[35] One of the functions of these typographic changes — at least in the blue and red sections — is to indicate different levels of Babs's consciousness. The opening blue section, for instance, is divided into three monologues printed mainly in three separate, standard typefaces: roman, italic, and boldface. With these typographic aids, we can separate the strands of Babs's thoughts roughly as follows: the roman sections deal with her memories about the past and her concern with words; the italic sections indicate her memories of her first sexual encounter; and the boldface sections present her views about the nature of bodily processes (another obsession of many of Gass's characters) and their relation to her aspirations for "saintly love." The blue section can be read largely as an ordinary narrative, from top to bottom, left to right; the different typefaces, however, enable us to read each of Bab's thoughts *as a whole* (by reading all the italics as a unit, then reading the boldface sections, etc.). In the olive and red sections, however, the graphics and typography destroy any linear response by the reader.

Gass's aim in using such techniques is to achieve, like Joyce in *Ulysses*, a freedom from many of our language's traditionally imposed rules of syntax, diction, and punctuation. To help emphasize the incredible versatility of human consciousness, Joyce relied on a wide range of linguistic parodies of earlier literary styles (most notably in the "Cyclops" and the "Oxen of the Sun" episodes). Like his fellow Irishman, Laurence Sterne, Joyce was also quite willing to use unusual typographical devices to help present his parodies. Such devices—Sterne's blank and marbled pages, Joyce's headlines, question-and-answer format, the typographic formality of the "Circe" episode—are foreign to the "pure" storyteller but are available to modern writers by the nature of books and print alone. Hugh Kenner persuasively argues that Joyce hoped to liberate the narration of *Ulysses* from the typographical conventions of ordinary narratives and notes that the linear, one-dimensional method of presenting most books simply could not do justice to Joyce's expansive view of language: "There is something mechanical, Joyce never lets us forget, about all reductions of speech to arrangements of twenty-six letters. We see him playing in every possible way with the spatial organization of printed marks."[36] Kenner's remarks are perceptive, although he overstates his case when he says that Joyce experimented with printed marks "in every possible way." Gass's more directly metafictional work, written fifty years later in the age of McLuhan (himself a Joyce scholar), carries the methods of typographical freedom to a much fuller development.

Gass's intentions in *Willie Masters* can be compared to Joyce's in other ways. Like Joyce's presentation of a parodic history of English styles in the "Oxen of the Sun" section, Gass's work is practically a history of typography. One of Gass's original intentions for *Willie Masters* was to reproduce the first-edition typefaces of any lines taken from other works, something which would have visually emphasized the highly diverse natures of those voices who have "used Babs" in the past. This intention proved to be impractical, but type styles can be found here from nearly every period since Gutenberg, ranging from pre-printing press calligraphy to old German gothic, Victorian typefaces, and modern advertising boldface.

In addition to mimicking typefaces, Gass presents many other typographic conventions, often with parodic intent. One amusing example is found in the olive section in which a one-act play is presented with all the rigid typographical formality usually found in a written transcription of a play. Babs provides asterisked comments and explanations about stage directions, costumes, and props. These remarks begin in a very small type, but as the play progresses the typeface becomes larger and bolder. Gradually the number of asterisks before each aside becomes impossible to keep up with, and the comments themselves become so large that the text of the play is crowded off the page—to make room for a page containing only large, star-shaped asterisks. Gass thus pokes fun at typographic conventions much as John Barth does with his manipulation of quotation marks in "The Menelaid." Gass also uses the asterisks for reasons we do not usually consider with a work of fiction: for their *visual* appeal. As Babs notes, "These asterisks are the prettiest things in print" (olive section). Throughout the olive and red sections there are many other examples of typographic variations: concrete poems, quoted dialogue inscribed in comic-book "balloons," pages which resemble eye-charts, a Burroughs-like newspaper "cut-up," and even the representation of coffee stains.

In addition to drawing attention to the visual qualities of words, Gass also forces us to reexamine the whole process of how we read words. In particular, Gass reminds us that the Western conventions of reading—left to right, top to bottom, from first page to last—are all merely conventions that can be altered. Indeed, as Michel Butor has pointed out, even in Western cultures we are probably much more familiar than we probably realize with books which do not rely on linear development (books like dictionaries, manuals, telephone directories, and encyclopedias): "It is a misconception for us to think that the only kinds of books are those which transcribe a discourse running from start to finish, a narrative or essay, in which it is natural to read by starting on the first page in order to finish on the last."[37] In *Willie Masters,* especially in the olive and red sections, Gass typographically makes ordinary reading procedures impossible. In the red section, for example, Babs begins four or five narratives on a single page. In order to follow these largely unrelated narratives, each presented in a different typeface, we cannot begin at the top of the page and read down; instead, we are forced to follow one narrative from page to page and then return to the beginning of the section for the second narrative. Like Joyce, who requires us to move backward and forward to check and cross-check references, Gass takes advantage of what Kenner terms "the book as book."[38] This disjointedness is an advantage; the use of asterisks and marginal glosses indicates

Gass's willingness to take advantage of the expressive possibilities of literature's form as words on the printed page. Kenner has pointed out the effect of using such typographical methods to deflect the eye from its usual horizontal/vertical network in a discussion of the use of footnotes:

The man who composes a footnote, and sends it to the printer along with his text, has discovered among the devices of printed language something analogous to counterpoint: a way of speaking in two voices at once, or of ballasting or modifying or even bombarding with exceptions his own discourse without interrupting it. It is a step in the direction of discontinuity: of organizing blocks of discourse simultaneously in space rather than consecutively in time.[39]

Throughout *Willie Masters* Gass never allows our eyes to move easily along the page from left to right and top to bottom; instead, we turn from page to page, moving backward and forward, moving our eyes up and down in response to asterisks or footnotes, from left to right to check marginal glosses, and occasionally standing back to observe the organization of the page as a whole (as when we note that one page is shaped like a Christmas tree, another like an eye chart). The effect is remarkably close to Kenner's description of "blocks of discourse" organized "simultaneously in space rather than consecutively in time."

The last and most significant method used by Babs to call attention to herself is also probably the least radical of her strategies. It involves the sensuous, highly poetic quality of the language which she uses to create herself. Of course, a fundamental aspect of most poetry is a focus on words, but in ordinary discourse and in the language of literary realism, the "utility function" of words is usually primarily emphasized. As Babs explains, "The usual view is that you see through me, through what I am really—significant sound" (red section). Babs, however, is extremely vain about her physical qualities and resentful when she is used but is not noticed. In suggesting that when words are placed into an aesthetic context their utility is sacrificed in favor of a unity of sound and sense, Babs is also paraphrasing one of the key features of Gass's own aesthetic stance:

Again there is in every act of imagination a disdain of utility, and a glorious, free show of human strength; for the man of imagination dares to make things for no better reason than they please him—because he *lives*. And everywhere, again, he seeks out unity: in the word he unifies both sound and sense; . . . between words and things he further makes a bond so that symbols seem to contain their objects.
(Red section)

A bit earlier in the same section, Babs even goes so far as to suggest that of all the methods of discourse available to man, only her language—"the language of imagination"—allows man to fully express his human qualities:

Well then: there's the speech of science and good sense—daily greetings, reminiscences and news, and all those kind directions how-to; there's the speech of the ultimate mind, abstract, soldierly, efficient, and precise; and then there's mine, for when you use me, when you speak in my tongue—the language of imagination—you speak of fact and feeling, order and spontaneity, suddenness and long decision, desire and reservation—all at once. It is the only speech which fills the balloon of the whole man, which proceeds not from this part or from that, in answer to this isolated issue or that well and widely advertised necessity, because, although it may have a focus . . . nevertheless, it is always—when right, when best, when most beautiful—an expression of a unity, and ideal and even terrible completeness—everywhere rich and deep and full—and therefore—let me warn you, let me insist—can only come from one who is, at least while speaking in that poet's habit, what we—what each of us—should somehow be: a complete particular man. That's why imaginative language can not be duplicated; why it is both a consequence of enormous skill, of endless art, but also a sign in the speaker of his awesome humanity.
(Red section)

But like Barthelme's Snow White, who says, "Oh I wish there were some words in the world that were not the words I always hear!"[40] Babs is bored with her own existence. "Why aren't there any decent words?" she exclaims in the blue section; and in a footnote to the play in the olive section, she compares the "dreary words" of ordinary prose to ordinary action in the theater which often loses all subtlety and beauty as it strains to make itself understood to an audience "all of whom are in the second balcony." Babs shares with Gass the opinion that both readers and writers are too often unresponsive to the body of literature—a body made of language. At one point she comments on the writer's necessity to accept the medium in which he works. The passage is typical of the lyrically expressive, highly poetic language favored by Babs throughout her monologue:

> You are your body—you do not choose the feet you walk in—and the poet is his language. He sees the world, and words form in his eyes just like the streams and trees there. He feels everything verbally. Objects, passions, actions—I myself believe that the true kiss comprises a secret exchange of words, for the mouth was made by God to give form and sound to syllables; permit us to make, as our souls move, the magic music of names, for to say Cecilia, even in secret, is to make love. (Olive section)

These remarks not only emphasize the purely verbal nature of the poet's enterprise, they also reinforce the sexual parallels between writing and lovemaking. Even as we read these words, we have "in secret" been making love to Babs—and one hopes our response has been better than Gelvin's.

If poetry is the language in which Babs tries to realize herself, she admits that she rarely finds lovers appreciative enough to create her properly. Apparently her encounter with Gelvin is a typically unsatisfactory one, for when he leaves, Babs says, "He did not, in his address, at any time, construct me. He made nothing, I swear. Empty I began, and empty I remained" (white section). Indeed, she even anticipates various inadequacies on our own part, as when she asks us, "Is that any way to make love to a lady, a lonely one at that, used formerly to having put the choicest portions of her privates flowered out in pots and vases?" (red section). The main problem, as Babs observes, is simply that we have forgotten how to make love appreciatively: "You can't make love like that anymore—make love or manuscript. Yet I have put my hand upon this body, here as no man ever has, and I have even felt my pencil stir, grow great with blood. But never has it swollen up in love. It moves in anger, always, against its paper" (red section). Today readers and writers alike approach lady language in the wrong spirit, looking for the wrong sorts of things.

And the pencil—the writer's phallic instrument of creation—grows great nowadays only with blood or anger, never with love. After intercourse, Babs is left alone to contemplate the sterile whiteness of the last section; here she sits and ponders her fate: "They've done, the holy office over, and they turn their back on me, I'm what they left, their turds in the toilet. Anyway, I musn't wonder why they don't return. Maybe I should put a turnstile in" (red section).

Lonely, misunderstood, and often ignored, Babs spends a good deal of her time considering her own nature and the relationship between words and the world. In the olive section, for instance, she half-quotes John Locke's discussion of the way in which language develops from sense to impression to perception to concept. Locke shows how our understanding sorts out our perceptions; he concludes that we give proper names to things "such as men have an occasion to mark particularly."[41] Babs has taken Locke's view to heart, for she constantly muses over the appropriateness of names in just this fashion. She wonders, for instance, why men do not assign proper names to various parts of their anatomy:

They ought to name their noses like they named their pricks. Why not their ears too?—they frequently stick out. This is my morose Slave nose, Czar Nicholas. And these twins in my mirror, Reuben and Antony, they have large soft lobes. . . . If you had nice pleasant names for yourself all over, you might feel more at home, more among friends.   (Blue section)

As this passage indicates, Babs confers upon language the same magical potency which Stephen Dedalus gave it in A Portrait of the Artist as a Young Man: she exalts the habit of verbal association into a principle for the arrangement of experience. And, of course, she is right—words do help us arrange and particularize our experience. In this sense words are connectors, for if we have a means of touching and naming something, then we are given a sort of power over it; we become master of a situation, in part, by simply being able to put it into words. Babs is also proud of the fact that although men die (both literally and sexually), language does not. "I dream like Madame Bovary," Babs says in the blue section. "Only I don't die, during endings. I never die." In the olive section she compares her own ethereal existence ("I'm only a string of noises, after all—nothing more really—an arrangement of air moving up and down") with the unfortunate, mortal condition of man: "You see? a man, a mere man, mortal, his death in his pocket like a letter he's forgotten, could not be that, could not be beautiful. . . . Oh you unfortunate animals—made so differently, so disastrously—dying." If it is immortality we seek, she tells us, we can find it only in the community of concepts: "Only here in the sweet country of the word are rivers, streams, woods, gardens, houses, mountains, waterfalls and the crowding fountains of the trees eternal as it's right they should be."

On the other hand, Babs is also haunted by what she terms "the terror of terminology" (blue section), that is, the failure of language to adequately express or suggest what it is supposed to. As noted earlier, words are one means of "touching" reality, embracing it, and just as Babs is made lonely by the failure of her lovers to embrace her ardently, so too is she continually depressed by the failures of language adequately to embrace reality. Tony Tanner summarizes the implications of this idea in *Willie Masters:*

We are creatures of ever-attempting, ever-failing modes of attachment. We try to adhere ourselves to other bodies through embraces and holdings and adhere to the world through words and concepts. Yet the text constantly touches on the dread involved in the sense of failure of all our adhesions and adherences.[42]

As might be expected, when Babs offers some examples of the way in which words fail us, they are typically drawn from sexual contexts: "Screw—they say *screw*—what an idea! did any of them ever? It's the lady who wooves and woggles. Nail—bang—sure—*nail* is nearer theirs" (blue section).

Because of her envy of poetic language, Babs is especially interested in circumstances—as with the language of any great poet such as Shakespeare—where the words become something more than simply Lockean devices for calling to mind concepts. Babs's concept of the poetic ideal coincides almost exactly with Gass's own view of the ideal language in literature: words in literature lie midway between the "words of nature" (which constitute reality) and the words of ordinary language (which are nothing in themselves but arbitrary symbols directing our minds elsewhere). In the olive section Babs explains her view of the qualities of ordinary words:

What's in a name but letters, eh? and everyone owns *them*. . . . The sound SUN or the figures S, U, N, are purely arbitrary modes of recalling their objects, and they have the further advantage of being nothing *per se,* for while the sun, itself, is large and orange and boiling, the sight and the sound, SUN, is but a hiss drawn up through the nose.

At times Babs exploits the sound of words at the expense of their sense (or referential quality) in a way which may remind us of Poe's poetry or that of the French Symbolists. For instance, she takes one of her favorite words—*catafalque*—and repeats it for several lines just because she likes the way it sounds.[43] She then creates a lovely-sounding but totally nonsensical poem: "catafalque catafalque neighborly mew / Ozenfant Valéry leonine nu" (olive section). What Babs really seems to be searching for, at least in her own creation, is the kind of fusion of sound and sense that can be found in the best poetry. As she says admiringly of Shakespeare, "Now the language of Shakespeare . . . not merely recalls the cold notion of the thing, it expresses and becomes a part of its reality, so that the sight and sound, SUN, in Shakespeare is warm and orange and greater than the page it lies on" (olive section). It is precisely this sort of fusion, of course, that Gass is searching for in his own writing.

Willie Masters, then, is one of the purest and most complexly developed metafictions to yet appear. If Babs (Gass) has succeeded, our attention has been focused on the act of reading words in ways we have never before experienced. As Tony Tanner puts it, "Gass's text takes us into the heart of the heart of the desolations of our corporeal existence, but it also takes us into 'the sweet country of the word'—writer and reader talking and dying alike, the lonesome self losing and recreating itself in language, the prisonhouse turning itself into the playhouse before our very eyes."[44] At the end of the book, we encounter a reminder from Gass stamped onto the page:

"YOU HAVE FALLEN INTO ART—RETURN TO LIFE." When we do return to life, we have, hopefully, a new appreciation of—and perhaps even love for—that lonesome lady in Gass's title.

In the Heart of the Heart of the Country and Other Stories

Turning now to an examination of Gass's stories and his one novel, *Omensetter's Luck,* we discover that they share remarkably similar personal and metafictional concerns. All of Gass's characters—from his earliest (Jorge in "The Pedersen Kid," the major figures in *Omensetter's Luck,* Babs in *Willie Masters*) to his most recent (such as Kohler in Gass's unfinished *The Tunnel*)—are driven, lonely people whose desire for contact with the living, breathing world is constantly thwarted by their fears and obsessions, by their environment, and, above all, by their tendency to use their art to engage reality rather than confronting it directly. It is this latter tendency—the inability of Gass's characters to "return to life" once they have "fallen into art"—which allows us to view most of his work from the metafictional perspective we have been using with Coover and Barthelme. Several of Gass's works (*Willie Masters,* as we have seen, "In the Heart of the Heart of the Country," *The Tunnel*) deal with metafictional concerns by directly using the fiction-about-the-construction-of-a-literary-fiction device. More subtly, however, even characters like Fender in "Icicles," the unnamed narrators of "Mrs. Mean," and "Order of Insects," and each of the main characters in *Omensetter's Luck* can be seen to be surrogate artist figures who have retreated inward to spin webs which are often wonderfully beautiful and intricate *as designs* but which ironically serve to further entrap them.

The stories collected in *In the Heart of the Heart of the Country and Other Stories,* arranged in the order in which Gass wrote them, show a definite progression in style, from the early, somewhat realistic methods of "The Pedersen Kid," which is still tied closely to chronology, plot, and character development, to the highly experimental, plotless arrangements of "In the Heart of the Heart of the Country." All of Gass's fiction has similar clusters of thematic and symbolic arrangements which are used to develop the relationship between his characters, reality, and their view of art:

PERSONAL CHARACTERISTICS	REALITY	PROMISE OF ART
Personal temerity	Threatening; destructive	Linguistic and imaginative bravery
Sense of personal isolation and imprisonment	Presence of walls, barriers and objects which reflect only the self (windows, mirrors)	Symbolic interaction with others via speech, gestures, imagination
Fear of sexual and imaginative impotence	Emotional and physical coldness; mocking emblems of sexuality and castration	Proof of potency via imaginative and artistic constructions
Obsession with bodily process and debilitating effects of time	Entropic	Triumph of spirit over body; establishment of permanence and beauty
Fierce internal conflict and sense of emotional chaos	Disordered and ambiguous	Creation of balance, order, harmony

In terms of the structure of these stories, it is important to see that Gass takes great pains to isolate his characters, to cut them off from others to the point where they are left alone to confront an impersonal and often threatening environment, themselves, and their imaginative projections of themselves. As Gass has said of this strategy, "Like Lowry, I want closure, suffocation, the sense that there is nowhere else to go. Also I think the voices tend to reinforce this impression of obsession because I often locate the work in a single consciousness."[45] Typically this sense of isolation and obsession is present at the very outset of Gass's stories, and the "events" serve primarily to drive the characters even further inward toward neurosis, loss of control, and personal destruction. "Events" is probably a misleading term in dealing with Gass's fiction, for with a few exceptions the *actions* of his characters tell us very little about them; it is their conscious and unconscious choice of *language* that truly reveals them to us. Loren Hoekzema provides a good summary of the way the inner psychologies of these characters are revealed through the symbols by which they depict themselves:

The descriptions of his narrators are not merely discursive filler but are significant in themselves. An individual's description of his reality—his method of forming his surroundings—is the construction of his own personality. When Gass says that descriptions are "only constructions," he is not denigrating the importance of constructions, rather he is attempting to readjust our perspective on the meaning of what we formerly viewed as unimportant. The way the self describes the space around him, the spatial metaphors he uses, becomes for Gass the method by which a self can be constructed, for Gass's characters must be seen more as linguistic than as psychological selves.[46]

Gass also gains a tremendous technical advantage by driving his characters so deeply inward, so near the edge: this allows him to free the language and open up their discourse to a wide range of poetic effects which would be unavailable to him if his characters were normal, stable individuals. As with Shakespeare's fools, then, or Lowry's drunken counsel in *Under the Volcano,* Gass's characters are freed by their positions *really* to say anything; consequently, the "events" which constitute the plot of Gass's fiction serve only as excuses to justify the language—a reversal of the priorities found in most realistic fiction.

Although somewhat disguised, these tendencies are present in Gass's first work of fiction, "The Pedersen Kid." In terms of plot, the story presents an almost classically rendered initiation formula, with the adolescent narrator, Jorge Segren, setting forth on a journey which releases him from his family ties and forces him to reevaluate himself and the nature of the world around him. The story opens after a snowstorm; Jorge is summoned by Big Hans (the family handyman and a sort of substitute big brother for Jorge) who has found the unconscious body of a neighbor's son (the Pedersen Kid) in the barn. After bringing the child inside and reviving him by rubbing and giving him whiskey, they are told a frightening tale of an intruder who invaded the Pedersen house and possibly murdered the family. The boy had escaped from the fruit cellar where the intruder was holding the family captive and fled into the snowstorm. Following the boy's account, Jorge, Big Hans, and Jorge's vicious, alcoholic father, goaded by a complex sense of mutual rivalry, set off for the Pedersen house. After discovering the intruder's abandoned horse lying dead in the snow, they first attempted to tunnel their way into the house through the snow. Digging this tunnel proves to be impractical, so Jorge—spurred on by a desire to assert himself and already nearly delirious from the cold—runs to the house. When his father tries to follow Jorge, he is shot by the intruder, hidden in the house. Hans runs away, and Jorge slips into the Pedersens' basement. Eventually Jorge hears the intruder leave, and he goes upstairs to wait out the blizzard. When the morning sun arrives, Jorge finds himself strangely and exuberantly making plans for the spring, feeling "warm inside and out, burning up, inside and out, with joy."[47]

Before turning to an analysis of the psychological and symbolic aspects of this story, we should note that here, as elsewhere in Gass's fiction, even the most seemingly realistic elements of the narration are so carefully controlled in terms of the individual sentences' reliance on rhythm, pacing, alliteration, and assonance, plus the overall orchestration of various patterns of sounds, symbols, and images, that the narrative ultimately loses any claim to realistic credibility. However, Gass is careful to disguise these artificial, musical qualities in what Bruce Bassoff has called a "fiction in which substance is clearly an illusion of imaginative reticulation."[48] Jorge, for example, is constantly creating vivid, elaborate metaphors and similes in his discourse that seem highly implausible coming from an uneducated adolescent. Consider the following passage from early in the story when Jorge is expressing his feelings for his father and Big Hans:

I hated Big Hans just then because I was thinking how Pa's eyes would blink at me—as if I were the sun off the snow and burning to blind him. His eyes were old and they'd never seen well, but shone on by whiskey they'd glare at my noise, growing red and raising up his rage. I decided I hated the Pedersen kid too, dying in our kitchen while I was away where I couldn't watch, dying just to pleasure Hans and making me go up snapping steps and down a drafty hall, Pa lumped under the covers at the end like dung covered with snow, snoring and whistling.   (P. 37)

When carefully examined, such language is obviously highly artificial: the startling similes and comparisons ("as if I were the sun off the snow," "burning to blind him," "like dung covered with snow"), the use of assonance, anapestic rhythm, and alliteration ("sun off the snow," "burning to blind him," "growing red and raising up his rage," "while I was away where I couldn't watch," "snapping steps and down a drafty hall") are all trademarks of Gass's poetic prose which can be found throughout Jorge's narration. This defiance of realistic norms makes Gass's employment of the interior monologue considerably different from its use by writers like Joyce, Faulkner, and Woolf, who are trying to create verbal equivalences for actual psychological processes. With Gass, however, such equivalences are largely beside the point (which is why Stein, and not Joyce and Faulkner, is really a more relevant comparison); Gass uses the interior monologue form *not* because he wants to recreate the way people *really think* under certain circumstances, but because it provides him with a formal situation which grants him considerable freedom to develop language objects of beauty and complexity. Thus the more we return to the sentences on the page—as Gass demands that we do—the more we realize that any sense of verisimilitude is an artistic sham, that, as with Nabokov's fictions, we are watching creatures composed only of language operating in wholly artificial worlds in which every detail of language and personality has been carefully selected for aesthetic rather than mimetic effects. Throughout the remainder of this discussion readers should keep this point in mind, for although I frequently analyze Gass's works as if they were traditional, psychological narratives, their existence as language-objects is always much more to the point.

   A further indication of Gass's disdain for realism in this story lies in the way he undermines the expectations created by the plot structure itself. Initially it appears that "The Pedersen Kid" is going to combine various aspects of the initiation format with those of a mystery story: the entire action of the story hinges on the Pedersen kid's mysterious tale and the efforts of the three males to discover what "really" happened to the family. But by the time the story is over, the focus has shifted dramatically. We never, for example, discover the identity of the intruder or his motive for invading the Pedersens' household. More crucially, we never find out what happens to the Pedersen family at all. Thus the basic mystery remains completely unresolved, and it becomes obvious that Gass has been using this mystery thriller format merely as an excuse to keep his *language* moving forward.

As Jorge unconsciously reveals in his unfolding narrative, his personality and family situation help us understand the full implications of the journey undertaken by these unlikely would-be saviors. Jorge's desire to assert himself, for example, stems in part from his unfortunate family situation and partially from the usual adolescent predilections and obsessions. Certainly the most evident thing about the relationship between Jorge and his parents is the lack of warmth and affection. Late in the story, while nearly delirious from shock and the cold, Jorge says of his father, "I was cold in your house always, pa" (p. 101). This coldness, reinforced in this story as in "Icicles" and "In the Heart" by the literal coldness of the environment, is what Jorge must escape by creating his own "burning space" in the landscape (p. 77). Of his mother, Hed, we know little except that her apparent weakness and passivity may at least partially be an attempt to escape the cruelty and irrational anger of her husband (she does, after all, surprise Jorge and Big Hans by knowing exactly where to look for Pa's bottle of whiskey). But largely she seems created, like many of Gass's women, out of familiar female stereotypes; she is, for example, worried about the "mess" being created when the Pedersen kid is brought into her kitchen, and she is squeamish about foul language. Apparently she has been unable to convince Jorge that she cares for him more than for her own narrow self-interest. Thus after her remarks about the mess being created in her kitchen, Jorge bitterly comments, "That's all she could think of. That's all she had to say. She didn't care about me. I didn't count. Not like her kitchen" (p. 52).

More relevant to Jorge's current crisis, however, is his relationship with his father and with Big Hans. Jorge's Pa is a vicious, animal-like man whose disposition is worsened by his incessant drinking in the wintertime ("He said once that whiskey made it summer for him," p. 98). In Jorge's long monologue in the latter third of the story, we are given a glimpse into the one time when Jorge and his father appeared to live together in relative harmony. Significantly, this period took place in the natural warmth of the summer:

Pa would stop the tractor and get off and we'd walk across the creek to the little tree Simon stood his bowed head under. We'd sit by the tree and pa would pull a water bottle out from between its roots and drink. He'd swish it around in his mouth good before he swallowed. He'd wipe off the top and offer it to me. I'd take a pull like it was fiery and hand it back. Pa'd take another drink and sigh and get on up. Then he'd say: you feed the chickens like I told you. I'd say I had, and then he'd say: how's the hunting? and I'd say pretty good.   (P. 97)

In this scene Pa drinks from a water bottle instead of a whiskey bottle and seems to show some affection and concern for Jorge. But in the preceding paragraph Jorge's early feelings of hostility for his father have already surfaced. Here Jorge likens an old broom he used to take with him into the meadow to "a gun"; he recalls that as he followed his father's tractor he would hide and then leap out "with a fist like a pistol butt and trigger, going fast, [he] shot him down" (p. 96)—prefiguring Jorge's later urges to kill his father during the course of their journey to the Pedersens'. The sources of Jorge's resentment and hatred for his father are easy to determine. Typical of Pa's cruel, insensitive treatment of Jorge is the way he hides and eventually destroys Jorge's favorite picture book. This book contained various pastoral scenes, including Jorge's favorite which depicted "a line of sheep . . . down a long green hill" (p. 94). That Jorge liked this scene best despite the fact that "there were no people in it" (p. 94) shows his own isolation and inward retreat. But his Pa hides the book and Jorge finds it torn asunder in the cold, stinking privy where Jorge eventually discovers his Pa's first hidden bottle.

With no friends or parental affection to sustain him, Jorge naturally turns for guidance and companionship to Big Hans when he is hired to help with the chores. At first Big Hans befriended Jorge, who looked up to this older, more experienced man with affection and admiration: "Big Hans was stronger than Simon [the family's horse], I thought. He let me help him with his chores, and we talked, and later he showed me some of the pictures in his magazines" (p. 97). But eventually Pa sees to it that even this small personal connection is stripped from Jorge. After telling Jorge not to spend so much time with Hans, Pa humiliates the hired hand one day by pouring the disgusting contents of a chamber pot over him, an act which embitters Hans, effectively serves to divide all three men from one another, and establishes the triangular set of intense, bitter rivalries that propels them outward into the snow.

Given this destructive, emotionally barren personal environment—which is perfectly reflected in the forbidding natural landscape—Jorge's desperate efforts to assert himself in the course of the story become much more understandable. Largely ignored or denigrated by the few people he comes in contact with, Jorge naturally seizes on every available opportunity to assure himself that he is the equal of those around him. As an adolescent, Jorge seems especially anxious to assert himself sexually, an effort which is closely linked to a more general attempt to demonstrate his potency as an individual. When Jorge first sees the Pedersen kid, he instinctively compares his own penis with the kid's and notes that, "I was satisfied mine was bigger" (p. 36). During the journey through the snow, Jorge's desire to favorably compare his own sexual potency with that of his rivals emerges in a more unconsciously phallic observation: "I wondered what color my nose was. Mine was bigger and sharper at the end. It was ma's nose, pa said. I was bigger all over than Pa. I was taller than Hans, too" (p. 71).[49] At the outset of the trip, Jorge had dreamed of asserting himself in a more literal fashion, although his reveries about confronting the mysterious stranger are also charged with the obviously phallic significance of the gun:

I dreamed of coming in from the barn and finding his back to me in the kitchen and wrestling with him and pulling him down and beating the stocking cap on his head with the barrel of the gun. I dreamed coming in from the barn still blinking with the light and seeing him there and picking the shovel up and taking him on. That had been then, when I was warm, when I was doing something big, heroic even, and well worth remembering. . . . I could only see him back where I wasn't any more—standing quiet in our kitchen with his gun going slowly up and down in ma's face and ma shooing it away and at the same time trying not to move an inch for getting shot.   (Pp. 63–64)

Jorge's constant worry about accidentally firing his gun (given him by Hans) also reflects his sexual anxieties. Later in the trip, Jorge's fantasy about killing everyone, even his mother, with his gun is a further indication of his deep-seated need to prove his potency and a direct expression of his bitterness toward his family situation.[50]

The fact that Jorge, Big Hans, and Pa decide to go out on this journey at all seems unlikely, for given their backgrounds there is little to indicate they would be willing to risk danger or discomfort to assist a neighbor. But in part one of the story Gass is careful to establish the harsh, immature sense of mutual rivalry that eventually forces these men out into the cold. Ma's discovery of Pa's whiskey bottle disrupts the carefully maintained balance in the household. Each of the three male rivals is jealous of whatever small area of pride they can maintain and, at the same time, each is constantly on the lookout for ways to embarrass or "one-up" the others. Hans, for example, is obviously proud that he has revived the Pedersen kid, although he is embarrassed that he had to rely on Ma to find the whiskey bottle. Pa, meanwhile, has little to feel good about except his ability to hide his bottles; and as Jorge realizes soon after his mother brings in one of Pa's hidden bottles, his father is surely going to be humiliated that a mere woman was able to discover his hiding place:

A fool could see what was going on. If he found out ma found it—that'd be bad. He took pride in his hiding. It was all the pride he had. I guess fooling Hans and me took doing. But he didn't figure ma for much. He didn't figure her at all. And if he found out—a woman had—then it'd be bad.   (P. 42)

Jorge, who has no apparent basis for pride at all, attempts to undercut Hans's feelings of self-satisfaction by suggesting that Hans will be unwilling to admit this, even though it would be much simpler for everyone if the kid were lying: "Hans didn't like that. He didn't want to believe the kid any more than I did, but if he didn't then the kid had fooled him for sure. He didn't want to believe that either" (p. 49).

Hans replies by reminding Jorge that he had allowed the kid's head to hit the table when they were trying to revive him — an implication that Jorge had been afraid. When Jorge repeatedly says that he wouldn't have run away as the Pedersen kid did,[51] Hans denies this with a smug retort: "'You'd have run all right,' he said, running his tongue across his lips. 'Maybe you'd be right to run'" (p. 52). This reply provides Jorge with a means of embarrassing Hans. To Hans's reminder, that he had saved the kid, Jorge shrewdly suggests that if Hans *really* believes the kid's story, it was time he did something (p. 53). In a series of sarcastic speeches, Jorge repeatedly challenges Hans to act on his belief in the kid's story:

I don't think they're freezing. You're the one who thinks that. You're the one who thinks he ran for help. You're the one. You saved him. . . . You saved him. That wasn't the kid's idea though. He came for help. According to you that is. . . . You've been feeling mighty, ain't you? thinking how you did it. Still feel like a savior, Hans? . . . I'm asking you what you're going to do. You believe it. You made it. What are you going to do about it?   (Pp. 53–54)

It now remains only for Pa to make his entrance and discover that Hans is sitting in the kitchen drinking his whiskey for the situation to tighten even further. As the three of them discuss what the kid's appearance may mean, Pa, who has been keeping his anger to himself, finally demands of Ma, "Who found it? Who found it? God Dammit, who found it? Which one of them was it?" Hans is anxious to exploit this development, in part to recoup his own pride in front of Jorge, and goads Pa on with tantalizing hints: "You're pretty good at hiding. . . . It hatched. . . . Or maybe the kid found it — had it hid under his coat." When Hans finally confronts Pa with the truth — "Oh Hed found it. You don't hide worth a damn and Hed found it easy. She knew right away where to look" — Pa responds by first knocking the whiskey glass out of Hans's hand and then announcing, "Okay, we'll go. We'll go right now, Hans. I hope to god you get a bullet in your belly" (pp. 61–63).

As part two of the story opens, the initiation or quest motif is immediately made apparent when Jorge announces that he feels this trip will give him an opportunity to prove himself: "It was like I was setting out to do something special and big—like a knight setting out—worth remembering" (p. 63). The fundamental movement of the story is closely tied to images of heat and cold, around which most of the other major imagery and symbolism (the color and seasonal imagery, for example) is centered. It is significant, for instance, that the story begins in the cold with the discovery of the Pedersen kid, moves inside for a while (during most of part one), moves back into the cold (part two, the journey to the Pedersen house), and then in part three gradually returns inside, where warmth is slowly restored to the point where the story ends with Jorge "burning up inside and out with joy" (p. 105). Throughout the story, despite the ambiguous "burning" qualities of the snow, Jorge tends to associate most positive aspects of his life with warmth and burning; as the story progresses, it is Jorge's role to go forth into the frightening "endless white space" (p. 69) to recover a sense of primal warmth which both the environment and his cold family life have deprived him of. For this reason, it is appropriate that when Jorge sets out with his momentary bravado about doing something "special and big," he unconsciously associates this with warmth: "I tried to hold the feeling but it was warm as new bath water and just as hard to hold" (p. 63). In a symbolic sense, Jorge has traded identities with the Pedersen kid, whose "rebirth" on the kitchen table was accomplished only after his own journey through the snow. This exchange of roles operates on other levels as well: not only does Jorge's journey have the effect of placing him in the same predicament that the Pedersen kid has escaped from but, in Jorge's mind at least, each is responsible for causing the death of his family—and hence each needs to expiate this guilt with "brave deeds." Jorge's desire to free himself from the destructive forces of his family is symbolically enacted on his journey when he pulls his gun on Big Hans and his father. And once they arrive at the Pedersen farm, it is Jorge's impulsive gesture of running through the "winded space of snow" (p. 89) to the side of the Pedersen house that causes his father to be murdered. Just as his father is fatally wounded with a second bullet, Jorge's sense of guilt manifests itself when he observes, "Pa bumped when I heard the gun again. He seemed to point his hand at me" (p. 90). Alone and cold in the basement of the Pedersen house, Jorge muses on the "exchange" idea:

I . . . wondered if everything had been working to get me in this cellar as a trade for the kid he'd missed. Well, he was sudden. The Pedersen kid—maybe he'd been a message of some sort. No, I liked better the idea that we'd been prisoners exchanged. I was back in my own country. No, it was more like I'd been given a country. A new blank land.   (P. 90)

Soon afterward, Jorge directly confronts the idea of guilt and once again directly relates it to the kid's culpability in allowing his family to die. But Jorge now already senses that he is going to find a way out, that his trip through the snow will end in warmth and security: "The kid for killing his family. But what about me? Must freeze. But I would leave ahead of that, that was the nice thing, I was already going" (p. 91).

Even before Jorge hears the stranger leave and goes upstairs to light the fire, he already is convinced that he has triumphed in his battle to assert himself, for both Big Hans and his father have failed in their mission. "Would they be dead already?" Jorge wonders. "Sure they'd be. Everybody was but me. More or less. Big Hans, of course, wasn't really, unless the fellow had caught up with him, howling and running. But Big Hans had gone away a coward. I knew that. It was almost better he was alive and the snow had him" (p. 92). Feeling that he is "on the edge of something wonderful," Jorge also realizes now that he isn't content with the kind of warmth and existence he previously had; even the idea of returning home to sit by the fire is no longer appealing: "By the stove I'd come to myself again. By it I'd be warm again. But as I thought about it, it didn't appeal to me any more. I didn't want to come to myself that way again" (p. 93). When Jorge hears a door slam, he decides to go upstairs and repeats his conviction that he is "on the edge of celebration" (p. 94). After warming himself by the fire, he decides that "it was good to be warm but [he] didn't feel so set against the weather as [he] had been" and reiterates his sense of triumph over Hans by saying, "Even if his cock was thicker . . . I was here and he was in the snow. I was satisfied" (p. 100).

After a delirious all-night vigil, Jorge awakens the next morning to re-build the fire and contemplate his newfound freedom created, as he sees it, by the force of his own brave deeds:

There was no need for me to grieve. I had been the brave one and now I was free. The snow would keep me. I would bury pa and the Pedersens and Hans and even ma if I wanted to bother. I hadn't wanted to come but now I didn't mind. The kid and me, we'd done brave things well worth remembering. The way that fellow had come so mysteriously through the snow and done us such a glorious turn—well it made me think how I was told to feel in church. The winter time had finally got them all, and I really did hope that the kid was as warm as I was now, warm inside and out, burning up, inside and out, with joy.   (P. 105)

Having journeyed through the cold, empty spaces—suggestive of the journey of narration as well as the literal journey—Jorge at last feels he has created his own warm, self-rewarding space in the landscape.

Although "The Pedersen Kid" remains Gass's most traditional story ("From the outset, however, I was far too concerned with theme," Gass admits in his preface, p. 17), it is much less conven-tional and realistic than it might initially appear. Certainly the range of poetic effects that Gass creates here is remarkable, and the influ-ence of Stein, Faulkner, and Joyce is very evident. Like the work of James Joyce, to which Gass's fiction can be most obviously com-pared in terms of its structural complexity and tight control, "The Pedersen Kid" exhibits a painstaking effort to create a rich and com-plicated verbal texture in which the words and images combine to produce a multilayered series of implications and associations which seem almost deterministic in their results. Because most of these resonances are clearly far beyond the control and intent of Jorge (just as they are for all of Gass's first-person narrators), the highly artificial, *constructed* nature of the story is emphasized in much the same manner that Nabokov's godlike presence is evoked throughout his fiction. And by refusing to "complete the picture" by solving the mystery which seems to be at the story's realistic center, Gass succeeds, in his own words, in "covering the moral layer with a frost of epistemological doubt" (p. 19). In the next story, "Mrs. Mean," this epistemological concern becomes more evident.

The unnamed narrator of "Mrs. Mean" is the first of many of Gass's major characters who lives life voyeuristically; like Furber, Fender, and the narrator of "In the Heart," this narrator is at once repelled by and attracted to the ordinary world around him. As a result, he erects a kind of barrier of abstraction—an artistic web or design—between himself and this world. Appropriately, "Mrs. Mean" opens with a paragraph dominated by verbs of observing and naming, a paragraph which immediately establishes the narrator's capacity for abstraction and imaginative projection:

I call her Mrs. Mean. I see her, as I see her husband, each of her four children, from my porch, or sometimes when I look up from my puttering, or part my upstairs window curtains. I can only surmise what her life is like inside her little house; but on humid Sunday afternoons, while I try my porch for breeze, I see her hobbling on her careful lawn in the hot sun, stick in hand to beat her scattered children; and I wonder a lot about it.   (P. 106)

This passage is followed by the narrator's admission that he is aware that such abstractions are inadequate in dealing with a living human being: "I don't know her name. The one I've made to mark her and her doings in my head is far too abstract. It suggests the glassy essence, the grotesquerie of Type" (p. 106). As the story moves forward, the narrator grows less and less content with such pleasures as his imagination or curtained windows can provide, and more and more recklessly he seeks a means to penetrate directly this self-devised veil of abstraction.

The specifics of this narrator's background are hazy and probably unimportant. Certainly we can tell by his many literary and philosophical references to such figures as Plato, Proust, and Melville that he is a man of considerable erudition. Because he is retired, we can assume that he is middle-aged or older, and his obsessional concern with death and bodily decay confirms this. His other obsession— his sexual curiosity—is less overt and is evident primarily in his unconscious choice of words and images which are filled with hidden sexual undercurrents.[52] When he offers an explanation of his existence, the parasitic nature of his imagination is vividly established: "I have chosen to be idle, as I said, to surround myself with scenes and pictures; to conjecture, to rest my life upon a web of theory—as ready as the spider is to mend or suck dry intruders" (p. 107). As a spider, then, spinning his own "web of theory" from the raw materials around him, this narrator is a type of artist-figure who, like Coover's Waugh, gradually involves himself in his own self-created projection as a substitution for direct contact with the world.[53] At this self-imposed distance from reality, he is free to manipulate others in his mind and to confirm for himself his own imaginative potency. He believes that his neighbors fear his powers of observation "as they would the supernatural" (p. 109). In discussing the sources of their fears, he reveals his deep desire to exert control and assert himself:

The people by me primitively guess that I am enemy and hate me: for I take their souls away—I know it—and I play with them; I puppet them up to something; I march them through strange crowds and passions; I snuffle at their roots. . . . Yet I somehow retained my mystery, my potency, so that [their] indifference was finally superficial and I fancy that they felt a compulsion to be observed—*watched* in all they did.   (P. 109)

Confident that he has "retained . . . [his] potency," the narrator is nonetheless aware of the limits of such power and is occasionally dissatisfied with its results. This partially explains his sadistic enjoyment of manipulating doddering old Mr. Wallace, whom he finds easy to puppet about. Realizing that his "budding world was ruined if he were free in it" (p. 112), the narrator cruelly decides to invade the innermost recesses of Mr. Wallace's private world, to allow himself to be swallowed like Jonah by the whale, in order to discover the mysteries that lay within. Relying on Mr. Wallace's superstitious nature and his fascination with death, the narrator sends him home to his wife to find out the nature and location of moles on her body, explaining that he can read in the moles indications of inner conditions: "Signs without are only symbols of the world within," he tells Wallace (p. 133). After some persuasion, Mr. Wallace begins to bring back reports about his wife's body, and soon the narrator's perverse sexual curiosity has taken over his imagination. Although the narrator at first claims, "Even now I dare not let my mind look upon the picture of that pair [of moles] peering beneath her lifted skirts," almost immediately he is describing imagined intimacies between Wallace and his wife in graphic detail:

He spies out her moles, creeps upon her dressing, at her bath, or he remembers lovelier days when he was whole and she was smooth and clean and there was flesh to glory in. Then those moles were yellow on her hip perhaps like beads inviting kisses. No. I see the moistened finger, the hiked skirt, the inquiring frown. I see it clearly, bright with color, dimensional with shadow.

(P. 136)

The narrator's plan is successful. In his words, "My triumph was complete. I broke the weaker vessel" (p. 137). When Mr. Wallace arrives with some final secrets about his wife, the narrator makes light of the whole affair and sends him back to his moles, gas, and falling hair.

Of course, most people are not so easily manipulated, and in fact the narrator's intense interest in Mrs. Mean is generated largely because he senses that he has no control over her, that she threatens his transcendence. Early in the story, after commenting on his success in manipulating Mr. Wallace, he proudly announces that he has "succeeded to the idleness of God" (p. 113). But he immediately qualifies this statement and suggests the real reasons for his fascination with Mrs. Mean:

Except in the case of Mrs. Mean. I am no representative of preternatural power. I am no image, on my porch—no symbol. I don't exist. However I try, I cannot, like the earth, throw out invisible lines to trap her instincts; turn her north or south; fertilize or not her busy womb; cause her to exhibit the tenderness, even, of ruthless wild things for her wild and ruthless brood. And so she burns and burns before me. She revolves her backside carefully against a tree.

(P. 113)

This description, with its highly sexual suggestiveness, is another indication of the narrator's dissatisfaction with the limitations of imaginative contact. And yet he takes considerable pride in his ability to project himself inward and see beneath the surface of outward, objective reality. Usually his wife acts as a kind of mediator, a restraining force for his imagination, and consequently the narrator is disdainful of her "failures of the imagination" (p. 129). In trying to conjure up a picture of what the inside of the Means' house must be like, he explains the difference between his own approach to reality and the more literal attitude of his wife:

I have tried to carry her but her sentiments are too readily aroused. Her eyes stay at the skin. Only her heart, only her tenderest feelings, go in. I, on the other hand, cut surgically by all outward growths, all manifestations, merely, of disease and reach the ill within.   (P. 128)

The narrator follows these remarks with a vivid, sexually charged description of the Means' house, with its closed windows, its dirtiness, its "damp" walls, and its satin-shaded lamps. He pauses for a moment to remember an incident that happened when he was a child that he associates with the Means and their house; the sexual repression present in so many of his descriptions is very evident in the association he makes between Mr. Mean and the semen-like slugs:[54]

I was playing with toy cars and digging roads around the supports of the family porch when I accidentally placed my hand upon a cold wet pipe which rose out of the ground there and saw near the end of my nose, moist on the ridge of a post, four fat white slugs. I think of that when I think of the Means' house and of pale fat Mr. Mean, and the urge to scream as I did then rises strongly in me.   (P. 128)

The narrator of "Mrs. Mean" seems to realize that his imaginative projections have a metaphorical appropriateness; but he also senses that the artist must be careful about trying to apply these constructions too literally, for the attempt to confirm these metaphors empirically misreads the nature of the artistic process and destroys the power of the artist to invent freely. As Gass observes in his essay "In Terms of the Toenail" (*FFL*, p. 76): "In a metaphor that's meant, the descent to the literal can never be made," for such forays into reality confuse aesthetic designs with the designs of the real world. In order to maintain his godlike power as an artist, then, the narrator is anxious to block any such descents to the literal. As he says, "My wife maintains that Mrs. Mean is an immaculate housekeeper and that her home is always cool and dry and airy. She's very likely correct as far as mere appearance goes but my description is emotionally right, metaphysically appropriate. My wife would strike up friendships, too, and so, as she says, find out; but that must be blocked. It would destroy my transcendence. It would entangle me mortally in illusion" (p. 129).

As should be evident, this narrator is involved in a kind of paradoxical struggle with his imaginative powers which Gass describes in his preface as being "at once escape and entry, an inside pulled out and an outside pressed in" (p. 27). A "shy and timorous man" (p. 127), he fears direct contact with the world and contents himself, at first, with an escape into his own projections. In an anecdote about a Russian woman named Tanya, the narrator shows that words are powerful vehicles but have the advantage of being immaterial and hence "unsoiled" by contact with reality. This is one reason why he is so taken with Tanya's tale: "I picture her moving lips. I roll the words on my own tongue—the lovely words, so suitable for addressing the world—but they roll silently there, as chaste as any conjunction" (p. 116). Very much like Jethro Furber, this narrator finds in words a "chaste" and protective means of escape; yet, also like Furber, he is also anxious to *penetrate* the wall of abstraction which he builds with the help of words—a "penetration" which is closely linked with his sexual curiosity. As the story concludes, the narrator is driven to more directly enter his neighbors' lives, and one evening he decides to prowl around "through the alleys by the backsides of the houses" (p. 139). That this invasion of the privacy of his neighbors is partially sexually motivated is obvious: not only does the image of the "backsides of the houses" bring to mind his earlier description of Mrs. Mean ("she revolves her backside carefully against a tree," p. 113), but his explanation of why he fears entering the Wallace's empty garage is overt in its sexual evocations:

I am at the entrance and frightened by it as a child is frightened by the bold air that drifts from a cave to damp the excitement of its discovery. Not since I

was very young have I felt the foreignness of places used by others. I had forgotten that sensation and its power—electric to the nerve ends.   (P. 139)

Although the narrator is both drawn to and excited by the power
that this entry into their lives provides, he also senses that he has
failed to heed the warning given by Gass at the end of *Willie Masters:* "YOU HAVE FALLEN INTO ART. RETURN TO LIFE." He compares this initial foray into his neighbors' world as being akin to "a
necromancer carrying a lantern" and further admits, "I have fallen
into the circle of my own spell" (p. 139). When he is almost discovered by a neighbor, Mrs. Cramm (whose name is another indication
of the sexual nature of his obsession), he jumps into Mrs. Mean's garage; he decides that this entry is but a *self*-entry and that what he is
really doing is burrowing further into his own imagination: "I realize
that I have breached the fortress, yet in doing so I lost all feelings for
the Means and sensed only myself. . . . This is not the world. I have
gone too far. It is the way fairy tales begin—with a sudden slip over
the rim of reality" (p. 140). Hiding in the garage the narrator thinks of
another couple who became lost within a fiction: "I think of Hansel
and Gretel. They were real and they went for a walk in a real forest
but they walked too far in the forest and suddenly the forest was a
forest of story" (p. 140). The danger being faced by this narrator, of
course, is falling under the same kind of fictional spell that so many
of Coover's and Barthelme's characters succumb to. The narrator
admits that he has been almost completely taken over by the power
of his urges. As he awaits his nightly adventures "with growing excitement," his description of his feelings of anticipation strikingly reveal the power which his imaginative involvement has created in
him: "The desire is as strong as any I have ever had: to see, to feel, to
know, and to possess!" (p. 141). The story's paradoxical movement of
escape and entry—a movement away from empirically observed reality into the realm of the imagination—is completed in the narrator's last words which bring together the central motif of sexual and
imaginative penetration: "Shut up in my room as I so often am now
with my wife's eyes fastened to the other side of the door . . . I know
the time is only days before I shall squeeze through the back screen
of the Means' house and be inside" (pp. 141–42).

Although the dramatic situation in Gass's next story, "Icicles," is very different from that found in "Mrs. Mean," the main character, Charley Fender, also moves away from contact with reality toward isolation and contemplation of his own imagination. Thus "Icicles" presents a similar kind of breakdown and withdrawal on the part of its main character. However, whereas "Mrs. Mean" portrayed its narrator's "approach and avoidance" strategy, "Icicles" shows a much more fundamental breakdown of the imagination's ability to deal with reality, for Fender is so pathetically weak and passive that even his imagination is overwhelmed by—and even contributes to—the destructive processes around him. The most important imaginative construct created by Fender—his identification between himself and the icicles—serves only to reinforce the inertness and sterility of his life and offers him no entry into the world of warmth and personal contact which he so obviously longs for. The very fact that Fender identifies so strongly with these icicles is a telling indication of the way his personality and character are intertwined with a dead, life-destroying environment. Bruce Bassoff's comparison of the themes of "The Pedersen Kid" and "Icicles" offers a good introduction to the important way these two stories differ: "While 'The Pedersen Kid' enacts a sacrifice, an expense that solarizes the world and restores our sense of intimacy, "Icicles" enacts the contrary process of reification, in which the boundaries between men and things break down."[55]

Charley Fender is a self-conscious, Prufrockian individual whose sense of personal destiny is too intimately related with *things* rather than people. Fender is a real estate salesman who has grown to believe literally in his boss Mr. Pearson's suggestion that "properties are like people" (p. 150). As his name indicates, Fender has become as inanimate as the objects around him. He is a man who has grown accustomed to absorbing the bumps that life has to offer; his main purpose is currently that of "fending off" those who would intrude into the private sanctuary which he has created for himself. In an early description of Fender's isolation and loneliness, Gass points to the interconnections existing between landscape and mental outlook, environment and man:

He hated winter. The same gray sky lay on the ground, day after day, gray as industrial smoke, and in the sky the ground floated like a street that's been salted, and his closets were cold, holes wore through his pockets, and he was lonely, indoors and out, with a loneliness like the loneliness of overshoes or someone else's cough.   (P. 144)

We are told very little of Fender's past life, but it is inconsequential enough that even the census ignored him in its last official report. Indeed, we learn that Fender's life had "vanished so completely, in fact, that at a party once, when he was asked as part of a game to compose his autobiography, he'd had to answer that he couldn't tell the story of his life because he couldn't in the least remember it" (p. 161). If his past is forgettable, his present is equally intolerable, with "the little energy he had" said to be "ebbing" (p. 155). The barrier between Fender and the world is symbolically introduced early in the story when Fender considers the possibility of cooling his hot tongue (he is eating a pot pie at home) by placing it to the window glass. This "kiss," however, is immediately rejected by Fender, who thinks, "Who would dare to . . . publicly? Even alone he felt constraint. As if Pearson might be passing and would see him apply such a kiss to the glass" (p. 145). In this passage, Gass uses the window as a symbolic focus in much the same manner as he will use it in "In the Heart of the Heart of the Country." The window separates Fender from the outside world much more than it joins him to it; even if he should apply a kiss to the window (as he eventually works up courage to do, later in the story), no real contact would be established, for such a kiss would actually be a *self*-kiss. The windowpane, then, can create only the illusion of contact between inner and outer worlds, and as such it serves as a perfect manifestation of the barrier of imagination which most of Gass's characters create to protect themselves from direct contact with the world.

The few meager relationships Fender has established at work are sadly revealing about the nature of his personal dilemma. For instance, his two fellow office workers, Glick and Isabelle, seem to be engaged in a secret conspiracy to humiliate Fender and destroy what little self-confidence he possesses. Fender is obviously and pathetically attracted to Isabelle, but his obsessive self-consciousness and sense of personal anxiety—which has evident sexual roots— makes it impossible for him to convey his attraction. Glick, meanwhile, is a younger officemate whom Fender had hoped to take in hand and educate in much the same way that he himself had been instructed by Mr. Pearson. But Glick refuses to acknowledge Fender's aid and even turns the tables on Fender by offering his own actions as a model, to which Fender can only mutter to himself, "Advice. From the start. Very wise. And Glick was the younger man. . . . No friend of his" (p. 145). Like everything else encountered by Fender, Glick's presence at the office further reduces his meager supply of life and self-confidence. Fender's unconscious habit of breaking down the distinctions between objects and people is fully evident in his thoughts of Glick, whom he constantly equates with a pickle—"Glick. A pickle. A pickly fellow" (p. 145). This identification is created in part by Glick's name and partially by the pickle's phallic shape, for Fender sees in Glick an embodiment of sexual aggression and competition which he cannot match. These feelings are evident not only in Fender's envy at the way Glick has so smoothly won Isabelle's confidence but also in his discomfort at the way Glick aggressively handles the dried flowers kept on his desk. Fender's sympathetic identification with these flowers is evident in his worried comments about the way Glick "kept thrusting stems in a vase, then yanking their heads" (p. 162). Worst of all, Glick shows no concern at all for Fender's precious icicles; "You should have seen the bunch I kicked off my car," says Glick casually to which Fender, "hardly able to speak," can only feebly reply, "I can bet" (p. 163).

By far the most important member of the office for Fender, however, is his boss, Mr. Pearson. Pearson's name suggests both "peer" and "person," indicating what Bassoff calls "the omniscience and *impersonality* of a god."[56] It also hints at the destructive effect his entry into Fender's life has been, for Fender's frequent concern about being observed by Pearson shows how easily his boss "pierces" his inner defenses. Pearson is clearly a sort of father figure for Fender who, at one time, viewed him as "a prophet, sometimes a god" (p. 152). Despite being completely dominated by his boss, Fender defends him in front of Glick and Isabelle, a loyalty pro-

duced in part because Pearson at least doesn't jeer at him and partially because of what Fender terms his boss's "beautiful belief" in
reification. This "beautiful belief"—the insistence that people are
like property—is Pearson's most important legacy to Fender, and ultimately it lies at the center of the dissolution process we see working throughout the story. Because nothing matters in his own life,
Fender is enormously impressed with Pearson's attention to detail,
and he feebly tries to mimic his boss's "devotion, his passion, his
love" for his work (p. 148). Assured by Pearson that the real estate
business is creative and fulfilling, Fender eagerly listens to his
lengthy harangues about the important connections between
people and the property they own, for he senses that only in his job
can he achieve any level of personal satisfaction. As a result, many
of Fender's fondest memories of his boss are of Pearson's impassioned advice about the real estate business. In one of Pearson's
speeches, he reassures Fender that the real estate business provides
an adequate creative substitute for personal involvements. And, as
the language of the passage implies, even sexual fulfillment can be
found in the profession:

It was important (it was everything!) to know properties—how they fared—
because properties were like people . . . you've got to be creative, Fender,
you've got to see . . . ideas! ideas! that's what this job is, it's creative . . . this is
your person, Fender—these streets, these buildings, this town—the body of
your beloved—yes, yes, yum—and you've got to know it . . . think, perceive,
consider and create . . . who were those biddies with the string? yeah, fates—
well that's our function, Fender, we're the fates . . . here she is, Fender, feel
her up, eh? . . . you've got to have everything at the tip—the tip. . . . Fender,
the thing is: it's moving and the thing to ask yourself is: am I going to create,
control, direct, manage, make that move, or is it going to manage and move
and make me?   (Pp. 149–51)

Pearson's unconsciously phallic suggestion—"you've got to have
everything at the tip—the tip"—only serves to reinforce Fender's
evident phallic anxieties. Fender recalls, for example, that for a time
"he'd had the same fear of the icicles he'd had from time to time of
sharpened pencils—that one might pierce his eye" (p. 161); he advises Glick to feed prospective clients "facts sharp as needles" and

then continues an imaginary conversation with a client by saying, "See this piece of pipe, Mr. Ransay, it's six feet long. You know how important that sort of thing is—I mean how far your water travels" (p. 160). Fender's past life is even described as disappearing "like a stick on a river," while he later thinks that "he has no history. Like a log in a stream" (p. 171). But it is Pearson's analogy between property and people that is utmost in Fender's mind as we watch his slide toward insanity and death. Fender's obsession with the icicles is not only a clear manifestation of his phallic concerns but also the end product of Pearson's suggestion that property is really an extension of the people who own it. "Listen," says Pearson at one point, "*property owns people*" (p. 152), and he also suggests that if you look at property carefully enough, you can even "pass judgment on it, read its future" (p. 150) as you can with people.

Physically and mentally falling apart, Fender gradually withdraws deeper and deeper within himself and desperately seizes on his imaginative identification with icicles as a means of self-protection. When the story opens, his reaction to the icicles forming on his house is normal enough—on his way to work, he sweeps them away with his arm, and when he returns he kicks the fragments from his stoop, thinking, "Multiply like weeds" (p. 143). But as the story progresses and Fender's various personal defenses are stripped from him, his curiosity and concern for the icicles correspondingly increase. Having been astonished by the "purity of the ice" the night before, Fender awakens the next day feeling depressed about everything. Almost as if to compensate for his own loss of substantiality, Fender is driven this morning "to see if his own string [of icicles] had survived the night." We are told that "he took no pleasure in anything" except for the "thought of the icicles and whether they were safe and whether he was picturing their lengths correctly" (p. 157). As the phallic nature of Fender's obsession becomes more complete, so too do his protective feelings toward the icicles. For instance, early in the morning of his last day, Fender thinks that "he could use his tape and if they [the icicles] were still there, he could measure them, that would be interesting—to know how large" (p. 158). Sitting in his car after his first, highly ironic "triumph" (he had managed not to look at his icicles on his way to the car), Fender proudly considers the superiority of his own icicles over those of his neighbors: "He could not help noticing that his were longer than any of his neighbors—they were grander in every way—and since the weather had been considerate enough to remain fine, they would certainly continue growing, they might even double themselves during the day" (p. 160). Fender's second triumph comes moments later when he refuses to allow himself to risk public humiliation by measuring his icicles with a tape measure. His thoughts at this point are extremely revealing about his paranoid self-consciousness ("What would people think if they saw him . . . anyone passing . . . Pearson conceivably?") and his thinly veiled castration anxieties ("He wished his icicles were growing on the other side—within—where he might measure them in private, examine them in any way he liked. But if one broke off. . . . The thought was dismaying," p. 161). These concerns are more dramatically presented later in the morning, as Fender shows a house to some prospective customers. When he notices a young boy cradling a huge icicle taken from the house, Fender rushes out into the snow shouting, "Those icicles, boy, you ought to know, they come with the house. They're part of the property" (p. 173). Later he fends off the postman's potential threat: "When he saw the postman coming, Fender hurried out and stood in front, painfully screwing a smile on, terrified lest the man push by him suddenly and knock them off" (p. 174).

In addition to unconsciously associating the icicles with his own sense of potency, Fender is attracted to the icicles because his belief in reification allows him to feel that their beauty somehow reflects his own unrecognized inner value. In a key passage (pp. 174–77) we are told that for Fender "the beauty of the icicles was a sign of the beauty of their possessor. . . . They were a mark of nature's favor, like fair skin, fair hair, blue eyes." Fender's growing sense of personal and spiritual regression and deterioration is reflected in his persistent concern that his icicles will soon be destroyed by the sun, the wind, or "the weight of their armor." Desperate to uncover some value or beauty in his debilitated existence, Fender observes in the growth of the icicles "laws that build beauty out of change." Although he admits to himself that he is "in a dull way . . . ugly, certainly deceitful, cowardly and disloyal, cheap and thin like the over-pressed and cleaned out clothes [he is] standing in," Fender takes heart in the fact that reification allows him partially to repair his shattered condition. "There is another law," he consoles himself, "the law that passes beauty into me, for I am growing like them, I am coming to deserve them." Of course, he must acknowledge that the icicles, like himself, are slowly dying—"Perishing is the word for them"—but they also manage to transform the process of their extinction into the kind of defiant production of beauty that Fender wishes for himself: "One day it's done. Even now you're melting down. True—but those icicles gather the snow as it softens, oppose their coldness to the sun, and turn their very going into . . . Isabelles."

Like all of Gass's other reclusive artist-figures, then, Fender's inability to deal directly with a hostile, threatening reality leads him to an inner retreat where his potency can manifest itself in private constructions expressly designed to provide a sense of protection and beauty. As is the case with Furber and the narrators of "Mrs. Mean" and "In the Heart," Fender is able to assert himself only in his imagination, for only in his carefully wrought fantasies can he transform his weakness and impotence into the kind of strong, purposeful activity that he desires. At work, he is constantly trying to muster up the courage to make snappy, confident replies to Pearson and Glick, but he can do so only in his mind. Likewise, Fender's anal-compulsive habit of counting the number of bits of peas, carrots, and beef in his pot pies leads him to imagine writing an aggressive letter of complaint to the pie manufacturer, a letter whose phrasing he takes pride in but which will obviously never be sent. The way that he is quick to transform his first negative impression of the streaked snow in front of his house ("like the urine of dogs by trees") into a vision of beauty (he later likens the snow to "a diaphanous robe" p. 155) is typical of the way he fights to rework the ugly, trivial details of his daily existence into something more worthy of his affection. At work he looks cautiously about his office and finds that its contents reflect the disarray of his life with its "lady's hanky in a wad, string of clips, glistening pen stem, ringlet of phone wire, pamphlets bent back savagely." Deciding that this vision is "wrong, wrong, wrong, everything wrong," he quickly substitutes a more pleasing and potent image which he flings at Glick (under his breath, of course): "a golden row of pencils coming to points, then Glick" (p. 165). But perhaps the most important example of these pathetic attempts by Fender imaginatively to recreate his environment occurs late in the story when he is shoveling his walk. We are told that "he would frequently rest to watch his icicles, the whole line, firing up, holding the sun like a maiden in her sleep or a princess in her tower— so real, so false, so magical. It was his own invention, that image, and he was proud of it" (p. 173). This image of which Fender is so proud—the sun like a sleeping maiden or a princess—is indeed lovely, but ironically it also suggests his own torpor, entrapment, and the distance that separates him from the world.

By the time we arrive at the last few pages of the story, the dismantling of Fender's psyche is all but complete. One strong indication of Fender's regression is the deterioration of his language into infantile babbling and playing with the sounds of words, such as the following naughty nonsense: "Well, it was fart smart to stand empty through the winter, that's all I say. . . . Pearson—jesus, he's piss bliss, Pearson is. . . . Selling's not all fuck luck, nossir. Not all fuck luck . . . fuckaluck. . . . Sure they'll laugh—pee hee hee. . . . A dog's house is a dog's house, to be cunt blunt" (pp. 177–80). Fender finally surrenders himself to Pearson's philosophy and takes inventory of his private, bodily property. Not unexpectedly, this list is dismal indeed: "How much room do you have around the ribs there—there in the cage? Many kidney malfunctions? They come on often, about your age. Your shoulders slope and we ought to burn that wart off your chin. . . . Um, your skin is sort of fibrous looking, I'm afraid, and pretty splotchy—scaly, thin—a sour diet" (p. 178). When this self-appraisal is completed nearly three pages later, Fender is left with the unhappy conclusion: "You got a place and nobody wants to live in it" (p. 180). In the last paragraph of the story, Fender sits helplessly entrapped in his chair, apparently ready to vacate his own body. It is here that he manages to conquer himself for the third time that day; but this triumph is only to open himself more completely to the forces of assault, symbolized by the crowd of children who rush down the hill toward him "like a snowfall of rocks" which engulfs him as the story ends. Thus, more than any of Gass's other major characters, Fender is a pathetic victim for whom the special qualities of art and the imagination offer no real consolation at all.

"Order of Insects" is the shortest of the fictions collected in *In the Heart of the Heart of the Country,* but Gass has indicated on several public occasions that he feels it is the best piece of fiction he has yet published.[57] It resembles the other stories in the collection in its examination of how imagination can infuse our relationship to reality with freshness and vitality. Once again Gass presents a central character—an unnamed female narrator—who is struggling against a variety of deadening forces in her everyday life. Eventually she discovers that only an imaginative transformation of the materials at hand into something more orderly and pleasing offers a viable means of escape from these forces. Before she began finding the bodies of large black bugs in her new house, this woman's main worries consist of what she calls simply, "the worries of our ordinary life. . . . The cat has fleas again, they will get in the sofa; one's face looks smeared, it's because of the heat" (p. 187). Her initial reaction upon finding these strange dead creatures is stereotyped disgust and revulsion, as is indicated by her first description of them:

Haphazardly, as earthworms must die on the street after a rain; looking when I first saw them like rolls of dark wool or pieces of mud from the children's shoes, or sometimes, if the drapes were pulled, so like ink stains or deep burns they terrified me.   (P. 182)

She subsequently adds that in her first encounters with the bugs she "saw only horror . . . turned, sick, masking my eyes" and that she "felt instinctively that the insects were infectious" (p. 185). But this initial revulsion almost immediately modulates into a type of aesthetic fascination:

The other, slimmer, had hard sheath-like wings drawn over its back like another shell, and you could see delicate interwoven lines spun like fossil gauze across them. The nymph was a rich golden color deepening in its interstices to mahogany. Both had legs that looked under a glass like the canes of a rose.
                                                                                          (P. 184)

Increasingly the housewife finds herself drawn to these bugs, although her use of such tentative phrases as "I suppose," "I suspect," and "I think" indicates that her absorption with them is more imaginative and speculative than literal. Apparently one of the main reasons for her growing enchantment is the absence of anything in her daily personal life to seize her interest. Thus, in explaining the sudden change in her attitude toward the bugs, she says, "As I consider it now, the whole change, the recent alteration in my life, was the consequence of finally coming near to something" (p. 185). Soon afterward, she says that she "came near often" and hints that she is drawn to a sense of intensity, order, and even beauty in the bugs that she feels is lacking in her dull, everyday routine. Now she says she

saw, for the first time, the gold nymph's difference; put between the mandibles a tinted nail I'd let grow long; . . . found an intensity in the posture of the shell, even when tipped, like that in the gaze of Gaugin's natives' eyes. The dark plates glisten. They are wonderfully shaped; even the buttons of the compound eyes show a geometrical precision which prevents my earlier horror. It isn't possible to feel disgust toward such an order.   (P. 186)

Despite this radical change in perception, however, the narrator is also quite self-conscious about the incongruity of her interest in these objects. It is supposedly a male characteristic to seek out the untamed of the world and become master of it, as the narrator is intensely aware. Thus even after a glowing description of the insects she pauses to note, "Nevertheless, I reminded myself, a roach . . . and you a woman" (p. 186). But soon she finds that not only has she grown to identify actively with the bugs themselves, but also her imagination has begun to "possess" her in a way her husband and family have failed to do. As she explains,

I no longer own my own imagination. . . . I used to rest by my husband . . . stiffly . . . waiting for silence to settle in the house, his sleep to come, and then the drama of their passage would take hold of me, possess me so completely that when I finally slept I merely passed from one dream to another without the slightest loss of vividness or continuity. Never alive, they came with punctures; . . . a soul so static and intense, so immortally arranged, I felt, while I lay shell-like in our bed, turned inside out, driving my mind away, it was the same as the dark soul of the world itself—and it was this beautiful and terrifying feeling that took possession of me finally, stiffened me like a rod beside my husband, played caesar to my dreams.   (P. 186)

This important passage not only suggests her passive reaction to her husband and her more active involvement with the insects, but also reveals her unconscious identification with the masculine images of potency (e.g., she is "stiffened like a rod" when possessed). In response to these feelings, she begins to seek out other bugs "with a manly passion." Now, instead of the previous fear and disgust, she observes in the insects "gracious order, wholeness, and divinity" (p. 188). Rather than being surrounded with disorder, death, and ugliness, she has created a type of artistic beauty which also possesses the permanence granted only to products of the imagination. "I had always thought that love knew nothing of order and that life itself was turmoil and confusion," she says, but she has now discovered something which opposes this view: "But this bug that I hold in my hand and know to be dead is beautiful, and there is a fierce joy in its composition that beggars every other, for its joy is the joy of stone, and it lives in its tomb like a lion" (p. 186).

The story ends with the narrator still trying to resolve the male-female struggle that she feels prevents her from giving herself over completely to the realm of the artistic imagination. Like the narrator in "Mrs. Mean," she senses that the imagination bestows a considerable power on those who use it; consequently, although she admits to a stereotypical feminine sense of timorousness about her new role (she says that she "trembles in her current point of view," p. 189), she also acknowledges her masculine potency when she says that this position "is the point of view of a god" (her choice of "god" rather than "goddess" makes this point even clearer). Her choice of language throughout the story has already demonstrated that the release of her imagination has produced a shift toward androgyny in her character; indeed, this fundamentally androgynous nature of the artistic impulse is Gass's main theme in this story. Unfortunately, her new androgynous character is stifled by her role as housewife and woman. She conjectures that her unresponsive husband, whose artistic powers are probably also blocked by a narrowly defined masculine role, may attempt to "comfort me blindly" by saying that her current impulses are only the product of a "bad dream"; but she is anxious to leave behind the "shell" of her previous existence and to emerge, transformed and ready to soar away into another, less restrictive realm: "I could go away like the wise cicada who abandons its shell to move to other mischief. I could leave and let my bones play cards and spank the children" (pp. 189–90). The last words of the story indicate her bitterly ironic attitude toward her imprisoning role: "How can I think of such ludicrous things—beauty and peace, the dark soul of the world—for I am the wife of the house, concerned for the rug, tidy and punctual, surrounded by blocks" (p. 190). These remarks, sadly enough, show no awareness of the possibility that her newly found artistic vision may have *already* created an escape from the "blocks" of her previous role. This escape into what Yeats has termed "the artifice of eternity" seems to be the only alternative for Gass's lonely, alienated characters who find themselves so easily crushed in jousting with the real world. Gass's next story, "In the Heart of the Heart of the Country," provides his most complex examination of the attractions and risks involved in such a flight and also serves to effectively focus many of the metafictional motifs and themes introduced in the previous stories.

Built out of thirty-six blocks of prose, each containing an identifying tag ("A PLACE," "EDUCATION," etc.), "In the Heart" is almost defiant in its refusal to tell a story in any conventional sense. Gradually a rather opaque "dramatic situation" is revealed to us: a middle-aged poet has moved to a small, decaying town in Indiana. Claiming that he is "in retirement from love" (p. 191), he apparently has left a former lover behind, preferring now to bury himself and his love for her in a depressing midwestern landscape which usually mirrors his own spirits. Although he says that he has come here "to see, and so to go out against new things" (p. 192), his "going out" is limited almost solely to excursions of perception and imagination, for he despises this town and its inhabitants and will have nothing to do with them. His response should be familiar by now: he retreats inward to build a work of art which he hopes will somehow redeem him and his petty, impotent existence. Devoid of any true plot development or transitional connectives, the individual sections can be seen to develop a complex network of themes, images, and symbolic patterns. Thus, as Loren Hoekzema suggests, "The town takes on the dimension of an organized construction of juxtaposed parts, not unlike spatial form."[58] "I must organize myself," says the narrator in a key section entitled "MY HOUSE, MY CAT, MY COMPANY" (p. 201), and his efforts to organize the disparate elements of his entropic existence are embodied in his attempt to organize these elements into the verbal space of a work of literature. These two efforts are really a single effort, for the town, the people, and the country he describes act as a sort of objective correlative which reflects the narrator's inner condition. Indeed, as Frederick Busch was the first to suggest, the entire description of "B., Indiana," with all of its realistic details, can be identified directly with the narrator's own state of existence. Referring to the story's opening lines ("So I have sailed the seas and come . . . to B . . . a small town fastened to a field in Indiana") which make an important allusion to Yeats's "Sailing to Byzantium," Busch notes:

If we reread the line "and come . . . / to B . . ." we might see "to B" as not only an abbreviation for Byzantium, but what in addition it *sounds* like: "to be." Then we have Gass's narrator having fled the world of flesh only to return to it—in fact, to *be* a part of it. Furthermore, every detail of the small town he goes on to describe will not only be an accurate portrayal of smalltown life in the heartland of America; it will be a description of *him*: he is the town, the town is he. The life he describes may be an imaginative construct, the refuge or prison he creates for himself.[59]

The opening allusion to Yeats also suggests a wide range of inferences about the narrator's self-conceptions, his attitudes about the landscape around him, and—more importantly—about his yearnings for the type of order, beauty, and permanence which art can provide. These lines refer, of course, to Yeats's opening lines which read, "And therefore I have sailed the seas and come / To the holy city of Byzantium." The persona of Yeats's poem is an aging artist who has journeyed to Byzantium because it represents for him the symbol of art as opposed to the natural world of change and inevitable decay. The first stanza immediately establishes the narrator's dissociation from the "sensual music" of those around him who are so caught up in their sensual activity that they "all neglect / Monuments of unaging intellect." Intensely aware of the destructive effect of time on all "those dying generations," the persona realizes that the only way to overcome his sense of mortality is through the operations of art. As he puts it:

> An aged man is but a paltry thing,
> A tattered coat upon a stick, unless
> Soul clap its hand and sing, and louder sing.

In the poem's final stanza, Yeats's narrator envisions for himself an escape "into the artifice of eternity":

> Once out of nature I shall never take
> My bodily form from any natural thing,
> But such a form as Grecian goldsmiths make
> Of hammered gold and gold enameling.

Once taken out of nature, then, the bird and song—artist and activity—are fused and achieve a timelessness denied to those who inhabit only the material world.

The narrator of Gass's story shares with Yeats's persona a similar alienation from the "sensual music" around him; he, too, has decided to distance himself from the world in order to build a work of art. He is also similar to Yeats's narrator in his hyperawareness of the decaying effect of time on the body and spirit and in his belief that only art offers a redemption from the disorganized, often ugly existence around him. But like most of Gass's characters, this midwestern narrator is also drawn in some mysterious fashion to what he claims to despise; it is this struggle, which Loren Hoekzema rightly calls a "voyage both out and in,"[60] that creates the peculiar tension in this actionless fiction. This tension is also generated by the fact that the narrator's "retirement from love" suggests not only the distance he has placed between himself and his former lover but his distance from the act of poetry itself.[61] ("It's impossible to rhyme in this dust," he says, p. 209.) Thus, as in the other stories in *In the Heart,* the concern with a loss of physical potency and communion is intimately linked with a loss of *imaginative potency*. The story we read, then, is not merely a wonderfully apt description of life in a small midwestern town but also both a description of the narrator's inner psyche as he struggles to "pull himself together" (p. 201) *and* the vehicle of his redemption, the proof of his current potency.

When we begin to look at the story's thirty-six individual sections, which correspond to the thirty-six lines in Yeats's poem, we discover that although they initially seem unrelated to one another they actually introduce various symbolic patterns and themes which are tightly unified and subtly developed as the story moves on. The opening section ("A PLACE"), for example, immediately establishes the poetic intensity of the language and introduces several of the story's important motifs. After the initial reference to "Sailing to Byzantium" with its disguised pun on "to be," the narrator lists the first bit of factual information of the story: "Twice there have been twelve hundred people here to answer the census." Such statistics and lists, scattered throughout the story, contrast sharply with the highly lyrical, more personal descriptions of the narrator, although, as Hoekzema indicates, "These statistical sections do achieve a lyricism of their own when they approach a Whitmanesque grand catalogue. Listing, then, can become a highly personal activity which asserts the individual's ability to organize."[62] As a result, the categories listed under such headings as "VITAL DATA" and "FINAL VITAL DATA" are not mere reportage but create an intensely *personal* vision of the town which belies their seeming objectivity. The rest of the first paragraph appears to be simply more neutral description, but it also hints at the hypocrisy and artificiality of the town: "The town is outstandingly neat and shady, and always puts its best side to the highway. On one lawn there's even a wood or plastic iron deer" (p. 191). Obviously, one cannot always trust appearances in this town. The tawdry efforts of the townspeople to imitate nature demonstrate their fundamental alienation from it; we later learn that even the farmers in this community "give not a hoot for the land" and that for the narrator "everything—sky, the cornfield, stump, wild daisies, [his] old clothes and pressless feelings—seem fabricated for installment purchase" (p. 209). Certainly, such artifacts

are extremely ironic when compared with what the narrator is hoping *his* art can produce. The last paragraph of this opening section
takes us "down the back streets" of the town where "the asphalt
crumbles into gravel" and "the sidewalk shatters." These images, as
Hoekzema notes, "suggest fragmentation and decay" and in showing the true nature of the town's collapse, they also "reflect the narrator's psychic fragmentation."[63]

As we move into the landscape of the town, then, we find that the
environment, the people, even the weather, directly reflect the narrator's own sense of entropy, loss of love and potency, and general
feelings of depression. For instance, looking around at the houses of
the town, the narrator comments that "these houses are now dying
like the bereaved who inhabit them; they are slowly losing their
senses—deafness, blindness, forgetfulness, mumbling, an insecure
giant, an uncontrollable trembling has overcome them" (p. 200). The
cold, threatening weather in "The Pedersen Kid" and "Icicles" served
as a convenient symbol of their characters' isolated, loveless lives;
the weather here likewise reflects the narrator's similarly bleak existence and even infuses the entire landscape with a gray, luckless slush:

That's how it is—for instance in the winter. The sides of the buildings, the
roofs, the limbs of trees—they are gray. Speech is gray, and the grass where it
shows. Every flank and front, each top is gray. Everything is gray: hair, eyes,
window glass, the hawkers bills and touters' posters, lips teeth, poles and
metal signs—they're gray, quite gray. Cars are gray. Boots, shoes, suits, hats,
gloves are gray . . . all are gray, everything is gray, and everyone is out of luck
who lives here.   (P. 199).

If there is any positive aspect of this oppressive weather, which
rarely "allows the heart up" (p. 192), it lies only in the way in which
the narrator uses it to ease his sense of responsibility for his current
condition. The following passage indicates his romantic desire to
shift his sense of guilt to the environment and once again reinforces
his identification with the cold, life-destroying landscape around
him. This passage, with its vivid metaphors, personification, and
heavy reliance on assonance and alliteration, also illustrates the lyrical and poetic qualities of Gass's finest prose:

I would rather it were the weather that was to blame for what I am and what my friends and neighbors are—we who live here in the heart of the country. Better the weather, the wind, the pale dying snow. . . . A cold fall rain is blackening the trees or the air is like lilac and full of parachuting seeds. Who cares to live in any season but his own? Still I suspect the secret's in this snow, the secret of our sickness, if we could only diagnose it, for we are all dying like the elms in Urbana.   (Pp. 209–10)

If the weather haunts the narrator's imagination, so too do the people he comes in contact with embody his own fears and obsessions, especially his concern with death and loss of vitality. Even his closest "companion," his cat, Mr. Tick (whose name reflects the narrator's obsession with time), painfully reminds him of the potential of a life lived directly and unselfconsciously with no responsibilities: "Mr. Tick, you do me honor. . . . You are alive, alive exactly, and it means nothing to you—much to me. You are a cat—you cannot understand—you are a cat so easily. Your nature is nothing you must rise to."[64] Mrs. Desmond is his eighty-five-year-old neighbor whose complete absorption with the past and with her own imminent death causes the poet to "sweat in wonder" at "the brevity of life" (p. 202). His descriptions of her emphasize not their communication but their separation, portraying her in lifeless, inanimate images which establish the barrier between them: "We do not converse. She visits me to talk. My task to murmur. Her talk's a fence—a shade drawn, window fastened, door that's locked" (p. 202). In a later paragraph that begins with the words "I do not work on my poetry," the narrator suddenly connects aesthetic impotency with all his other losses: "For I am now in B., in Indiana; out of job and out of patience, out of love and time and money, out of bread and out of body, in a temper, Mrs. Desmond, out of tea." This is followed by a vicious, powerful address to Mrs. Desmond which vividly suggests what she symbolizes:

So shut your fist up, bitch, you bag of death; go die, my dearie. Die, life-deaf old lady. Spill your breath. Fall over like a frozen board. Gray hair grows from the nose of your mind. You are a skull already. . . . I wanted to be famous, but you bring me age—my emptiness. What is *that* which I thought would balloon me above the rest? Love? where are you? . . . love me. I want to rise so high, I said, that when I shit I won't miss anybody.   (Pp. 206–07)

An even more important representation of the narrator's feelings of alienation and decay is his psychic double, Billy Holsclaw. Billy is mentioned far more than any other person in the town, and it is clear from the outset why the narrator so closely identifies with him. In the first section devoted to him, the poet describes the "vacant lots on either side of Billy Holsclaw's house," a passage which immediately establishes the physical nature of Billy's separation from others. Next the narrator tells us: "From spring through fall, Bill collects coal and wood and puts the lumps and pieces in piles near his door, for keeping warm is his one work. . . . I notice he's squinting a little, which is perhaps the reason he doesn't cackle as I pass" (pp. 192–93). Like the narrator, then, Billy attempts to maintain an inner warmth by gathering the decayed elements of his environment around him, although he is an arranger of things rather than words. Billy's "squinting" and failure to notice others also suggests an inward turn to his vision which is characteristic not only of the narrator but of the other dying old men found in a later section entitled "PEOPLE": "Where their consciousness has gone I can't say. . . . Our eyes have been driven in like the eyes of old men" (p. 195). Just as the town's physical characteristics reveal the poet's inner condition, so too does Billy's environment: "His house . . . shed its paint with its youth, and its boards are a warped and weathered gray. So is Billy" (p. 192). After a chance meeting with Billy at the post office, the narrator says, "Our encounter drives me sadly home to poetry—where there's no answer" (p. 198)—an admission that his poetry is unable to effect any *outward* change in his situation. Nevertheless, the narrator reveals in a later discussion of Billy what he hopes his poetry can achieve: "Nevertheless, I keep wondering whether, given time, I might not someday find a figure in our landscape which would serve him faithfully, and furnish his poverty and loneliness richly out" (p. 208). Clearly this is exactly the kind of "furnishing" that the narrator hopes to construct for himself.

In his last description of Billy, whose title ("THE FIRST PERSON") underscores their relationship as doubles, the poet's sense of physical and imaginative impotence, as embodied in Billy, is further developed. The section begins with a summary of the narrator's view of Billy: "Billy's like the coal he's found: spilled, mislaid, discarded. The sky's no comfort. His house and his body are dying together. His windows are boarded up" (p. 218). This depiction, with its hints about sexual decline, about the related decay of house and body, and its suggestion (in the "boarded up" windows) that perception and imagination have been blocked and driven inward, could be applied to the poet as well as to Billy. The connection between sexual loss and the loss of poetic potency, evident throughout the story in the narrator's unconscious castration fears,[65] is more directly apparent later in this same section when he laments his loss of physical potency, saying of his testicles that "they weren't so flat in those days, had more round, more juice." He then links sperm with words: "And over here's the sperm I've spilled, nicely jarred and clearly labeled. Look at this tape like lengths of intestine where I've stored my spew, the endless worm of words I've written, a hundred emissions or more" (p. 219). Earlier the narrator had stated that his ideal had always been to experience via perception — "It's as though I were living at last in my eyes, as I have always dreamed of doing," (p. 192) — while welcoming the release of his pent-up "emissions": "There are moments — foolish moments, ecstasy on a tree stump — when I'm all but gone, scattered I like to think like seed, for I'm the sort now in the fool's position of having love left over which I'd like to lose" (p. 192). Now, however, the poet more honestly acknowledges a dissatisfaction with his inability to feel with his body and with the loss of his "seed." Admitting that his potency has always been more imagined than literal ("Oh I was quite a man right from the start . . . though mostly, after the manner approved by Plato, I had intercourse by eye"), he goes on to get at the "root" of his problem: "My organs are all there, though it's there where I fail — at the roots of my experience" (p. 219). Consequently, he is even willing to wonder if blinded Billy, who must "know" through his fingers rather than through sight, is not a more complete individual than he is: "I'm inclined to say you aren't half the cripple I am, for there is nothing left of me but mouth" (p. 219). This separation between mind and body and the related inability to *feel* because of an overreliance on thought and abstraction will be one of the major concerns of *Omensetter's Luck;* Gass has summarized some of the results of this opposition in "The Evil Demiurge":

We take walking for granted, elementary seeing for granted, yet we find we cannot feel. Thought seems to remove us; we cannot enjoy life; the mechanics of the car are so demanding, we cannot have the pleasure of the ride. . . . We have fallen out of our bodies like a child from a tree; bruised, forlorn, we bellow at the foot of it and wish we were back there among the leaves, and wish at the same time never to suffer such risks again.   (*FFL*, p. 261)

As the poet of "In the Heart" seems to realize, then, even a successful escape into the realm of art and language may not prove to be a satisfactory compensation for the direct, sensual pleasures which Mr. Tick, and possibly even Billy, experience without the burdens of self-consciousness.

Just as Billy is associated with the condition of his warped and weathered house, so too does the narrator closely identify himself with his own house. Indeed, he views his house much as he views his body—as a place of refuge, a source of protection from contact with the world, a sanctuary to which he can retire and attempt to organize the elements of his life which he feels are "spilled, bewildered, quite mislaid" (p. 219). "I live *in,*" he tells us in a section whose title—"MY HOUSE, THIS PLACE AND BODY"—immediately establishes the relationship between body and dwelling place; he adds that when he is well, "I occupy myself . . . completely—to the edge of both my house and body. No one notices, when they walk by, that I am brimming in the doorways" (p. 198). The paradoxical nature of his retreat to a *decaying* environment in order to resurrect and reorganize his flagging powers is indicated by the poet when he says of his "house, this place and body": "I've come in mourning to be born in" (p. 198). Although he wishes to "possess" the elements of the reality around him in much the same way that Fender and the narrator of "Mrs. Mean" did, the poet nevertheless senses his inability to *touch* what lies outside; and although his windows (by extension, his eyes) allow him to observe reality, they also serve as a barrier preventing direct contact. In this they function much like the wires near his house which serve to "prevent [his] going out" (p. 193), but which also act as "bars of connection" (p. 209). In perhaps the most important single section in the story, "HOUSE, MY BREATH AND WIN-

DOW," the poet explores the paradoxical qualities of his house as both tomb and birthplace, agency of access and enclosure, doorway and barrier. Standing in front of one of his forty-one windows, the poet finds that on the window glass the inside and outside meet, as his own reflection joins with the images of the outside world to form a peculiar union: "Ah, my friend, your face is pale, the weather cloudy; a street has been felled through your chin, bare trees do nothing, houses take root in their rectangles, a steeple stands up in your head" (p. 213). A kiss when applied to this glass is, like Charley Fender's in "Icicles," really a narcissistic gesture; and when he comments that "the pane is cold," we understand the difficulty of achieving warmth from self-love, especially because this window is said to be "a grave, and all that lies within it's dead." Later in this section, when the poet comments, "We meet on this window, the world and I, inelegantly, swimmers of the glass," we see how this window, with its two-way reflections, serves as an analogue of the pages he is composing. On the window glass, as on the page, the outer reality merges with the inner reflection or, as the narrator puts it, "the world beyond my window, me in front of my reflection, above this page" (pp. 213–14).

The struggles of this poet-narrator to rescue his past and present experiences by transforming them into a work of art may recall the similar attempts by Faulkner, Proust, Stein, Colette, and Valéry which Gass found so interesting in his critical studies. Like the warmth Billy receives from the coal and the "caresses" and "kisses" the poet receives from his contact with the bug-infested fruit in the HOUSEHOLD APPLES section, there are benefits to be reaped from the release of energy that exists within decaying things. Haunted by a sense of loss and driven inward by his alienation from his current surroundings, the poet in this story resembles Nabokov's Humbert Humbert, who similarly attempts to rely on the transforming powers of art to immortalize a depressing series of events. The resulting works of art—Humbert's "Confession of a White Widowed Male" and the poet's short story—offer no real salvation for their creators here on earth: Humbert dies, lonely and publicly humiliated, while we last see Gass's narrator at Christmastime "alone, leaning against a pole" with "no one in sight" (p. 223). But we should also remember

that both Humbert and the narrator in Gass's story have succeeded
in leaving behind enduring works of surpassing beauty. We are surely
meant to feel embarrassed and sorry for Gass's poet in many instances: he is often self-indulgent, pompous, and too quickly projects his own self-loathing onto the environment around him. However, as Tony Tanner points out, "Even this world of deprivation and
near-death bestirs him to language, and where there are words there
is life—that is the feeling . . . he cultivates his language until, amidst
the drab aridity of the Midwestern plains, flowers bloom in what we
may probably call his lexical fields."[66] As with the best of metafictions, this story allows us to observe the important function that the
fiction-making process plays in allowing man to synthesize even the
worn-out detritus of a life into an artistic, fictional unity. Thus, Humbert's final words in *Lolita* might well have been spoken by Gass's
poet about his own lost love—"I am thinking of aurochs and angels,
the secret of durable pigments, prophetic sonnets, the refuge of art.
And this is the only immortality you and I may share, my Lolita."[67]

Omensetter's Luck

There can be no doubt now that the publication of Gass's *Omensetter's Luck* in 1966 was one of the most important literary events in
the United States since World War II. As with other difficult, innovative masterpieces in this century (one thinks of Joyce's *Ulysses* or
Gaddis's *The Recognitions*), the acceptance of Gass's work by the literary community has been only gradual. But even the book's first reviewers immediately sensed that the novel was a stunning achievement. Richard Gilman, for example, began his review of the book for
the *New Republic* by calling it "the most important work of fiction
by an American in this literary generation." He went on to claim that
it provided "the first full replenishment of the language we have had
for a very long time, the first convincing fusion of speculative
thought and hard, accurate sensuality that we have had, it is tempting to say, since Melville."[68] Other early reviewers were almost
unanimous in their praise, frequently comparing Gass's achievement
with that of Joyce and Faulkner. Certainly the book provided a daz-

zling display of Gass's talent for language. As Paul West summarized in his review for *Book Week,* "One would have to be criminally tone-deaf and almost snowblind not to register the sonic and visual brilliance of the language . . . a pregnant, swaying physicality with an undertow of festive and smutty limericks: a delight to say aloud and a continuing sound in the mind."[69]

Before David Segal agreed to get the novel published for the New American Library, Gass had labored on the book for a dozen years and had seen the book rejected by a long list of publishers. Although two lengthy sections of the novel appeared in *Accent,*[70] Gass was hampered in his efforts to complete the book when, shockingly, the only completed copy of his manuscript was stolen by one of his colleagues at Purdue University.[71] In a frantic and powerful burst of energy, Gass rewrote the entire manuscript from notes and memory during a six-month period which followed the original's theft. The rewritten manuscript still differs considerably from the book which was eventually published; essentially, it concentrated on the Pimber-Omensetter relationship, with Jethro Furber only being a name in the background. But with Gass's realization that the book was still unsatisfactory, the focus of the novel began to change away from Pimber and Omensetter, while emphasizing the role of Furber; eventually Furber's dense, highly experimental narrative took over nearly three-fourths of the book's development.

Although *Omensetter's Luck* is clearly headed in the direction of the plotlessness found in "In the Heart," its basic movement is fairly easy to summarize. Set in Gilean, a small Ohio river town, in the 1890s, the book revolves around the reactions of various townspeople to the arrival of Brackett Omensetter and his family. Omensetter is a "wide and happy man" (p. 31) who shares with the prelapsarian Adam a sort of naturalness and unselfconsciousness that makes him appear admirable to some and suspicious to others. As Gass himself comments in a letter to David Segal, "Three figures grouped themselves around Omensetter: the devoted chronicler, the worshiper, the opponent. All must see an extraordinary power in him, otherwise they would not stop to chronicle, worship, or oppose." These three characters also give Gass a chance to move through the major artistic modes of language, for, as Gass explains,

"Tott took on the responsibilites of narrative, Pimber the responsibilities of the lyric, Furber those of rhetoric, and finally, since he is pivotal, the dramatic as well."[72] At the level of language, then, the book presents a metafictional investigation into the nature of differing styles. And as with each of the main characters in *In the Heart,* it is also at this *linguistic level* that these characters most readily reveal themselves—a factor which helps us understand Gass's remark that "each of the major characters in *Omensetter's Luck* represents a different artistic type, and they're all bad as far as I'm concerned."[73] In addition to these central metafictional concerns, there are other familiar themes and symbolic patterns developed in the novel. Indeed, Gass has said that he began the book planning to examine a variety of the "stock materials" of American fiction:

I think I had something in mind very like a desire to tackle some of the basic themes in American literature that have become clichés in standard works. So I chose to write about the kind of allegorical conflict that occurs particularly in the earlier literature in America, such as in works by Hawthorne and Melville. You see, I was still interested in the mileage that could be gotten out of the standard, traditional modes and themes.[74]

These "stock materials"—the initiation motif, the arrival of Omensetter as a kind of Second Coming, the corruption of the New Eden pattern, and so on—are obviously present in the novel's development, although Gass is anxious to exploit them for his own purposes. Indeed, as is true of all of Gass's work, much more important to the book than the themes he develops is the enormously rich and sensuous language he uses to embody these ideas.

The novel opens with a relatively brief introductory section called "The Triumph of Israbestis Tott" which acts in much the same way that an overture does for a musical composition; here all of the novel's major characters and events are introduced briefly and obliquely, along with most of its important symbolic and thematic patterns. The narrator of this section is Gilean's unofficial historian, Israbestis Tott, an ancient, doddering old man who loves to tell stories about the past but whose illness and incipient senility cloud his narrative with confusion and ambiguity. As we watch Tott—whose name derives from the German *tod,* death—wander from the auction which opens the section to several chance encounters with various people, to his final, highly ironic "triumph" in which he kills a spider, we are given glimpses into the major actions of the novel which will be developed and clarified later on. Many of the names and anecdotes Tott repeatedly returns to—the arrivals of Omensetter and Furber in Gilean, Sheriff Curt Chamlay's search through the "snowy weeds" (p. 13) for Pimber, the instances of Omensetter's "luck," Pimber's bout with lockjaw, and so on—turn out to be key events in the novel's subsequent development. But just as many names and events are red herrings, mysteries which will never be directly taken up or later unraveled: Bob Stout's fall from the Methodist steeple, the hunt for Hog Bellman, the Hen Woods' burning, and several others. In much the same fashion that Benjy's section serves to preview the rest of *The Sound and the Fury,* then, "The Triumph of Israbestis Tott" provides an ambiguous overview of all that will follow in *Omensetter's Luck,* although Tott's fading memory and tendency to "storify" history makes us reevaluate everything he tells us as we progress through the novel.

Tott's section opens on a fall day at an auction of Lucy Pimber's personal belongings; this is an appropriate setting, for Tott is a relic as useless and forgotten as most of the items being sold. Naturally the sale of these familiar items bothers Tott because they remind him of his own past and the past of Gilean—both of which he is anxious to preserve. This is Tott's first excursion out into the town after a long illness, and we quickly realize that his first "triumph" is simply that of being still alive: "He'd said he'd see the summer under and he had" (p. 9). But throughout his section, we are given plenty of reminders that Tott's initial triumph is only temporary and he will soon be dead: the hints of approaching winter; Tott's perilous connection to the past slipping through his fingers as Lucy Pimber's things are auctioned off; his resting "under an elm that was dying of disease" (p. 22); the remembrances of all his friends who have died and the repeated references to Uncle Simon, a huge tree that had perished in a fire. As the auction drones on, Tott's eager attempts to provide some stories and background information for the townspeople are met only with impatience and indifference. It also quickly becomes apparent that, as Tott admits, "He was out of touch" (p. 10)—a phrase which holds true for Tott's relationship to the past as well as to the present.

In the course of his wandering, Tott is able to engage only the interest of a few children. While engaged in these dialogues, Tott unknowingly introduces several of the book's major symbolic motifs. For example, in one conversation with a young boy, Tott raises the key idea of the pleasures of the natural, unselfconscious life and directly relates this idea to Omensetter:

[Israbestis]   Ever watch a cat stretch? Cats know how to live.
[Boy]   I know it.
[Israbestis]   Cats beat us at it bad. Now Brackett Omensetter, though—
                                                            (P. 26)

This passing reference to Omensetter's animal-like ease and naturalness anticipates the important comparison that Furber makes in the second section of the novel, when he is attempting to prove to the townspeople how peculiar is Omensetter's relation to the world: "'That man,' he declared, 'lives like a cat asleep in a chair. . . . A cat's a pretty thing, of course. How pretty a man? Is it attractive in a man to sleep away his life? . . . The cat's an unmitigated egotist, a slothful beast, slave to its pleasures'" (p. 41). When Tott continues the conversation, the child raises the problem of the relationship between words and reality and unwittingly introduces the nominalist position that words somehow are responsible for the existence of objects in the world. The boy begins the exchange:

Did Kick's cat have a name?"

A name? . . .

What was Kick's cat's name? Molly's turtle's Sam, which is dying.

His name was Kick's cat.

If he didn't have a name you couldn't find him. I know a kid got his name
    erased and he went away forever.   (P. 26)

This whole question of the relation between symbols and their referents and between names and reality lies at the center of Furber's metaphysical and religious speculations, as we shall see. In fact, Furber often seems to share the child's opinion that words are directly connected to their referents, as the following passage indicates. Furber is musing to himself:

Didn't a man grow like his name in the long run, and wasn't there a piece of him wedged in it, between the syllables, like meat in a sandwich? How else could you know that the noises fit? It's what finally does those famous people in, his father used to say, wagging a long, plump finger; every time you're thought of, a part of you gets used. . . . If each man were in his syllables somewhere, he could be reached that way. And touched. . . . There was Backett Omensetter, then. He'd worn that man to a shadow, if this was true; his name could only call a ghost.   (Pp. 132–33)

Ironically, of course, Furber's continual mispronunciation of Omensetter's name (he refers to him as "*Backett*") is one of the key indications that he is *not* in touch with Omensetter's true nature.

A bit later in this same conversation, when Tott explains Kick's cat's love of milk, he raises another ontological issue that will haunt Furber—the problem of definition and the necessity of earthly beings following the laws of nature set up by God:

That's a way cats have. They've got to love milk and fish and chase mice and rats and birds. Otherwise they ain't cats. It's what they call a law of nature.

                    . . . .

My cat hates milk.

You don't have a cat and if you did he wouldn't hate milk, but if he hated milk he'd be a beaver and bite you in half like a log.   (P. 28)

Another important motif is introduced when Tott first tries to kill the spider. We are told that "Israbestis put the shadow of his hand over the spider" (p. 21), a description which foreshadows the death of the spider later in the section by Tott's hand and which also suggests Tott's inability to engage directly the reality around him. More importantly, this description introduces the shadow symbolism that is developed throughout the Furber section and which reaches its culmination in Furber's memory of being able to make love to the girl on the train only with his shadow. In a similar fashion, Gass uses many of the seemingly inconsequential episodes and descriptions throughout "The Triumph of Israbestis Tott" to present obliquely many of the major themes and symbolic patterns that will be more fully developed later in the novel.

Tott's difficulties in finding an audience for his stories is only one of several indications of his basic failure as a historian and as an artist. In his role as the "devoted Chronicler," as Gass calls him,[75] Tott obviously wishes to hold on to the past, to explain and clarify it. But his grasp on history is feeble indeed, as his confused efforts to explain one of his stories to an onlooker suggest:

He [Bob Stout] fell on the iron fence that used to go around it. Parson Peach, he'd just come then—no, no, it was longer ago than that, Huffley's day it was—Huffley was a builder—took Furber's place. . . . Lutie Root? It was her lot across the street. Was that the one her old man got in a swap for a flock of geese? Yes. There was a story. No. That wasn't Lutie Root.   (P. 11)

Tott's interjection—"There was a story"—also hints at another of his tendencies: he is more interested in the past for its literary potential in his stories than he is for its historic reality. Tott's jealous guardianship of these stories and his disregard for the *reality* of events except as they help him manufacture stories is further revealed when he meets an old friend on the street and listens to him ramble on about the misfortunes of some mutual friends. After listening for a moment, Tott thinks to himself, "Dull old fool . . . he's got no flair. I know these stories. Most of them are mine, my mouth gave each of them its shape, but I've no teeth to chew my long sweet youth again" (p. 13).

Tott, then, is an artist who transforms the people and events of his cherished past into mere elements of stories. As Gass explains, this process is destructive but at least has one consolation: "By putting people in stories he destroys them as people; but he also preserves something—he preserves history—a record of what is no longer alive."[76] Furber's judgment of Tott in a later section of the novel is a more eloquent condemnation of this dual tendency:

Young, yet ancient like his sister, he was a button collector already, a museum director, a digger of dry earth, a peeler of print from old paper, feeder upon the past, despoiler of the slain, bugger of corpses. Save oh save. Preserve. Oh redigest.   (P. 106)

Thus the major problem for Tott is the familiar one for Gass's characters—he can live only in his imagination, through his words, while the real world drifts on beyond his reach.

Although Tott is the first artist-figure in the novel, he betrays the artistic impulse in various ways, at least according to Gass's own aesthetic principles. As a historian, of course, Tott's love of his "storied past" (p. 19) is constantly coming in conflict with the necessity of relying on facts rather than the imagination. That Tott is willing to abandon the imagination is symbolically suggested at the conclusion of the section when Tott's highly ironic "triumph" occurs; in his childish, egotistical action of squashing the spider—a symbol of the artistic imagination—Tott has demonstrated his own artistic sterility. Just as important as this last destructive gesture are the uses to which Tott has put his imaginative powers as he lies alone in his room. Gass is always contemptuous of those who use art to confront what they haven't the nerve to deal with in reality. In a passage we have already examined from *Fiction and the Figures of Life* (p. 37), Gass says: "We are so pathetically eager for this other life, for the sounds of distant cities and the sea; we long, apparently, to pit ourselves against some trying wind, to follow the fortunes of a ship hard beset, to face up to murder and fornication, and the somber results of anger and love; oh, yes, to face up—*in books*—when on our own we scarcely breathe." For Gass, such an approach mistakes the beauties and the complexities of life for those of fiction. Thus we are probably supposed to see Israbestis's life in the wall as a trivialized application of art. Certainly the description of Israbestis's "restfully confining" adventures of the imagination is filled with dramatic irony and calls to mind the passage just quoted from *Fiction and the Figures of Life*:

The days that he was in the wall he thought of himself primarily as a sailor. He conjured up bright images of sail, green swells on the reaches of the ocean, the brown slabs of river mouths and the awesome blue chop and the trailing spray of troubled water. . . . In this way he visited the ports of the world. He was a Chinese, a Hindoo, a shiek; he rode on wild Asian horses and on the backs of elephants in India, while on camels he crossed the African wastes.

(P. 17)

But even in these fictitious adventures designed purely for escape, Israbestis suffers from a fundamental failure of his imagination to produce the kind of realism he desires. Unlike the true artist, who realizes that what he creates need have no necessary connection to the world, Israbestis blames his lack of education for being unable to supply the *facts* to support his fancy: "He was conscious, always, of the inadequacy of his details, the vagueness of his pictures, the falsehood in all his implicit etceteras, because he knew nothing, had studied nothing, had traveled nowhere. Consequently he was never fully in the wall, he was partly clenched in the bedclothes" (p. 18). Unable to create the kind of work which keeps us "kindly imprisoned" (as Gass advises us a good artist will do), Israbestis betrays himself both as a historian and a storyteller, sailing the seas of his imagination in a very leaky boat indeed. Near the end of his section, Tott says to himself in a rare moment of clarity, "Tott—you've shut your house. In effect, you've shut your house. You can't forget, and you don't dare remember" (p. 30); as this house metaphor suggests, Tott is indeed "shut in"—by language, by senility, and by the basic failure of his imagination which, as with Charley Fender, makes it impossible for him to create any alternatives for himself.

The second section of *Omensetter's Luck,* "The Love and Sorrow of Henry Pimber," introduces the dramatic situations which will be worked out near the conclusion of the novel: Omensetter's arrival in Gilean, the town's mixed reactions to this event, and Henry Pimber's decision to commit suicide. From the outset it is clear that Brackett Omensetter (this name suggests not only the "omen-setting" aspect of his character but "Brackett" indicates the way others group themselves around him) is seen by most of Gilean's townspeople as being a kind of Adam before the Fall. To the townspeople, Omensetter appears free from sin or guilt and possesses an animal-like sense of ease and unselfconsciousness; he is therefore capable of living in the world without the various burdens and anxieties that humanity has had to endure since the expulsion from the Garden. The "luck" which Omensetter possesses, then, is merely an outer manifestation of the state of grace which governs his life. The opening paragraph of the section immediately establishes Omensetter's prelapsarian oneness with nature:

Brackett Omensetter was a wide and happy man. He could whistle like a car-
dinal whistles in the deep snow, or whirr like the sky 'white rising from its
cover, or be the lark a-chuckle at the sky. He knew the earth. He put his hands
in the water. He smelled the clean fir smell. He listened to the bees. And he
laughed his deep, loud, wide and happy laugh whenever he could—which
was often, long, and joyfully.   (P. 31)

Unlike the rest of Gilean, Omensetter possesses what Gass refers to
as "a gargantuan capacity for life,"[77] a quality which is heightened
by his obliviousness to the concerns and obsessions of his fellow
men. Although when Omensetter does speak his words are said to be
"happy and assured" (p. 33), he is ordinarily content to respond more
directly, allowing his actions to do his talking. When he makes his
first appearance in town looking for a job, for example, he goes
directly to Matt the blacksmith and *shows* his ability, his hands
dominating his presence.

The response of the townspeople to Omensetter is predictably of
two kinds. On the one hand, many people have a sense of admiration and awe for his free spirit and his harmonious relations with nature. After his near-miraculous cure of Henry Pimber's lockjaw, the
entire town begins to openly gossip about "Omensetter's Luck" in
terms of both envy and suspicion. The more positive, practical side
of these feelings is expressed by Maggie Scanlon who scoffs at talk
of magic by saying, "Don't he always get what he wants. . . . He's
happy, ain't he, the sonofabitch. I wish to god I was" (p. 46). To others,
however, Omensetter's luck and naturalness make him seen, at best,
subhuman and, at worst, an agent of the devil. Furber, for example,
is quick to make the connection between Omensetter and Adam,
noting that "whatever Omensetter does he does without desire in
the ordinary sense, with a kind of abandon, a stony mindlessness
that makes me always think of Eden" (p. 126). As we shall see, Furber
eventually begins to see Omensetter as a much more sinister and
dangerous foe.

By far the most complex reaction to Omensetter presented in the
second section, however, is that of his landlord, Henry Pimber. According to Gass, Pimber should be seen as "the worshipper,"[78] and it
is Pimber's despair in discovering that Omensetter is not going to
play the role of his personal savior that leads him to commit suicide.

Basically, Pimber sees in Omensetter the lost potential of his own meager life. To Pimber, whose "artistic temperament" derives directly from his romantic view of man's relationship to nature, the love which Omensetter evokes is produced because he possesses man's original potentials—a freedom from sin and guilt and a capacity to live life directly and joyfully. As Richard Schneider summarizes, Pimber admires Omensetter "because he has not yet felt man's separation from God and nature. Omensetter lacks the tragic sense of quiet desperation that fallen men have."[79] Obviously Pimber is hopeful that Omensetter will rescue him from his fallen, debased condition. "Was that why he loved him," Henry ponders just before taking his life, "It lay somewhere in the chance of being new . . . of living lucky, and of losing Henry Pimber" (p. 58). As a result, Pimber views Omensetter as "more than a model. He was a dream you might enter" (p. 43).

The nature of this "dream" and the degree of Henry's sense of separation from it is immediately established in their first meeting, when Omensetter arrives at Pimber's house asking for a place to rent. Henry's first impressions are of Omensetter's "muddy clothes" and his genuine, natural ease: "To Henry he seemed fat and spoke with hands which were thick and deeply tanned. . . . His dark hair fell across his face and he'd tracked mud on the porch, but his voice was musical and sweet as water, his moist lips smiled around his words" (p. 34). Although symbolically protected from Omensetter in this first encounter by a screened porch, Pimber quickly realizes that "Omensetter had nevertheless instantly overpowered him" (p. 34) by his very presence. Thus "the screen was no protection" for Pimber, who gazes out and "received the terrible wound of the man's smile" (p. 34). Until this moment, Pimber has been able to hide his dissatisfactions within his daily routine; but this meeting with Omensetter awakens him to possibilities he had not permitted himself to consider—possibilities that ultimately lead Pimber to destroy himself when he decides he will never realize them. In effect, Pimber is Omensetter's psychic opposite or, as Richard Schneider suggests, they "seem to be a pair, opposite halves of the same man—Omensetter with his healthy carelessness and fertile wife, and Pimber with his weak will and barren bitchy wife."[80]

The full implications of Henry's condition are illuminated for him when a fox accidentally falls into a well which has been left uncovered. Omensetter and his daughters respond to the fox's plight with laughter, fully content to let nature do with the fox as it will—a response which directly parallels Omensetter's passive reaction to his son's illness late in the novel. Pimber's horrified reaction to their willingness to let the fox perish in the well obviously results from his sympathetic identification with what is happening to the fox, whose life is now as enclosed and threatened as Pimber's own existence. Henry's imaginative recreation of how the fox feels trapped in the well—"At best, the fox must be badly bruised, terribly cramped, his nose pressed into the damp well wall" (p. 39)—is an apt projection of his own imprisonment; Henry senses the similarity of their "falls" as he rushes home to get a gun with which he can put the fox out of its misery. "Suppose he'd fallen there himself" (p. 41), he wonders, and then extends this analogy with several childish ditties:

> Ding dong bell
> Pimber's down our well.
>
> Who'll pull him out?
> Nobody's about.   (P. 42)

In his letter to Segal, Gass explains that the main source of Pimber's disturbance in this situation is that he has been hoping so strongly that Omensetter will be able to rescue him from his own condition. Gass outlines Pimber's "metaphorical conclusion to a metaphorical argument" in syllogistic form:

> I am in this well like the fox is.
> Only Omensetter can save me.
> Omensetter won't save the fox.
> Omensetter won't save me either.[81]

Pimber also identifies the fox's natural unselfconscious qualities with Omensetter, and his gesture of shooting the fox not only prefigures his own suicide ("Murder would be suicide," he says, p. 40), but is also a means of striking out against Omensetter for his callous refusal to be a savior. Thus after killing the fox Henry admits, "He knew, of course, it was Omensetter he had struck at" (p. 43). As Henry sees it, Omensetter, like the fox, is perfectly at ease with everything he does because he is so completely devoid of self-awareness; Omensetter also lacks the capacity for abstractions that create in man the concepts of sin, sorrow, and the destructive movement of time. Consequently he says that "What Omensetter did he did so simply that it seemed a miracle. It eased from him, his life did. . . . He had an ease impossible to imitate, for the moment you were aware, the instant you tried" (p. 42). Omensetter's naturalness, then, is impossible for others to duplicate because the very act of pursuing this condition implies the development of self-consciousness and abstraction—qualities which preclude the direct involvement with the world that Omensetter has. Standing over the trapped animal, Pimber wonders if perhaps even the fox has been made self-conscious, a possibility which Henry revealingly calls a "reversion":

The fox, he felt, had never seen his past disposed of like a fall of water. He had never measured off his day in moments: another—another—another. But now, thrown down so deeply in himself, into the darkness of the well, surprised by pain and hunger, might he not revert to an earlier condition, regain capacities which formerly were useless to him, pass from animal to Henry, become human in his prison, X his days, count, wait, listen for another—another—another? (P. 42)

Henry's ensuing lockjaw allows Omensetter to once more demonstrate his magical powers; although Pimber is attended to by Doc Orcutt—who is said to represent "science"—and by Furber—"God" or religion (p. 46)—it is Omensetter's beet poultice that most of Gilean feels is responsible for Henry's miraculous recovery. Like Lazarus, Henry feels reborn in a new and liberating existence governed by the senses rather than the intellect: "There was no mistaking Omensetter's likeness; Henry was newborn in that waltzing body now; he had joined it as you join a river swimming" (p. 47). But Henry's romantic desire to return to his primitive, natural origins, to sink into the "dream" represented by Omensetter, is destined to be shattered for, as Richard Schneider observes, what Henry wants is made unattainable by the inescapable fact of his own humanity: "To deny thought would be to deny our humanity, our very essence; thus, Pimber seeks a solution to the most basic human dilemma: to enjoy our bodies fully, we must eliminate or at least subordinate thought; yet to be human, we must cling to perception and thought. We seem not to be able to have it both ways."[82]

Before departing on his last trip into the forest where he will hang himself, Pimber talks with his wife who anticipates the failure of his hopes by saying, "What do you want from him? You'll never get it, whatever it is. He cares for no one, don't you know that? Not even you, Henry" (p. 55). Since his illness Henry has felt that he shares with Omensetter the "painful beauty" of direct perception "in which all things were dazzling, glorious, and terrifying" (p. 57). But as he and Omensetter begin their walk, Henry feels "abandoned" by his growing conviction that his savior has taken on the same qualities of abstraction and human knowledge that he has abandoned since his bout with lockjaw. "The blasted fellow understood his luck. He knew," thinks Henry (p. 57), who senses that by being made aware of his luck, Omensetter has forever lost his ability to rest in what Furber later calls "the sweet oblivion of the animal" (p. 175). On their journey deeper into the forest, Henry and Omensetter appropriately find it impossible to communicate, their efforts blocked by the trees which interfere with their vision and by the howling wind, which makes it impossible to talk. Possessed with "an immense weariness," Pimber begins to realize that Omensetter is not going to respond to his current crisis any more than he was willing to help the fox: "Of course—he'd been a fool—Omensetter lived by *not* observing—by joining himself to what he knew . . . he's going to leave the fox where he has fallen" (pp. 60–61). As the chapter comes to its eloquent and lyrically expressive conclusion, Henry makes it clear that the dream he saw as residing in Omensetter was the romantic's ideal of a life lived simply and naturally. "It seemed to me," he says, "that you were like those clouds, as natural and beautiful. You knew the secret—how to be." In trying to decide what happened to destroy this dream, Henry wonders if possibly he "had . . . simply been mistaken" about Omensetter's special qualities or whether "Omensetter had been robbed already"—robbed of his naturalness by being made aware of it and by now trying to preserve it. This latter possibility lies at the center of the book's development, for in one sense *Omensetter's Luck* is a novel which presents another version of the Fall: Omensetter gradually changes from a privileged, prelapsarian innocent to an ordinary human being. In the end, Henry angrily decides that Omensetter "had been a miracle . . . not to be believed," and that he has now been changed, contaminated: "And now he had to defend against the world like everybody else. No miracle, a man." The key here to Pimber's view—and Furber will echo it in his section—lies in the difference between *having* the secret of life and in *knowing* it, with the latter destroying the former, at least in Henry's mind. "If Brackett Omensetter had ever had the secret of how to live," thinks Henry, "he hadn't known it. Now the difference was—he knew. Everybody at last had managed to tell him, and now like everybody else he was wondering what it was" (pp. 62–63).

Despondent over the fact that he's "scarcely been alive" (p. 60) and abandoned by the one person he hoped could save him, Pimber inverts the image of his earlier symbolic suicide—the fox destroyed in the darkness of the well—by hanging himself "high-up" in a tree. That this inversion is in his thoughts is clear by Henry's remarks that he is "off to kill a fox. But I'll not die as low as he did, for I could ornament a tree like the leaves of a maple" (p. 63). A gesture of defiance, a desire to escape in death from the lowly position he suffered in life, Henry's decision to die in the freezing weather also allows him to escape into the stone-like, wordless oblivion which he had earlier longed for when he said, "I shall be my own stone, then, my dear, my own dumb memorial, just as all along I've been my death and burial, my own dry well—hole, wall, and darkness" (p. 60). Even as he tests the belt to be used for the hanging, he finds himself taking some small pleasure in the act of language, as he creates puns: "There was beauty in the pun: leave-taking," and names the trees as he passes them: "He went by cherry and by black gum trees calling their names aloud. He was the Adam who remembered them" (p. 63). Ironically, however, the very act of naming or creating puns emphasizes the distance Henry remains from the "stony mindlessness" he desires, for as Schneider summarizes, "Naming is as close as Pimber can come to nature, but even that act implies separation from it."[83] In trying to make up for an utterly wasted life by inventing phrases,

Pimber resembles both Tott and Furber who similarly remain locked-in by language.

Part 3 of *Omensetter's Luck,* "The Reverend Jethro Furber's Change of Heart," is a dense, extraordinarily musical section that is remarkable in the complexity of its thematic development and its tight interlocking of symbols and ideas. It also introduces the Reverend Jethro Furber, one of American literature's most diabolic and perverse inventions. In many respects, Furber is the culmination of a long list of Gass's lonely characters who have chosen to retreat into the pleasures and securities offered by art because of their inability to involve themselves more actively in the world. Furber's situation, however, is much more difficult to summarize because he is a clergyman (and thus is supposed to preach the virtues of spiritual rewards over those of the flesh) who has an insatiable hunger for sexual fulfillment. He is also an exceptionally subtle and complex thinker whose training in theology and philosophy, mingled with his rhetorical abilities, enables him to create convincing lies and to disguise motives, even to himself. As a result, Furber emerges as Gass's most complex and fully realized character, although the stylistic difficulties of his section — and they are great — create formidable problems for the reader in understanding his consciousness and personality.

The action in this lengthy third section of the novel is minimal, and Gass himself provides a clear summary of most of it:

Furber has been sent to Gilean by his church for unspecified but guessable misdemeanors. He is bitter and revengeful to begin with. His memories include flashes of his early life, his parents, etc., as well. He arrives during a dry spell, preaches an inflammatory and misguided and confused sermon, antagonizes everybody. Over the years, however, though he's never liked, he does gain a certain ascendency over the people. This he attributes to a series of confessional sermons (I have done wrong) which he preaches following a "religious experience" he has in the garden of his church. His success is far less than he imagines, and when Omensetter arrives on the scene, his belief that Omensetter is undermining his position is largely imaginary. He destroys his own position with his increasingly insane efforts to discredit Omensetter.[84]

Near the end of the novel, Furber finally realizes that Omensetter is only another man and not the devil's agent. He also admits to himself the evil he has been perpetrating and acknowledges the truth of his earlier observations about the primacy of body over spirit—truths he has proposed, played with, and contradicted throughout his section but which, like every other of his beliefs, he had never accepted except rhetorically. Eventually the townspeople, who have suspected Omensetter of murdering Pimber, allow him to leave Gilean, a "mere" man now who has been initiated into the world of knowledge and guilt like everyone else. After a period of madness, Furber also leaves.

The opening of Furber's section finds him wandering through his church garden, now appropriately doubling as the parish cemetery, which is clearly representative of a fallen, withered Eden to which mankind can never return. The rich symbolism of the lengthy opening paragraph introduces many of the section's most important symbolic and thematic motifs:

Rough dogs, barking, splashed into the river chasing sticks. Coats and ties had been hung in the trees and men were hurling stones at soda bottles or skimming pieces of slate and loudly counting the skips. He picked out squealing children and the laughter of the women. If there hadn't been a wall he would have seen them scuffling on the edge of the water. . . . The bench was damp and cold, shadowed all morning by the elms, and he slid his Bible under him. It was a poor garden, given over to ground ivy and plants that preferred deep shade, for the sun reached it only at the top of the day. . . . The shadows of the elm leaves passed gently over the vines and grasses. In winter one could see quite easily through the gate at the end of the garden to the river lying placidly in its ice—leaden, grave, immortal. He had never learned when the key had been lost but the lock was rusted now and the double gates were bound. By spring, when the ivy leafed and thickly curtained the pickets, his blindfold was complete. It wasn't true, but Jethro Furber felt he had spent his life here. . . . The rough cold bench was as familiar to him as his skin, and the garden, with its secret design and its holy significance, was like himself.

(Pp. 64–65)

Here, then, sits Furber, walled off from the sensual pleasures of laughing women and squealing children that lie just beyond him, anxiously staring outwards but largely blinded to the living reality around him. If the "poor garden" in which he sits on his "damp and cold" bench suggests a debased Eden, it is an Eden now securely bound from man by its "rusty" lock and "double gates." Almost immediately we are made aware of several of the section's most important motifs: the skipping of stones, the shadows cast by corporeal objects, the claustrophobic sense of Furber's imprisonment and blindness, his tendency to deny truth in favor of aesthetics (or what "feels" right), the secretive inner workings of his heart.

Among the most significant features of Furber's character are his devotion to acting, disguise, and aesthetics at the expense of honesty and the truth, his preference for words and symbolic gestures instead of action which is coupled with a paradoxical longing for fleshly gratification. In addition, Furber possesses a perverse self-consciousness of these same tendencies—an awareness which deepens his muddle, makes him rail out at himself for his posturing, and emphasizes what Gass describes as "the distance between his feelings and his actions, of the contrast between his inner and outer life."[85] Furber is, above all, a sophist, an artist who uses words not to present the truth but to persuade. "Believe nothing that does not sound well," Furber is told in one of his imaginary conversations with his predecessor, Reverend Pike, and he responds by saying, "By god Pike you have something there" (p. 96). But as Gass points out, the acceptance of this dictum "is essential to the artist, but is disastrous in a preacher, for Furber literally has no beliefs."[86] Furber therefore is an artist too self-conscious about his artistry, a liar who knows himself to be lying, and this partly accounts for his bizarre theological and philosophical positions, his blatant self-contradictions, his tortured attempts to resolve his desire for verbal eloquence with what he knows he should be preaching. For example, early in his section we are told that in rehearsing a sermon Furber is completely willing to "change its meaning if need be, anything, so that it might be eloquent" (p. 73). A bit later his daily routine is described:

Sometimes while he walked he would break into wild half-whispered words instead, and turn with open arms to the walls and leaves, his gaze fixed ecstatically on heaven, adopting the posture of saints he'd seen in prints. . . . Or unable to stomach his own acting, he would turn to mockery. *Oh give us a dramatic speech.* And often he would oblige, charming himself with his rhetoric like a snake playing the flute.   (P. 74)

This sort of deliberate acting and self-indulgence makes it impossible for Furber to believe anything of his own devising for, better than anyone else, he knows these opinions are lies.

Also disastrous to Furber is his inability to reconcile his hidden sexual desires with the Christian doctrine that bodily matters are unimportant or evil. This conflict leads Furber to wage within himself what Richard Schneider has termed "a kind of Machiavellian war between Spirit and Body, which he equates at first with Good and Evil."[87] We see this equation, with its evident Platonic roots, when Furber reminisces about his religious training: "In the seminary they'd been called The Great Hypothesis. The One and the Other. The Spirit and its Enemy. Yes and No. A and B. Truth against The Adversary, Father of Lies. A always won, while B . . ." (p. 200). Needless to say, Furber is not nearly so certain about the ultimate victor of this struggle—or at least he likes to *express* his uncertainty in well-turned phrases or analogies such as, "Is it two falls out of three? God wins the first but the Devil takes the next one. There has not yet been a third to anybody's knowledge" (p. 202). Furber likes to imagine that he has conquered these bodily impulses: once, when thinking about the women in Gilean with their "red hands and peasant bodies" he quickly halts these musings by muttering, "Not that it mattered. He'd forsaken all that" (p. 70). But immediately following this disclaimer, Furber goes on to imagine graphically the sexual blossoming of two adolescent girls whose "maidenly garments" (p. 70) he has long been conjuring up in moments of weakness. In another imaginary discussion with Reverend Pike, Furber at first parrots the church doctrine to the effect that, "Ghosting's what we're always called for. Be above yourself, that's what we're urged—Pike, you and I—the hanker for the other side" (p. 118). Characteristically, however, Furber goes on to question this ideal, wondering if man wouldn't be better off feeling at home with his body; he has grown to envy Omensetter in much the same way that the poet in "In the Heart of the Heart of the Country" grew to covet Mr. Tick's ability to feel at ease with his body. Thus Furber questions whether Omensetter might, "in his fashion," be defying nature's tug—a tug which leads to rot and decay—with his gesture of skimming stones over the water:

What ease instead to melt into the body's arms and be one's own sweet concubine. And Omensetter? Is he, in his fashion, like us? Is it cruel to tease stones so? What's your [Pike's] view now you've splashed under? Whatever he gives them, it lasts only a moment. There's no help for it, they have to come down to a stone's end.   (P. 118)

The stones which Furber here associates with the body (in Pimber's section they were similarly connected, with Henry's death called "a stone's end") are one of the important symbols in the novel. Furber has earlier been fascinated with the effortless way Omensetter makes his stones skim over the water, seemingly hovering free of nature's downward pull. In his typically diffuse manner, Furber sees an analogy between the stones' momentary flight into space—a type of transcendence—and the way the spirit allows the body to rise above its nature as a corporeal essence:

How different we give the semblance of life to the stone, he thought. And it did seem a stone until it skipped from the water . . . effortlessly lifting . . . then skipped again, and skipped and skipped . . . a marvel of transcending . . . disappearing like the brief rise of the fish, a spirit even, bent on escape, lifting and lifting, then almost out of sight going under, or rather never lifting from that side of things again but embraced by the watery element skipping there, skipping and skipping until it accomplished the bottom. . . . Omensetter threw horseshoes the same way. He sent them aloft and the heart rose with them, wondering if they'd ever come back they seemed so light.   (P. 117)

But unlike the Chinese painter who managed to paint a picture into which he finally disappeared, Omensetter manages to create this miracle of transcendence only "for things, for stone and horseshoes, while doing nothing to untie or lighten himself" (p. 118). Furber's elaborate analogy necesarily leads him to a despairing conclusion, for a stone's flight is only momentary, and like the flesh, it must eventually sink. As Furber explains, "Omensetter's stones did not skip on forever either, though they seemed to take heart, or did they renew their fear? from their encounter with the water; but despite this urging each span was less, like that shortness of breath which grows the greater, the greater, the greater effort is required—and plip . . . . plip . . . plipplippliplish was their hearts' register and all they were" (p. 118). This highly rhetorical "sermon of stones" directly anticipates Furber's more honestly derived admission of man's inalterably mortal condition, made after Pimber's frozen body has been recovered from the trees.

In response to this inner turmoil, Furber continually delights in verbally toying with various traditional and self-devised metaphysical and theological issues. Although he hopes these inner debates will provide solutions to his problems, there are numerous contradictions which torment and undermine his ideas concerning his favorite topics: the relation of mind and body, symbol and essence, the nature of perception, and the related topic of words and language. Like the transcendentalists, Furber has convinced himself that reality is a series of symbols created by God. Yet his attitude toward these symbols often seems ambiguous: on the one hand, he frequently spouts the familiar Christian platitude that "the body of any symbol was absurd, as ridiculous as Christ's body was" (p. 65); but he justifies his intense fascination with the material world by rationalizing that his job as a clergyman is to be a "watchman": "Jethro Furber felt that Nature was the word of God as certainly as scripture was— his task, therefore, to watch and listen, to interpret and bear witness. We should all be watchmen, and pray that God will open our eyes to evil and burn our hearts to admonish the ungodly" (pp. 66–67). Thus while guiltily watching the luscious body of Omensetter's wife who is bathing in a river, Furber thinks of the "joy to be a stone" (p. 67), for without perception the stone cannot sin. Furber shares with Pimber the conviction that "vision is no kindly injury" (p. 214), because vision leads man to create abstractions—abstractions which generate our sense of otherness and separate us from the world. More importantly, the ability to think—to possess the "knowledge" that Pimber feared Omensetter was developing—can therefore be seen as a necessary result of man's fall. Furber, like Pimber, senses that Omensetter represents the desire hidden in all of us to return to our earlier condition of complete intimacy with nature. This desire is, in effect, an attempt to deny the essence of what makes us human:

There is everywhere in nature a partiality for the earlier condition, and an instinctive urge to return to it. To succumb to this urge is to succumb to the wish of the Prince of Darkness, whose aim is to defeat, if possible, the purposes of God's creation. . . . For the most part men look upon their humanity as a burden, and call the knowledge of what they are a simple consequence of sin. Men, like all things, resist their essence, and seek the sweet oblivion of the animal—a rest from themselves that's but an easy counterfeit of death. . . . Yet when Adam disobeyed, he lit this sun in our heads. Now, like the slowest worm, we sense; but like the mightiest god, we *know*.   (P. 175)

When mankind ate from the tree of knowledge, then, he fell; but because Omensetter seems so free of the burdens haunting the rest of humanity, Furber reasons that he must be an agent of the devil. Gass provides a simplified version of Furber's patently absurd dialectical syllogisms in his letter to Segal: "God is omnipotent and omnipresent; He made and is in all things. What, of all these things, show him to us best? He cannot display his power best in making good, because he is good. Only by making evil. God is evident most in the Devil. And the Devil, being a master of deceit, hides himself in the God. So what appears good is evil, and what is evil is most like God."[88] It is the end product of this syllogism—"He [Satan] hides himself . . . oh ho! in the butt and body of the best" (p. 75)—that leads Furber to find in Omensetter the embodiment of Satan himself. The crux of this application occurs when Furber thinks to himself:

Omensetter seems beyond the reach of God. He's truly out of touch. . . . Sin's nothing but exile. It occurs when God withdraws. Should exile seem so blessed and free? . . . We know that men are evil, don't we? Don't we? Oh god haven't we observed it often? Haven't we bruised our eyes and stunned our hearts to discover that truth? Yet Omensetter doesn't seem to be. . . . And what shall we conclude from all of this then?
    We must conclude he is the worst.
    He is the worst.
    Therefore.   (P. 126)

In addition to these highly musical but logically ridiculous speculations, it is easy to understand why Furber is so suspicious of Omensetter, for Omensetter, with his lack of self-consciousness, his healthy sexuality, and his tendency to *live* life rather than to talk about it, clearly represents everything that Furber is not but wishes to be. Furber's current psychological hangups can be partially explained by his unhappy experiences as a child. We discover, for instance, that Furber was a weak, sexless adolescent with a peculiar "affinity for fear so pronounced that he had driven his parents nearly out of their wits with it." As a result "they tried to shelter him from the noise and violence," efforts which only served to cut him off from contact with the world around him (pp. 86–88). Gradually young Furber increasingly turned inward for his experiences, especially to the exciting and often sexual world of the Bible. Significantly, one of his favorite fantasies involved being martyred by stones; these stones are here associated with words, for like the pebbles which skim above the surface of the water, words also provide an example of momentary transcendence, a flight above mundane reality. After withdrawing as an adolescent to the Bible to contemplate the "wild times and his own terror" (p. 90), Furber, in effect, never returns to the world at all, except for some pathetic, childish sexual dalliances with his Aunt Janet and with a young girl in the neighborhood named Ruth. Furber's complete separation from normal family affection and concern is probably most touchingly revealed near the end of the book when he tells Omensetter, "Listen, when I was a little boy and learning letters—A . . . , B . . . , C . . . , love was never taught to me, I couldn't spell it, the O was always missing, or the V, so I wrote love like live, or lure, or late, or law, or liar" (p. 233).

By the time Furber arrives in Gilean, his loss of contact with the world is complete and he is now able to interact with reality only symbolically, through his eloquent speeches and his lusty, powerful imagination. Consequently, he retreats into "his beautiful barrier of words" (p. 183) which allows him to keep "everything at word's length" (p. 182). This retreat has the same appeal for Furber that it did for Henry Waugh and most of the characters in *In the Heart*: it permits him to frolic in a clean, vibrant world of aesthetics without risking the embarrassment and disgust he might feel if he were engaged with the real world. In one especially telling passage which describes the joy Furber receives as he "capered in the garden," we are told:

He knew how the orator, the actor, felt; what they sought in their success. He could tickle [his female parishioners] and they would laugh; he could spank them and they'd howl; he could caress . . . and sighing, they'd respond. He was an honest preacher at last. Through this thicket, now, he could thrust his stick to stir the soul. It was better, he felt, touching them this way, than all the ways he had imagined would bring on rapture if he had only dared to reach out to employ them, boldly to stare or boldly speak, harshly to grasp and greedily to seize . . . yes, words were superior; they maintained a superior control; they touched without touching, they were at once the bait, the hook, the line, the pole, and the water in between.   (Pp. 112–13)

But as nearly all the metafictional writers seem to agree, there is a considerable danger in becoming so absorbed with this world of words, for eventually our response mechanisms may grow confused. In "The Medium of Fiction" Gass notes of the literary artist that "if I describe my peach too perfectly, it's the poem which will make my mouth water . . . while the real peach spoils" (*FFL,* p. 32). For Furber, who is "fearless in speech" but "cowardly in all else" (p. 164), this is precisely what happens: his mouth waters for sexual contact, but even when most aroused he only has "made love with discrete verbs and light nouns, delicate conjunctions" (p. 162). The most vivid demonstration of Furber's inability to reach people directly occurs on his train trip to Gilean where he makes love to a young girl sitting next to him with his shadow—an event rightly termed a "sad testimonial to love" (p. 109), and a clear indication of how imprisoned Furber is within his own powers of perception and language.

Because Omensetter represents a direct threat to him both personally and theologically, Furber sets out to destroy him by suggesting he may be responsible for Pimber's unexplained disappearance. Furber also undermines Omensetter's position by spreading various rumors about his strange, magical behavior and powers. But Omensetter himself finds Pimber's body up in the trees, and he naively and ironically comes to Furber for assistance. This is the key moment in Furber's "change of heart," for it is here that he realizes that Omensetter is an ordinary man whose confused acceptance of his "luck" has very real and serious implications. When Omensetter reaches out and touches Furber on the shoulder (p. 188), the transformation or initiation of both men has begun in earnest. Here, for the first time in the novel, Furber is forced to engage someone on a direct, personal level. Amazed and touched by Omensetter's innocent assumption that he is a friend who can be trusted, Furber bluntly tells Omensetter, "Where—where have you been? My god. My god. A friend. I've spent my life spreading lies about you" (p. 190). After Omensetter humbly mutters, "All that matters is you trust me," Furber is shocked into confessing, "What a godforsaken soul I have. Ba—Brackett—what a shit I am" (p. 191), referring to Omensetter for the first time by his correct name to underscore the new insight he has received. This encounter finally makes Furber see that people may be more important than abstractions. As Richard Schneider suggests, "What Omensetter now reveals to Furber is love, an ability to accept the life and people around him with complete trust, to care for people rather than principle."[89]

The episodes of the near-death of Omensetter's child and of facing up to the physical reality of Henry Pimber's death also awakens Furber to the very *real* implications of some of his earlier, purely rhetorical discussions. These discussions had centered around what Furber called "The Great Alternative" to his religious theology—that when the body dies, the spirit dies with it, sinking to a grave the same way that stones wind up at the bottom of a river no matter how skillfully thrown. Sitting in Omensetter's house while baby Amos lies dying of diphtheria and the townspeople are out hunting for Pimber's body, Furber admits to himself the final reality of death: "So it is with us. So it is with me. . . . Buried in this air, I rot. Moment by moment, I am not the same" (p. 201). This recognition is followed by a brief, epiphanic moment when Furber acknowledges the sensual realities that surround him; the agency of this awareness is nothing more than the sound of Lucy Omensetter's chair rocking—a sensual experience which Furber has blocked out the same way he has all others:

Up and down, yes and no, A and B. She rocked. Suddenly it struck him—added up. It was as though he had been jumped at from the dark. Chilled. The rocker creaked. Its legs rubbed in their sockets. All this time a sound—each time the same—had issued from its motion. Yet he'd never heard it. Where was it when he'd watched the shadow pulsing.   (P. 201)

Aroused for the first time by a heartfelt rather than by a merely rhetorical conviction, Furber experiences a momentary desire for the freedom to respond sensually, "to dance, to whirl while kicking his leg in the air" (p. 202). Meanwhile, Omensetter and his wife exchange remarks which outline the "fall" Omensetter has undergone. When Lucy demands that he go for a doctor to save their child, Omensetter's reaction parallels his earlier decision to let nature take its course with the fox and with Henry Pimber. "We've got to trust my luck," he replies. Lucy, however, seems to sense that Omensetter's original state of grace has departed and that now, like everybody else, he is going to have to rely on human knowledge and perception. Thus Lucy says to him, "What do people do when their baby's sick? That's all I want—what anyone would want—what you'd have wanted once—nothing strange or new or put on—just what's ordinary—decent—human" (pp. 204–05).

Genuinely moved by this exchange, Furber is now anxious to do something actual rather than symbolic. After his first effort in this direction fails—"Furber extended his arms, but they careened down the hall" (p. 207)—he makes a central confession of his sins:

He had fathered every folly, every sin. No goat knew gluttony like his, no cat had felt his pride, no crow his avarice. He had said the psalm against envy, the psalm against anger, the psalm against sloth and the loss of hope, but they were no defense. He had wanted women. He had imagined them in every posture. . . . He had lied—his single skill. . . . Touch me not, he'd always cried; do not burden me with love. Even now he made himself a monster, overblew his vices so his charge would lack conviction. Was that not, admittedly, the maneuver of a monster? So often clever. Note how sweetly I pronounce her, musically wig-wag my ringalingling tongue.   (P. 206)

Ironically, even this bitter catalogue of failures is undercut by Furber's artistry with language—his "ringalingling tongue"—which makes it difficult for him to accept his sins with conviction; indeed, this difficulty lies at the heart of Gass's attack on the purely rhetorical artist who uses his skills to persuade without caring about what is true or humanly significant. Still, Furber's newfound sense of guilt and desire to right his wrongs seem geniune enough as he wonders, "Had he sinned so much that innocence should suffer this from him?" (p. 206). When Omensetter leaves the house, Furber chases him out into the night and finds him gathering stones in a circle, apparently in some sort of primitive ritual of prayer. Omensetter's gesture, which brings together many of the book's associations with stones (with death, with words, with lack of perception), is seen by Furber at once to be futile, empty. All along, it has been Furber who has surrounded himself with stones (words) and useless symbolic gestures, and now he strikes out against them by running around the circle, kicking at the stones, and thus destroying the barricade Omensetter was constructing.[90] When he is finished, he rails at Omensetter by saying, "You call this feeble nonsense trusting to your luck? Is asking me to pray—is that trusting to your luck or just more madness? Neither's the use. You've got to go for Orcutt, the baby's nearly dead of your confusion. . . . I think you're a monster and you are proving me right. . . . I've been right about everything all along . . . if only I had believed myself" (p. 207). Furber, of course, *has* been right about Omensetter all along, at least in a basic sense. Like Henry Pimber, Furber has recognized that Omensetter represents the promise of a life lived without guilt, responsibility, or reason; but not sharing Henry's romanticism, Furber feels that such a life is dangerous and potentially destructive. At last able to believe the opinions he has been expressing, Furber yells after Omensetter, who is stumbling away down the beach, "You've got to go—there's no luck in this world and no god either" (p. 208). Later, riding back in the wagon with Pimber's frozen corpse, Furber is moved to summarize the lessons he has learned about man's fallen condition, his separation from God, and the unkindly gift of man's knowledge and perception. The soliloquy is one of the most moving and musical passages in the novel:

You may call the soul our best, but this, our body is our love. . . . How simply is our fondness for it guaranteed: we can't live outside of it, not as we are, not as we wish. . . . What power have You, if You can't continue us, and what cruel nature have You to refuse? The moist soul hangs about the body, too heavy to rise. How cleverly, Henry, you avoided that. Henry, listen, Omensetter was nothing, only another man. Now he is given to despair beyond any of yours. Well there you are—we all despair. . . . We wish to be so like the dead, we living. But we shiver from the cold in spite of ourselves, and we hate your liberty of lying like a stone enough to envy the birds who pecked your eyes.

Most of all, we envy you—that you should open them unfeeling to their bills. My god! my eyes are every minute pained by what they see. I should take strength from being blind, if I were you. Vision is no kindly injury. . . . Why have You made us the saddest animal? He pushed himself off and felt the jar in his bones. He cannot do it, Henry, that is why. He can't continue us. All He can do is try to make us happy that we die. Really, He's a pretty good fellow.

(Pp. 213–14)

These unsettling experiences turn out to be too much for his unstable personality; his incipient madness—evident in his joyful but often nearly insane word play and smutty limericks throughout the section—now manifests itself more directly as he loudly proclaims his sexual desires in various childish rhymes and jingles. In one moment of clarity, however, Furber provides a near summary of the meaning of Omensetter's arrival in Gilean and its outcome in words which echo Pimber's final sentiments, "No—come to Gilean, the child, the river, told him—come to Gilean, the capital of human nature. And now he knows. There's no further injury that we can do them. . . . They will live on like we live most likely" (p. 235). The book's central allegory, then, has been completed, with both Furber and Omensetter having visited "the capital of human nature" and having grown to share in the mixed blessings of humanity.

THE CONTEMPORARY **5**
META-SENSIBILITY:
A PERSONAL CONCLUSION

As we move in the 80's, what is happening to fiction? Is it becoming more realistic and less experimental? Are writers more concerned with historical and
nonfictional material and less interested in being "self-referential," in writing
about writing? Are we really living, as one critic put it, in the Golden Age of
the American Novel?

New York Times Book Review, 14 Dec. 1980

For a while we had . . . *self*-consciousness, and now we have more of a self-
consciousness. The two terms are not yet separated, but they have achieved a
different kind of balance, so that we are going to have much more *consciousness,* much more reflexiveness (in the sense of thinking), much more awareness in the novel, with a lesser emphasis on the self. In this sense the novel
will reconnect with the outer world, not necessarily with reality, but with
history — history which is, of course, also a form of fiction.

Raymond Federman

If story-telling is central to the human experience, stories about story-telling,
or stories which talk about themselves as stories, become central too. For a
while anyway. I think, as a fashion, it's passing, though more self-reflexive fictions will be written.

Robert Coover

November 1981. One of the hazards of being a critic of contemporary fiction is that, somewhat like the authors I've been discussing in
this study, I've grown to suspect that reality is outstripping my ability
to write about it, that the patterns, definitions, and systems I've devised to generate some sense of coherence out of things are either
too rigidly conceived or absurdly overgeneralized. Like John Barth
and Tristram Shandy, I'm occasionally overwhelmed with the infinite
regress that faces all writers who wish to discuss the way the past
moves into the present: no matter how many words I put forth in the
hope of conveying my sense of the recent past, the very act of for- **251**

mulating my ideas and writing them down takes up time—time during which new events serve to qualify my impressions, or even make them obsolete. Others who have struggled with this problem have concluded that the best policy in such cases is simply to acknowledge it and keep on writing, hoping that the gap between word and reality can at least be narrowed. We'll see.

I began preliminary work on this study almost ten years ago. At that time I was a graduate student at the University of Illinois, and I was anxious to write my Ph.D. thesis on some aspect of recent fiction and literary theory—a virtually taboo area in those days. In examining the fiction of my three favorite writers from the late 1960s—Robert Coover, Donald Barthelme, and William Gass—I gradually realized that their fiction shared certain qualities and that a thesis could be developed which would analyze the nature and sources of these common features. All three writers, for example, were obviously interested in developing nonmimetic literary styles, in using typography and other formal means to restructure the relationship between reader, author, and text; all three frequently created fictions which either reflexively analyzed their own creative processes or which could be read as allegories about the writing process; more generally, and most importantly, all three appeared to center their works on the elaborate series of fictional systems which humanity has devised to stabilize our hold on reality.

During the early part of my investigations, in 1972 and 1973, I found very little critical assistance with these works. With one or two exceptions—Tony Tanner's *City of Words* (1971), Robert Scholes's *The Fabulators* (1967), Richard Gilman's *The Confusion of Realms* (1969), a few essays here and there—critics in the early 1970s were largely unsympathetic or (more usually) entirely unaware of the explosion of literary experimentation which had already begun to take place. Even critics specializing in contemporary American fiction often appeared to have never heard of writers like Coover, Barthelme, Gass, Reed, Sukenick, or Pynchon. When they did turn their attention to these writers, most scholars seemed uncomfortable with the playfulness and reflexivity of this fiction and consequently were uncertain what to say about it. It wasn't until the mid-1970s, when my dissertation (now focused solely on Coover) was nearly completed, that the first tentative attempts at defining the chief characteristics of this new wave of fiction appeared, together with a proliferation of critical terms used to designate it: "fabulation," "surfiction," "parafiction," "super-fiction," "post-contemporary fiction," and (the most persistent) "postmodern fiction." Thus it was not literary criticism at all that provided me with the basis of my own pet theory of metafiction, upon which this book is based. Rather it was my investigations into the philosophy of language, science, anthropology, mathematics, logic, religion, and semiotics that created the view of man-the-fiction-maker which is so essential to *The Metafictional Muse.*[1] I was already familiar with the notions of metalogic and metamathematics before I first encountered the phrase "metafiction" in William Gass's *Fiction and the Figures of Life.* It immediately struck me that an analogous notion of metafiction might be usefully applied to a great deal of contemporary writing, although such a notion, to be really useful, would need to be more flexibly applied to fiction than to the rigidly determined parameters of logic and mathematics. My thesis, which examined what I termed the "fiction-making process" in Robert Coover's works, began from the premise that literature was merely another metaphorical device developed by man to help him understand the world. Such a view inevitably led me to question and reject any theory of fiction based on a narrowly conceived mimetic basis. Indeed, since nearly all the other disciplines I had examined had gone through an early, naively mimetic period in which the disciplines' underlying subjectivity and metaphor-making were mistaken for truth and direct insight, it seemed plausible that the novel was going through a similar process of reevaluation.

Meanwhile this initial spark of insight was being reinforced almost daily by the contemporary novels and stories I was reading. The period from 1965 until 1975 was an extraordinarily rich one for literary experimentalism — comparable, perhaps, only to the 1920s in the quality and quantity of works produced. And during these years there was also an obvious emphasis on fictions-about-literary-fictions — or "metafiction" in its most narrow sense. As I picked up books by Ronald Sukenick (*Up,* 1968), Raymond Federman (*Double or Nothing,* 1971), Steve Katz (*The Exagggerations of Peter Prince,*

1968), Thomas Williams (*The Hair of Harold Roux,* 1974), Ursula Le-Guin (*The Left Hand of Darkness,* 1969), Alan Friedman (*Hermaphrodeity,* 1972), John Seelye (*The True Adventures of Huckleberry Finn,* 1970), Jerome Charyn (*The Tar Baby,* 1973), John Irving (*The 158-Pound Marriage,* 1974), Kurt Vonnegut, Jr. (*Breakfast of Champions,* 1973), Terry Andrews (*The Story of Harold,* 1974), John Barth (*Chimera,* 1972), and Steven Millhauser (*Edwin Mullhouse,* 1972)—the list could be considerably expanded—it seemed for a few years that practically every new, exciting book I encountered was either about a writer writing a novel or was a reassemblage of an earlier work of fiction. Once I had accepted the idea that science, history, politics, religion, and mathematics were fictional systems or metaphors, an obvious extension of metafiction became *any* work which examined the subjective systems through which man relates to the world. All these factors helped convince me that the concept of metafiction could serve as a very useful starting point for the discussion of postmodern fiction in general, and the works of Coover, Barthelme, and Gass in particular. The end result of this conviction is *The Metafictional Muse.*

Since I began to formulate these insights, of course, a great deal has happened, both in the world and in the world of words. Coover, Barthelme, and Gass have naturally continued producing new works while this book was being shaped into final form. Although William Gass published no new books of fiction during this period, he was continuing work on his long-awaited novel, *The Tunnel,* which promises to be the crowning work of his career. Donald Barthelme has published a retrospective collection entitled *Sixty Stories* (1981), which also contains several previously uncollected works, and *Great Days* (1979), perhaps his finest collection since *Sadness.* After the publication of *The Public Burning* in 1977, Robert Coover has published five novellas in hardback editions (*The Hair O'the Chine, After Lazarus, A Political Fable, Charley in the House of Rue,* and *Spanking the Maid*), one of which—*Spanking the Maid*—should eventually achieve recognition as one of Coover's most perfectly realized fictions.[2] But although these new works reveal certain new preoccupations—writers, after all, can hardly be expected to remain static while we critics devise our own metaphors to deal with their works—these new preoccupations have not, I think, lessened the usefulness of metafictional approaches to the bulk of their work. Indeed, the emergence of metafiction as a major category of postmodern literature is really but one indication that meta-approaches are increasingly influencing nearly all of today's major art forms in ways that are just now growing to be understood. I would even argue that this "meta-sensibility" is evolving into the characteristic sensibility of our age, the inevitable product of our heightened awareness of the subjectivity and artifice inherent in our systems, our growing familiarity with prior forms, our increased access to information of all sorts. As I outlined in my first chapter, our contemporary sensibility is saturated not only with self-consciousness but also with the realization that concepts such as play, games, fiction-making, artifice, and subjectivity lie at the very center of what makes human beings civilized. Life-as-theater, man-as-fiction-maker or game-player—these can no longer be considered *postures* which we should avoid when engaged in "serious" pursuits, but are now accepted as aspects of our basic nature. Hence we find in the contemporary sensibility a much greater tolerance for and enjoyment of those aspects of art, music, literature, film, television, and other cultural artifacts which investigate their own nature, parade their artifice, and refuse to provide the illusion of having arrived at final truth and absolutes.

Also crucial to the development of this metasensibility have been the effects of the public's rapidly increasing access to information and entertainment forms of all sorts. This proliferation of information and artistic reproductions—created by the computer and xerox revolutions, the developments in cable television and in the home video and sound recording industries, media bombardments of various kinds—has created an ideal situation in which meta-situations can flourish. With the ready availability of means of reproducing primary sources, there inevitably arise artists anxious to explore new ways to manipulate the public's relationship to this material. Of course, this is not to say that the self-consciousness and reflexivity which underlie these meta-approaches found in modern entertainment and culture are unique to our own age. On the contrary, as with fiction, most artistic genres have devised metaforms early in their development; think of the familiar musical comedy formula, dating from the 1930s, of the musical comedy "about" the making of a musical comedy, or the sophisticated juggling of illusion and reality in such old-time radio and television shows as *Burns and Allen* and the *Jack Benny Show*. But metaforms are obviously much more suited to an age in which the general public has an astonishing array of films, recordings, and television shows literally at their fingertips. One result of this push-button availability is the growing familiarity on the part of audiences with the content and form of these media — a familiarity which contemporary artists can exploit by means of extrapolation, satire, parody, or meta-treatments. Certainly the tens of thousands of Americans who already own their own personal videotapes of *Gone with the Wind* or *Citizen Kane* are potentially better able to appreciate and understand these films than audiences who saw them in movie houses forty years ago; likewise average home sports fans today, with the advent of instant replay, multiple camera shots of all plays, and (for those who own a Betamax or VHS system) video cassette recordings of important games, almost certainly have a more sophisticated understanding of the games they watch than even the most ardent game-going fans of previous generations.[3]

As proof of my argument for increased audience self-consciousness and the development of a contemporary meta-sensibility, I submit the following examples of contemporary popular culture: cinema: *Young Frankenstein, Bugsy Malone, Love and Death, Star Wars, Flash Gordon, Superman, Raiders of the Lost Ark, Pennies from Heaven;* television comedies and revues: *Mary Hartman, Mary Hartman* and *Fernwood Tonight,* most of the material on *Saturday Night Live* and *Fridays;* television commercials: Lite Beer from Miller commercials, various others such as current advertisements for Atari and Goodrich Tires, which rely on the audience's awareness of other commercials; popular music: the Blues Brothers, David Bowie's "Ziggy Stardust" persona (among others), Bette Midler, Leon Redbone, Tom Waits, Elvis Presley and Beatles imitators; comedians: Steve Martin, Andy Kaufman, Martin Mull; popular magazines: *Mad Magazine* and *The National Lampoon.*

The above examples of recent popular culture were produced in response to the meta-sensibility I have been describing — that is, each is really a meta-artifact designed to imitate, to parody, to examine, and often to playfully comment upon another artifact or artist. The production and dissemination of such entertainment phenomena becomes possible (and profitable), of course, only after the public has become familiar enough with the first-level artifact to understand the nature of the meta-treatment they are encountering. One does not have to possess such knowledge to enjoy the meta-artifact on some level, just as it isn't absolutely necessary for a reader to be familiar with the Snow White fairy tale to enjoy Barthelme's *Snow White;* but the nature of audience response and appreciation of any meta-artifact is clearly different *in kind* when such prior knowledge is absent. Obviously, for example, viewers watching Mel Brooks's *Young Frankenstein* who have never seen any of the 1930s *Frankenstein* films might still find Brooks's movie funny and enjoyable; and even a person who has never seen a 1930s musical might find Herbert Ross's *Pennies from Heaven* (1981) intriguing. But such viewers would be missing the "meaning" (in terms of parodic reference) of much of what is happening in both films, just as viewers totally unfamiliar with the conventions of soap operas or talk shows or news broadcasts would respond very differently from those familiar with the conventions to television's meta-treatments of the forms in *Mary Hartman, Mary Hartman, Fernwood Tonight,* and the "Weekend Update" portion of *Saturday Night Live.* Much the same point can be made of films like *Star Wars* (1977), *Superman* (1978), *Flash Gordon* (1980), *Raiders of the Lost Ark* (1981), and *Body Heat* (1981), all of which are clearly a species of meta-cinema, created with the self-conscious intent of mimicking the methods and techniques of a previous era's "straight" approaches to film making.[4]

These examples illustrate an important fact about virtually any formal system, one examined by Douglas Hofstadter in exhaustive detail in his brilliant study of reflexivity, *Godel, Escher, Bach: An Eternal Golden Braid.* Hofstadter shows that once any formal system reaches a certain threshold level of complexity—a computer system, a language, a literary text, a piece of music, or a system of mathematics or logic—reflexivity and self-reference necessarily emerge within that system. Although Hofstadter mainly discusses complex meaning systems such as logic, computer languages, and musical structures, his analysis is highly useful in explaining why certain forms eventually evolve meta-treatments of their materials. For instance, the history of television advertising seems to parallel what has been developing in fiction and cinema: the relatively simplistic "mimetic" techniques we have become familiar with, such as testimonials and direct demonstration of the product, are giving way to highly successful "meta-advertisements" such as those for Miller's Lite Beer, which use as their starting point motifs and characters from previous commercials.

This sort of self-conscious manipulation of audience expectations— which, as we have seen, is one of the defining features of metafiction— produces fascinating and unusual formal situations whose novelty modern audiences seem to embrace enthusiastically. The amazing popularity of the "Blues Brothers," a meta-musical act (from *Saturday Night Live*) in which television stars Dan Ackroyd and John Belushi re-create the music and personality traits of blues musicians, is another testimony to the contemporary audience's delight in meta-forms. After their routine was warmly received on *Saturday Night Live,* the Blues Brothers actually went on several highly successful national concert tours and released three albums, one of which, *Briefcase Full of Blues,* became the nation's best-selling album for a period. The Blues Brothers' use of the musical conventions associated with the blues plus Ackroyd's and Belushi's private zaniness produced some wonderfully incongruous audience reactions—amusement, genuine musical appreciation, an aesthetic response to the clashing forms— which would be impossible to generate in a straight comedy or musical routine. Much the same complex performer/audience dynamics are produced in the meta-comedy routines of entertainers like Steve Martin, Martin Mull, and Andy Kaufman. Martin, the most successful comedian of the 1970s, usually presented himself to concert audiences in the guise of an outlandish version of a cool, arrogant, bad comedian. Martin's typical routine heavily relied on what could be called meta-jokes: jokes about joke-telling, deliberately bad jokes, jokes which adopt the *form* of familiar joke conventions but which substitute an absurd element for the familiar one, and so on. Again, the essence of audience appreciation for this type of an act is a self-consciousness about the medium itself, an awareness of the established conventions and forms which Martin is mimicking and deriding. Uninitiated audience members who are unaware that Martin is *imitating* the conventions of bad comedians, for example, are likely to regard Martin as merely a bad comedian.

Even more radical than Martin is comedian Andy Kaufman (probably best known for his bit part in the weekly television series *Taxi*), who occasionally concocts his various roles so convincingly that the reality/illusion distinction becomes blurred and concert audiences become genuinely angry or bored. He is—variously—an obnoxious, smug, truly awful night club performer named "Tony Clifton"; an odious male chauvinist who challenges women to wrestle with him and then taunts them when he defeats them; a Polynesian bongo player who cannot speak English and sings songs in an unintelligible language; an obsequious born-again Christian. Actually, in creating these roles, Kaufman is conducting some fascinating explorations into the nature of familiar public formulas as well as examining the relationship between art and reality, between audience and performer, between wit and dullness. He is a perfect example of the extremely sophisticated, self-conscious artist who challenges conventional notions of comedy, popular music, film, television entertainment, among other artistic forms, much as metafictional writers are doing.

Having thus briefly summarized my views about the importance of meta-art in contemporary culture, I would like to make a few final observations about the role of metafiction in the evolution of postmodernist literature. A predictable result of the significant role that self-conscious, reflexive experimental techniques played in contemporary fiction has been a reaction against such strategies by critics and by fiction writers themselves in recent years. Such a reaction is a natural result of literature's slow dialogue with itself; as in politics— and literature's development often is political in nature—whenever one group dismantles the authority of a prior group, the new group in power is soon going to be counterattacked by opponents who inevitably arise to challenge its authority. Although a complete analysis of this process lies beyond the scope of this study, it seems obvious that some such dialectical struggle has been taking place in this country, with the radicalism of the sixties and early seventies—

apparent not just in literature, of course—giving way to more conservative attitudes by the late seventies and early eighties. It doesn't
require any particular social, political, or aesthetic acumen to see
the results of this dialectical swing. In 1972, as I began to focus on
the experimentalism characterizing the literature of the period, the
Democrats nominated George McGovern for president, miniskirts
for women and long hair for men were accepted fashions, and people
were experimenting not only with literature but also with drugs, sexual mores, and life patterns generally. Today, of course, Ronald Rea-
gan is our president; conservatives like Jerry Falwell, Phyllis Schlafly,
and Anita Bryant have replaced Abbie Hoffman, Jerry Rubin, and
John Lennon as media figures; Bob Dylan sings more about Christianity these days than about social protest; and the most controversial decision facing people in 1982 seems to be whether or not to
open up an IRA (individual retirement account) as a tax shelter.

At first glance, this growing conservatism would seem to provide
a hostile environment for the development of meta-forms, which are
essentially nontraditional. Yet they have gained widespread popularity. Perhaps the reason is that the striking technological advances
within the entertainment and news media have at least partially nul-
lified the influence of political and social conservatism. This has
been especially true in media such as the cinema, television, and
electronic music, which often depend inherently on technological
developments to stimulate formal experimentation. A film such as
Stanley Kubrick's *2001: A Space Odyssey* was experimental more for
the technology which went into its production than for its story line
(and much the same case can be made for *Citizen Kane*). Albums
which revolutionized popular music in the 1960s, such as Bob Dylan's
collection *Bringing It All Back Home* and the Beatles' *Sergeant Pepper's Lonely Hearts Club Band,* boldly incorporated the new technology available to musicians. Films and recorded music, then, are genres which are still rapidly evolving, which are technological by their
very definition, and which have not yet had a chance to formulate
sacrosanct conventions. (In the early eighteenth century, the newly
developed genre of the novel enjoyed a similar period of experimentalism in what was otherwise a fairly conservative literary climate.)
But the novel has gradually established a set of formulated guide-

lines—traditionally tied to mimesis and to art's obligation to instruct as well as entertain—and has not been directly affected by recent technological developments; therefore the conservatism of our times is reflected in contemporary fiction and criticism. Thus the emergence in the early 1970s of a recognizable body of radical postmodern texts and aesthetic principles, together with the concurrent development of a criticism which explicated and supported this movement, has most recently given way to more traditional fictional approaches and a body of critical texts which attack the theory and practice of postmodernism in fiction. As often happens in such debates, the real, important issues underlying these arguments frequently have become obscured by rhetorical hot air and absurdly oversimplified positions—as when John Gardner's stimulating but carelessly conceived study, On Moral Fiction (1978) had the effect of creating illusory polarities (moral versus immoral fiction, experimental versus committed fiction, for example). On the other hand, some more carefully worked-out critical texts, like Gerald Graff's Literature Against Itself and Alan Wilde's Horizons of Assent identify many of the central issues in the debate and may serve as useful starting points for serious discussion.

Just as inevitable as the dialectical nature of the debate between advocates and opponents of the radical literary strategies of postmodernism has been the synthesis that has begun taking shape in fiction and criticism in the late 1970s and early 1980s. My sense that such a synthesis is occurring is based not only on the fiction I have been recently reading, but also by dozens of formal interviews and late-night discussions I've held with writers from 1978 until 1980.[5] The most important conclusion I've reached is that experimentalism per se—especially experimentalism in the direction of reflexive, nonreferential works—is not nearly as important to writers today as it was a decade ago. The reasons for this shift in emphasis are not too difficult to understand: so-called artistic revolutions have a natural life span, and they are inevitably succeeded by a new artistic climate generated by practitioners who do not share the enthusiasms of a previous group and who are anxious to define themselves as artists in new ways. Then, too, the energy and hard work of any significant creative movement will eventually produce, in the course of its development, works of surpassing and even intimidating success. Finally, a sense develops among the artists who have defined themselves as part of a movement that most of its possibilities have been explored (or have become "exhausted" in Barth's famous phrase)—perhaps even explored as fully and successfully as they can be explored: think of the role of Proust or Joyce for the modernist period; of Mallarmé and Valéry for the symbolist movement; the same case can be made for the effect of Pynchon's *Gravity's Rainbow* and Barth's *Letters* on the contemporary literary sensibility. Of course, some of the sense of the decline in experimentalism results from our greater familiarity with the innovative strategies which once seemed so challenging and bewildering. Because later fiction which uses these experimental strategies seems more familiar, and hence less threatening, its subsequent appearance is less to be remarked upon—is, in fact, no longer even considered "experimental" at all. To take an obvious example, it might not occur to most readers or critics to talk about John Irving's *The World According to Garp* (1978) as an "experimental novel," although it obviously employs many of the same metafictional devices—the book-within-a-book, the interweaving of fiction and reality, playful self-references to its author's previous works—that other, seemingly more radical texts were using back in the 1960s. This is not to say that Irving's book isn't experimental or metafictional—it clearly is. It just may seem beside the point to label it as such today.

Much the same point can be made of many of the best novels that appeared in America in the last four or five years. Books like Tim O'Brien's *Going After Cacciato* (1978), E. L. Doctorow's *Loon Lake* (1980), John Gardner's *Freddy's Book* (1980), Toni Morrison's *Song of Solomon* (1977), Alexander Theroux's *Darcville's Cat* (1981), and Kurt Vonnegut, Jr.'s *Jailbird* (1979) incorporated postmodern experimental strategies into their structures so smoothly that they have often been seen as quite traditional in orientation. Naturally, more radically experimental works continued to be written during this period. But with a few notable exceptions—the remarkable prose fictions of Ron Silliman and Bob Perleman, Gilbert Sorrentino's *Mulligan Stew* (1979), Kathy Acker's "punk novels," a number of works published by the Fiction Collective—most of the important vital works of the late

1970s and early 1980s are neither exclusively experimental in a narrowly reflexive sense, nor representational in a traditional, realistic fashion. Rather, they belong to what Alan Wilde has termed "midfiction" (still another label!)—that is, fiction which develops its own brand of experimental structures but which does not depend primarily on reflexive methods that abandon the attempt to deal with the world outside of literature.[6] Wilde lists the recent fiction of Stanley Elkin, Max Apple, and Donald Barthelme as examples of midfiction, and suggests that such fiction operates on a middle ground between realism and reflexivity—the two poles which "mark out the extremes of contemporary literature, leaving between them . . . yet another class of works whose mood is one of interrogation: a questioning of, among other things, the validity of certainties—both those that take the world for granted and those that set it at naught."[7] Most of the fiction of Coover and Barthelme (though probably not of Gass, for obvious reasons) could probably be viewed as belonging to this midfictional form which shares neither the reflexivists' tendency to ignore the world absolutely nor the realists' desire to reproduce it.

If the fiction of Coover and Barthelme can be placed into some sort of midfictional zone, this does not mean that metafictional impulses do not also underlie their work. As I have repeatedly suggested, metafictional works may indeed be primarily reflexive, but the term "metafictional" is not limited to works which are wholly self-contained or which explore only their own nature. Coover's *The Public Burning,* for all its attention to its own artifice, to American lingoes, and to traditional fictional formulas, is also very much a novel about the mood and political climate of America in the 1950s. Similarly, Barthelme's works interest me most as they explore the contemporary language process, incorporate the words of our daily existence into new shapes, and satirize various fictional systems. But although I have not emphasized Barthelme's works as political and social commentaries, his fictions have obviously had much to say about such topical issues as the Vietnam War, the Watergate scandal and other political controversies, the social realities of modern urban life, contemporary sexual behavior, and other aspects of the world outside fiction. Thus, my aim in *The Metafictional Muse* is not to deny the ability of metafiction to engage the world outside of fiction, though its sophisticated awareness of the fiction-making process and the limits of objectivity makes the nature of this engagement very different from that found in traditional realistic fiction. Given the complexity in intent and achievement of the postmodern literary imagination, it would be foolish for a critic to insist on relying upon narrowly conceived critical categories to deal with it. Thus throughout *The Metafictional Muse* I have attempted to apply my definition as flexibly as possible without losing the thrust of what this term signifies.

It also seems relevant to this literary synthesis I am describing that the most admired living writers of the 1970s were probably Günter Grass, Garcia Marquez, and John Fowles—all genuine literary experimenters whose fiction is clearly "midfictional" in Wilde's terms—with Marquez's *One Hundred Years of Solitude* (translated into English in 1970) perhaps having more influence on contemporary American fiction than any other single work. Marquez's masterpiece is a perfect embodiment of the literary tendencies I've been pointing to: on the one hand, *One Hundred Years of Solitude* is an obviously nonrealistic novel, with its magical, surreal landscape, its dense reflexive surface, its metafictional emphasis on the nature of language and how reality is storified from one generation to the next, its labyrinthine literary references. Yet, for all this undeniably postmodern experimentalism, *One Hundred Years of Solitude* also tells a highly readable and coherent story peopled with dozens of memorable characters, and it speaks to us powerfully about real political and historical realities. It has thus become a kind of model for the contemporary writer, being self-conscious about its literary heritage and about the limits of mimesis, developing its own organic form of experimentalisms, but yet managing to reconnect its readers to the world outside the page.

Lastly, I would hope this study will not be viewed as a polemic, of which literary criticism has had too many recently, but as a tentative beginning to the investigation of an enormously rich period in American literature. As I noted at the outset of this "Personal Conclusion," I am aware that critics, like the characters in many metafictional works, are themselves frightened by chaos and disorder and are anxious to stabilize the flux of literary reality by creating categories and assigning names. Thus, inevitably, "metafiction" will be lumped together with all the other critical barbs recently thrown out in the hopes of latching on securely to that great leviathan, literature. But certainly Ahab's example should warn us of the dangers of literalizing our metaphors, lest they entangle us and we drown. What I hope to have done is to suggest a common tendency in much of the most significant postmodern fiction: the tendency of writers, grown ever more uncertain about their ability to describe and analyze reality accurately, to turn inward to investigate the subjective systems at our disposal in organizing and understanding our lives. This is not a phenomenon exclusive to our own age—Cervantes and Melville, to take two obvious examples, were engaged in much the same process and produced metafictional inquiries of matchless beauty and complexity of execution. Still, I remain convinced that the metafictional impulse is one of the defining features of postmodern fiction distinguishing it from the fiction of the thirties, forties, and fifties. Meanwhile, great fiction continues to be written and continues to defy our most lovingly created categories. My study, then, is inevitably a failure, for one of its premises is that there can never be any easy congruence between categories and reality. But it is, I insist, a failure born out of respect and admiration, not out of a desire to reduce some very great works of literature to a formula.

NOTES

Preface

1. John Barth, "The Literature of Exhaustion," *Atlantic Monthly,* August, 1967, p. 29.

2. Jerome Klinkowitz, *Literary Disruptions: The Makings of a Post-Contemporary American Fiction* (Urbana: University of Illinois Press, 1975).

Chapter 1: Fiction Making and the Metafictional Muse

1. Mas'ud Zavarzadeh, *The Mythopoeic Reality* (Urbana: University of Illinois Press, 1976), p. 39.

2. Frank Gado, *First Person: Conversations on Writers and Writing* (Schenectady, N.Y.: Union College Press, 1973), p. 142.

3. Ibid.

4. William Spanos, "The Detective and the Boundary: Some Notes on the Post-modern Literary Imagination," *boundary 2* 1 (Fall 1972), 150.

5. The range of this topic is, of course, enormous. The notion of man-as-fiction-maker has immediate and obvious connection with thinkers as varied as Freud, Jung, Frazier, Durkheim, Lévi-Strauss, Wittgenstein, Cassirer, and Chomsky—to name only a few prominent examples of theoretitians who are accused by more empirical opponents of being fiction-makers themselves.

6. Frank Kermode, *The Sense of an Ending* (New York: Oxford University Press, 1967), p. 36.

7. Ronald Sukenick, "The Death of the Novel," in *The Death of the Novel and Other Stories* (New York: Dial Press, 1969), p. 41.

8. Ronald Sukenick, "The New Tradition," in *Surfiction,* ed. Raymond Federman (Chicago: Swallow Press, 1975), p. 41. Sukenick's reference is to Robbe-Grillet's remarks in "Time and Description," in *For a New Novel* (New York: Grove Press, 1965), p. 156, where he says, "For, far from neglecting him, the author today proclaims his absolute need of the reader's cooperation, an active, conscious, creative assistance. What he asks of him is no longer to receive ready-made a world completed, full, closed upon itself, but on the contrary to participate in a creation, to invent in his turn the work and the world—and thus to learn to invent his own life."

9. Edward Said, "Contemporary Fiction and Criticism," *TriQuarterly* 33 (Winter 1975), 237.

10. William H. Gass, "Philosophy and the Form of Fiction," in *Fiction and the Figures of Life* (New York: Alfred A. Knopf, 1971), pp. 24–25.

11. For a complete discussion of metasystems, the implications of self-reference, and some of the applications of these notions to modern art and thinking, see Douglas R. Hofstadter, *Godel, Escher, Bach: An Eternal Golden Braid* (New York: Basic Books, 1979).

12. Said, "Contemporary Fiction and Criticism," p. 239.

13. The best analysis of this rapid change in American literary values can be found in Jerome Klinkowitz, *Literary Disruptions: The Making of a Post-Contemporary American Fiction* (Urbana: University of Illinois Press, 1975). Although I could argue with Professor Klinkowitz on several specific points, I generally agree with his basic contention that American fiction broke with its realistic heritage in the 1960s. See my review-essay, "Fiction in a 'Post-Contemporary' Age," *boundary* 2 5 (fall 1976), 137–52.

14. Alain Robbe-Grillet, "Time and Description," in *For a New Novel,* trans. Richard Howard (New York: Grove Press, 1965), p. 32.

15. Ibid., p. 162.

16. Ibid., pp. 31–32, emphasis added.

17. Stephen Kock, "Premature Speculations on the Perpetual Renaissance," *Tri-Quarterly* 10 (Fall 1967), 5.

18. Gass, "Philosophy and the Form of Fiction," p. 17.

Chapter 2: Robert Coover and the Magic of Fiction Making

1. Colin Turbayne, *The Myth of Metaphor* (Columbia: University of South Carolina Press, 1970), p. 56.

2. Robert Coover, *Pricksongs and Descants* (New York: New American Library, 1970), p. 77. Cited in the text as *PD,* if identification is needed.

3. Roger Shattuck, *The Banquet Years* (New York: Vintage Books, 1968), p. 327.

4. See my Robert Coover entry in the *Dictionary of Literary Biography* (Detroit: Gale Research Co., 1978), pp. 106–21.

5. Robert Coover, *The Origin of the Brunists* (New York: G. P. Putnam's Sons, 1966), p. 428. Cited in the text as *OB.*

6. Frank Gado, *First Person: Conversations on Writers and Writing* (Schenectady, N.Y.: Union College Press, 1973), p. 148.

7. The only book which Coover has openly acknowledged as a direct influence on *The Brunists* is *Moby Dick* (see Gado, *First Person,* p. 146), although in a letter to me, Coover has indicated that he read Pynchon's *V.* soon after it was published in 1963 and that he was enormously impressed with it.

8. Jackson I. Cope, "Robert Coover," in *Contemporary Novelists,* ed. James Vinson (New York: St. Martin's Press, 1972), p. 305.

9. Coover has stated that two of the men who most contributed to his understanding of this process are Emile Durkheim and Karl Jaspers. Both Durkheim's view of the sociological function of religion and Jaspers's idea that religious history should be ex-

amined solely from a mythic perspective are evident everywhere in *The Brunists* and are discussed by Coover in his interview with Gado (*First Person*, pp. 153, 156).

10. Interestingly enough, the quantum theory has altered many scientific and logical notions about causality to the point that some of our notions today are, in many respects, closer to those of "primitive man" than they are to those of scientists in the nineteenth century. Quantum scientist Erwin C. Schrodinger provides an excellent summary of these changes in *Science Theory and Man* (New York: Dover Publications, 1957).

11. Ernst Cassirer, *Mythical Thought,* vol. 2 of *The Philosophy of Symbolic Forms,* trans. Ralph Manheim (New Haven, Conn.: Yale University Press, 1946), p. 45.

12. Noted by Neil Schmitz in "Robert Coover and the Hazards of Metafiction," *Novel* 7 (1974), 215. Other stories in which this strategy of "self-exposure" is evident include "Panel Game," "McDuff on the Mound," "The Marker," and "The Magic Poker."

13. Leo Hertzel, "What's Wrong with Christians?" *Critique* 11 (1969), 17.

14. Mark Taylor, "Baseball as Myth," *Commonweal,* 12 May 1972, p. 237.

15. Robert Coover, *The Universal Baseball Association, Inc., J. Henry Waugh, Prop.* (New York: Random House, 1968), p. 35. Cited in the text as *UBA* if identification of the novel is needed.

16. Gado, *First Person,* p. 149.

17. This view of God as a "dice player" was the subject of considerable debate during the furor over the quantum theory. This theory seems to indicate that indeterminacy governs certain events and that chance does determine specific fundamental operations of the universe. For an examination of how Coover's metaphorical structures in *The UBA* relate to quantum physics, see Arlen J. Hansen's essay, "The Dice of God: Einstein, Heisenberg, and Robert Coover" in *Novel* 10 (Fall 1976), 49-58.

18. Ibid., p. 54.

19. Cassirer, *Mythical Thought,* pp. 40-41. In volume 1 of *The Philosophy of Symbolic Forms (Language),* Cassirer makes much the same point when he states that for mythic thought, "The name of a thing and the thing itself are inseparably fused; the mere word or image contains a magic force through which the essence of the thing gives itself to us" (p. 88).

20. In Jackson I. Cope, "Robert Coover's Fictions," *Iowa Review* 2 (1971), 94-110, Henry's adoption of Sewanee Law in the second bout with Hettie has a further significance: Cope feels that this indicates that "Waugh has joined the Legalists, as his assumption of Law's persona for his love games told us. He is an angry God of the Old Testament" (p. 97).

21. Cf. Hansen, "The Dice of God," pp. 49-55.

22. Cope, "Robert Coover's Fictions," p. 108.

23. In his interview with Gado (*First Person,* p. 149), Coover mentions that the eight chapters of *The UBA* correspond to the seven days of creation, with an eighth "apocalyptic" day implied.

24. Richard Gilman, "News from the Novel," *New Republic,* 17 Aug. 1968, p. 36.

25. J. L. Borges, "Partial Enchantment of the Quixote," *Other Inquisitions 1937–1952* (New York: Washington Square Press, 1965), p. 48.

26. Coover's epigraph is taken from Kant's *The Critique of Judgment*, trans. J. H. Bernard (New York: Hafner Press, 1966), p. 256.

27. Kant, *The Critique of Judgment*, p. 248. In describing the nature of the *intellectus archetypus*, Kant also points out an interesting distinction which we can apply to Waugh. Like the hypothetical God of Kant, Waugh knows no distinction between reality and possibility, for anything that he imagines in his Association immediately becomes "substantial." In this he differs from animals, who do not have the power to imagine at all, and man, whom we usually view as being able to imagine but not able to make this imagination assume substantiality (again, this situation differs from the writer, who creates beings and situations from his imagination). Kant discusses this distinction in sections 76–77.

28. Hansen, "The Dice of God," p. 55.

29. Henry earlier seemed to grasp this idea for a moment when he thought to himself after Damon's death, "First of all, . . . the circuit wasn't closed, his or any other; there were patterns, but they were shifting and ambiguous and you had a lot of room inside them. Secondly, . . . the game on his table was not a message, but an event; the only signs he had were his own reactions" (p. 143).

30. Hansen, "The Dice of God," p. 55.

31. See, for example, Ernst Cassirer's remarks in *Mythical Thought*, p. 25, that "the beginnings of creative art seem . . . to partake of a sphere in which creative activity is still embedded in magical representations and directed towards specific magical aims."

32. Quoted in Gado, *First Person*, pp. 149–50.

33. Cited by John Weightman, "Refrigerated Dream," *New York Review of Books*, 1 June 1972, p. 6.

34. Quoted in Gado, *First Person*, p. 150.

35. "The Reunion" appeared in the *Iowa Review* 1 (1970), 64–69. It was originally supposed to be included in *Pricksongs* but for reasons which Coover has never explained, it was omitted.

36. Alain Robbe-Grillet, "Nature, Humanism, and Tragedy," in *For a New Novel* (New York: Grove Press, 1965), p. 53. Coover seems to be mimicking or parodying Robbe-Grillet's stylistic mannerisms in several other works such as *The Origin of the Brunists* and "The Babysitter."

37. Ibid., p. 70.

38. The entire epigraph, taken from Felix Maria Samaniego's "La Lechera" fable in his *Fabulas Morales* (1781), reads: *Llevaba en las cabeza / una lechera el cantaro etcetera futuro; / mira que ni el presente esta seguro.* Freely translated, this passage says, "A milkmaid was carrying a pitcher on her head, and so on, into the future; look, not even the present is secure."

39. See my essay, "Robert Coover's Cubist Fictions," *Par Rapport* 1 (1978), 33–39.

40. Interestingly, the nonrealistic experiments by such contemporary writers as Coover and Barth also seem to be derived in part from a rediscovery of a sort of primitive art—in this case, the highly artificial, prenovelistic strategies of such literary forms as fairy tales, fables, and the epic.

41. Robert Rosenblum, *Cubism and Twentieth Century Art* (New York: Harry N. Abrams, 1966), p. 9.

42. Weightman, "Refrigerated Dream," p. 6.

43. Quoted in Gado, *First Person,* p. 151.

44. Ibid.

45. Schmitz, "Robert Coover and the Hazards of Metafiction," p. 214.

46. Ibid., p. 218.

47. Ibid.

48. Geoffrey Wolff, "An American Epic," *New Times,* 19 Aug. 1977, p. 54.

49. Cited in the Viking Press prepublication sheet distributed to reviewers.

50. Thomas R. Edwards, "Real People, Mythic History" [Review of *The Public Burning* by Robert Coover], *New York Times Book Review,* 14 Aug. 1977, p. 26.

51. Wolff, "An American Epic," p. 57.

52. Ibid., p. 54.

53. Ibid.

54. In *The Origin of the Brunists,* Tiger Miller notes that the main efforts of historians and journalists are to make "a good story": "Somebody with a little imagination, a new interpretation, a bit of eloquence, and zap—they're off for another hundred or thousand years" (p. 264). This view is echoed in *The Public Burning* when Cecil B. De-Mille explains to practical-minded Warden Denno, "See, life and the real stuff of life aren't always the same thing, Warden—like, one don't always give you the other, you follow? So sometimes, to get your story across, you gotta work a different angle or two, use a few tricks, zap it up with a bit of spectacle—I mean, what's spectacle? It's a kind of *vision,* am I right?" (p. 281). These remarks about "spectacle" also apply directly to Coover's own fictional strategy; it should be emphasized that many of the points Coover makes about the nature of such systems as history, journalism, myth, politics, and religion also apply directly to literary fictions.

55. Wolff, "An American Epic," p. 54.

56. P. 139. Coover psychologically sets the stage for these feelings by introducing a variety of elements from Nixon's childhood and early courtship days—for example, we learn that he was "farmed out" to relatives by his parents when he was a child and that a hired girl allowed him to suffer a traumatizing fall from a carriage ("her big lap, big to me, yet not big enough," p. 146).

Chapter 3: Donald Barthelme: The Aesthetics of Trash

1. See, for example, Alan Wilde, "Barthelme Unfair to Kierkegaard: Some Thoughts on Modern and Postmodern Irony," *boundary 2* 5 (Fall 1976), 45–70.

2. Ibid., p. 51.

3. The following passages are taken from Donald Barthelme, *City Life* (New York: Farrar, Straus & Giroux, 1970), p. 84; *Come Back, Dr. Caligari* (Boston: Little, Brown, 1964), p. 177; *Sadness* (New York: Farrar, Straus & Giroux, 1974), pp. 9, 93–95; *Unspeakable Practices, Unnatural Acts* (New York: Bantam, 1969), p. 3; henceforth these works

will be abbreviated as *CL, CB, S,* and *UP.* Also cited will be *Snow White* (New York: Bantam, 1968) and *Guilty Pleasures* (New York: Farrar, Straus & Giroux, 1974), abbreviated as *SW* and *GP.*

4. Wilde, "Barthelme Unfair to Kierkegaard," p. 56.

5. The fullest critical treatments of "The Balloon" are R. E. Johnson, Jr., "'Bees Barking in the Night': The End and Beginning of Donald Barthelme's Narrative," *boundary 2* 5 (Fall 1976), 71–92; Maurice Couturier, "Barthelme's Uppity Bubble: 'The Balloon,'" *Revue Française d'Etudes Americaines* 8 (1979), 183–201.

6. William H. Gass, in interview with Larry McCaffery.

7. Jerome Klinkowitz, *Literary Disruptions: The Makings of a Post-Contemporary American Fiction* (Urbana: University of Illinois Press, 1975), p. 69.

8. Ibid., p. 72.

9. Thus R. E. Johnson's remark that "almost anything the reader might determine about a Barthelme sentence will be taken away from him by some contrary movement in that sentence or another" (p. 83).

10. Klinkowitz, *Literary Disruptions,* p. 70.

11. Wilde, "Barthelme Unfair to Kierkegaard," p. 52.

12. *UP,* p. 153. This statement has often been quoted as a statement of Barthelme's own aesthetics, something which he objects to in an interview with Jerome Klinkowitz when he says, "No. It's a statement by the character about what he is feeling at that particular moment. I hope that whatever I think about aesthetics would be a shade more complicated than that." (In *The New Fiction,* ed. Joe David Bellamy [Urbana: University of Illinois Press, 1974], p. 53.) John Leland examines the role of fragments and meaningful wholes in Barthelme's fiction in "Remarks Re-marked: Barthelme, What Curios of Signs!" *boundary 2* 5 (Spring 1977), 795–811.

13. Wilde, "Barthelme Unfair to Kierkegaard," p. 52.

14. For a more complete treatment of this issue, see my essay, "Meaning and Non-Meaning in Barthelme's Fictions," *Journal of Aesthetic Education* 13 (1979), 69–80.

15. Donald Barthelme, "After Joyce," *Location* 1 (Summer 1964), 14.

16. Tony Tanner in *City of Words* (New York: Harper & Row, 1971), p. 404, suggests that these opening words imply a "strong feeling of being distinctly not at home in the trash age." He also adds that "although the idea is mocked, like every other idea offered as idea in Barthelme, this note of yearning for an unknown somewhere else sounds throughout his work." Alan Wilde suggests, however, that Barthelme is "less seriously attracted by an escape into the realm of total otherness than by the temptation to find *within* the ordinary possibilities of a more dynamic response" ("Barthelme Unfair to Kierkegaard," p. 59).

17. Tanner, *City of Words,* p. 403.

18. *CB,* p. 4. Betty Flowers uses this doctor-patient analogy as the starting point for her discussion of *Snow White* in "Barthelme's *Snow White:* The Reader-Patient Relationship," *Critique* 16 (Spring 1975), 33–43.

19. Wilde discusses this attitude of acceptance in further detail in "Barthelme Unfair to Kierkegaard," pp. 48–50.

20. The motif of disguise appears throughout *Dr. Caligari* (in addition to "Florence

Green" and "Hiding Man," it also figures prominently in "The Big Broadcast of 1938"), possibly to reinforce the basic "uncertainty principle" that Barthelme wishes to develop.

21. See Manuel Puig's translated works, *Betrayed by Rita Hayworth, Heartbreak Tango, The Buenos Aires Affair* and *Kiss of the Spider Woman*.

22. *CB,* p. 109. Henry Mackie, in "Marie, Marie, Hold on Tight," is another Barthelme character who understands how we are deceived in our role as ordinary citizens. Recognizing that most people are unable to stand back and look at their situation for what it is, he says, "It's a paradigmatic situation exemplifying the distance between the potential knowers holding a commonsense view of the world and what is to be known, which escapes them as they pursue their mundane existences" (pp. 119–20).

23. These "commercial messages" seem remarkably similar to the balloon which the narrator of "The Balloon" sends aloft as "a spontaneous autobiographical disclosure, having to do with the unease I felt at your absence, and with sexual deprivation" (*UP,* p. 21). I suspect that many of Barthelme's stories may be obscure, often painful "messages" of this private sort which the reader can never hope to understand.

24. George Steiner, "Silence and the Poet," in *Language and Silence* (New York: Atheneum, 1967), p. 46.

25. Ibid.

26. Richard Gilman, "Donald Barthelme," in *The Confusion of Realms* (New York: Random House, 1969), p. 45.

27. Robert Scholes discusses this parodic use of myth by contemporary writers (especially with regard to Barth's *Giles Goat-Boy*) in *The Fabulators* (New York: Oxford University Press, 1967).

28. Leland, "Remarks Re-marked," p. 804.

29. Gilman, "Donald Barthelme," p. 50.

30. Leland, "Remarks Re-marked," p. 801.

Chapter 4: William H. Gass: The World Within the Word

1. "A Symposium on Fiction: Donald Barthelme, William Gass, Grace Paley, Walker Percy," *Shenandoah* 27, no. 2 (Winter 1976), 22.

2. William H. Gass, *Willie Masters' Lonesome Wife, TriQuarterly Supplement* 2 (Evanston, Ill.: Northwestern University Press, 1968), white section. Gass's novella is unpaged into four sections printed on blue, olive, red, and white paper, respectively; hereafter cited as *WM* if identification is needed.

3. Thomas LeClair, "Interview with William H. Gass," *Paris Review* 70 (Summer 1977), 80.

4. For Gass's personal commentary on this experience, see his essay, "A Memory of a Master," in *Fiction and the Figures of Life* (New York: Alfred A. Knopf, 1970); hereafter cited as *FFL* if identification is needed.

5. Gass, *Fiction,* p. 27.

6. Gass attended Kenyon College as a philosophy student, where many of the

leading New Critics were teaching at the time. Gass reports that he even audited some courses taught by John Crowe Ransom, but it is difficult to determine whether this exposure to New Critical theories had any lasting effect on his literary opinions.

7. LeClair, "Interview with William H. Gass," p. 63.

8. Gass received his Ph.D. degree in philosophy from Cornell, where he did his dissertation on "A Philosophical Investigation of Metaphor" under Professor Max Black; Gass currently teaches at Washington University, St. Louis, where he has a dual appointment in philosophy and literature.

9. For the most significant recent attack on this position, see John Gardner's *On Moral Fiction* (New York: Basic Books, 1978), which takes Coover and Barthelme to task as well.

10. For a different view, see Ned French, "Against the Grain: Theory and Practice in the Work of William H. Gass," in *Iowa Review* 7 (Winter 1976), 96–106. French basically claims that Gass's nonmimetic literary theories go "against the grain" of his fiction, which is primarily realistic in orientation.

11. Interview with Larry McCaffery, December 1977.

12. Valéry discusses this idea in a number of essays. See, for example, his extended discussion of this subject in "Aesthetic Invention," *Aesthetics,* trans. Ralph Manheim (New York: Random House, 1967).

13. Gass develops this analogy at considerable length in his essay, "Carrots, Noses, Snow, Rose, Roses," in *The World Within the Word* (New York: Alfred A. Knopf, 1978), pp. 280–307.

14. Ibid., p. 283.

15. Paul Valéry, *The Art of Poetry,* trans. Denise Folliot (New York: Vintage, 1961), p. 70.

16. Valéry, "Reflections on Art," in *Aesthetics,* p. 158.

17. LeClair, "Interview with William H. Gass," p. 69.

18. Ibid., p. 70.

19. Paul Valéry, "Discourse on the Declamation of Verse," in *Selected Writings* (New York: New Directions, 1964), p. 157.

20. See Max Black's study of this topic in *Models and Metaphor* (Ithaca, N.Y.: Cornell University Press, 1962).

21. Marcus B. Hester, *The Meaning of Poetic Metaphor* (Paris: Mouton, 1967), pp. 19–20.

22. Black, *Models and Metaphor,* p. 43.

23. Ibid., p. 237.

24. Ibid.

25. Valéry, "Philosophy of Dance," in *Aesthetics,* p. 211.

26. LeClair, "Interview With William H. Gass," p. 71.

27. Ibid., p. 64.

28. Ibid., p. 62.

29. Ibid., pp. 63–64.

30. "The Clairvoyant" appeared in *Location* 1, no. 2 (1964), 59–66 (a journal edited by Barthelme), while "The Sugar Crock" appeared in *Art and Literature* 9 (Summer

1966), 158-71. Gass apparently intends these two pieces to be parts one and two of a longer work entitled "Cartesian Sonata"; part 3 will be his recently published piece, "I Wish You Wouldn't," *Partisan Review* 42, no. 3 (1975), 344-60.

31. Gass, "The Sugar Crock," p. 62.

32. In Tony Tanner's examination of *Willie Masters*, "Games American Writers Play," *Salamagundi* 35 (Fall 1975), 110-40, the suggestion is made that the specifics included on the front and back of the book—the breasts and buttocks—are significant: "This is not incidental, for orifices, nourishment and excrement, are central concerns of the book. We are, it reminds us, constantly taking things in and as constantly secreting them, as excrement, saliva, dirt, semen, and words" (p. 118).

33. For a different reading, see Charles Caramello, "Fleshing Out *Willie Masters' Lonesome Wife*," *Sub-Stance*, 27 (1980), 56-69.

34. Ibid., pp. 117-18.

35. Gass worked closely with Lawrence Levy, the book's graphic designer, to create these visual effects.

36. Hugh Kenner, *Flaubert, Joyce and Beckett: The Stoic Comedians* (London: W. H. Allen, 1964), p. 47.

37. Michel Butor, "The Book as Object," in *Inventory* (New York: Simon & Schuster, 1968), p. 44.

38. Kenner, *Flaubert, Joyce and Beckett*, p. 47; Butor refers to basically the same thing with the term "the book as object" in *Inventory*.

39. Kenner, *Flaubert, Joyce and Beckett*, p. 40.

40. Donald Barthelme, *Snow White* (New York: Bantam, 1968), p. 6.

41. John Locke, "An Essay Concerning Human Understanding," bk. 2, ch. 11, sec. 9 of *Selections* (Chicago: University of Chicago Press, 1956), p. 144.

42. Tanner, "Games American Writers Play," p. 119.

43. Tanner suggests that Babs's choice of "catafalque" may have a further significance: "Catafalque, perhaps not entirely coincidentally, is the structure on which the coffin rests which holds the body. The body dies: language, which to a large extent sustains and constitutes the body throughout its life, remains. Like a catafalque" (ibid., p. 119).

44. Ibid., p. 121.

45. LeClair, "Interview with William H. Gass," p. 77.

46. Loren Hoekzema, "Two Readings of Lyrical Space: William Gass's *In the Heart of the Heart of the Country* and Donald Barthelme's *City Life*," (Ph.D. diss., Miami University [Ohio], 1976), p. 71.

47. William H. Gass, *In the Heart of the Heart of the Country and Other Stories* (New York: Pocket Books, 1977), p. 105.

48. Bruce Bassoff, "The Sacrificial World of William Gass: *In the Heart of the Heart of the Country*," *Critique* 18 (August 1976), 37.

49. A scene of similarly powerful phallic implications occurs a few pages earlier. It begins with Hans describing his view of what might have happened at the Pedersen house: "He's got me and your ma and pa lined up with our hands here back of our necks, and he's got a rifle between them yellow gloves and he's waving the point of it

up and down in front of your ma's face real slow and quiet." Hans is next said to have "got up and waved the bottle violently in ma's face. She shivered and shooed it away" (p. 51).

50. Pp. 79–80. The connection between the gun, his sexuality, and his resentment is also suggested by Jorge's description of his imaginary murders: "Shooting Hans seemed like something I'd done already. I knew where he kept his gun — under those magazines in his drawer" (p. 79).

51. Bassoff feels that Gass may be punning on the phrase "to run": "If the colors run [the colors of the towels used to warm the Pedersen Kid], Jorge wants to convince everyone that he . . . would not have run" ("The Sacrificial World of William Gass," p. 39).

52. In his introduction to the Pocket Book edition of In the Heart, Gass comments that "'Mrs. Mean' is a story of sexual curiosity translated, again, into the epistemological" (p. 21).

53. Spiders appear regularly in Gass's fiction. In an interview Gass said: "I am very fond of spiders. I am as fond of them as my family allows me to be. I used to have a house out in the country and it sheltered many spiders. Once quite a large handsome spider spun his web in the john where I could conveniently watch him. . . . I regarded it as a convenient symbol of the imagination: spinning, lying in wait, sucking dry" (Leclair, "Interview with William H. Gass," p. 78).

54. Bassoff's essay, "The Sacrificial World of William Gass," is especially useful in identifying the many instances of imagery suggesting sexual repression in "Mrs. Mean."

55. Ibid., p. 42.

56. Ibid., p. 43.

57. See, for example, Gass's remarks about "Order of Insects" to LeClair, where he says this story is "the best thing [he] ever wrote," ("Interview with William H. Gass," p. 89).

58. Hoekzema, "Two Readings of Lyrical Space," p. 129.

59. Frederick Busch, "But This Is What It Is Like to Live in Hell: William Gass's 'In the Heart of the Heart of the Country,'" Modern Fiction Studies 20 (Autumn 1974), 99–100.

60. Hoekzema, "Two Readings of Lyrical Space," p. 132.

61. As with Barthelme, the estrangement of Gass's characters from both words and personal love is a major theme found throughout his work; it is the primary point of departure, for example, in Willie Masters, as it is also in Omensetter's Luck and The Tunnel.

62. Hoekzema, "Two Readings of Lyrical Space," p. 133.

63. Ibid., p. 134.

64. P. 203. The attractions of the life lived "directly" are elaborately developed in Omensetter's Luck.

65. See, for example, the narrator's description of the "headless maples behind my house" and the trees which have been "maimed to free the passage of wires" (pp. 192–93).

66. Tony Tanner, City of Words (New York: Harper & Row, 1971), p. 271.

67. Vladimir Nabokov, Lolita (New York: Capricorn Books, 1972), p. 311.

68. Richard Gilman, "Review of Omensetter's Luck," New Republic, 7 May 1966, p. 23.

69. Paul West, "Finnegan's Ache," *Book Week,* 20 March 1966, p. 907.

70. "The Triumph of Israbestis Tott," *Accent* 18, no. 1 (Winter 1958), 35–58; "The Love and Sorrow of Henry Pimber," *Accent* 20, no. 2 (Spring 1960), 67–95; all references to *Omensetter's Luck* (1966; rpt. New York: New American Library, 1972) will be given in the text.

71. Details of this episode are still sketchy, but Gass reported to me that his colleague stole the manuscript with the intent of publishing sections of it in dramatic form. Gass was alerted to who had stolen it (although he had earlier suspicions) when a friend reported that a portion of *Omensetter* had been submitted to the *Tulane Drama Review* as a play.

72. "A Letter to the Editor" [David Segal] in *Afterwords,* ed. Thomas McCormack (New York: Harper & Row, 1969), pp. 95–96.

73. Interview with Larry McCaffery.

74. Ibid.

75. Gass, "A Letter to the Editor," p. 95.

76. Ibid., pp. 96–97.

77. Ibid., p. 97.

78. Ibid., p. 96.

79. Richard J. Schneider, "The Fortunate Fall in William Gass's *Omensetter's Luck,*" *Critique* 18 (Summer 1976), p. 6.

80. Ibid., pp. 10–11.

81. Gass, "A Letter to the Editor," p. 98.

82. Schneider, "The Fortunate Fall," p. 11.

83. Ibid., p. 12.

84. Gass, "A Letter to the Editor," p. 101.

85. Ibid., p. 100.

86. Ibid.

87. Schneider, "The Fortunate Fall," p. 13.

88. Gass, "A Letter to the Editor," p. 102; Furber's more convoluted discussion of this issue appears on pp. 74–75 of the novel.

89. Schneider, "The Fortunate Fall," p. 17.

90. As a child, Furber had imagined a "circle of stones" surrounding him as a punishment—a circle which suggests the barrier of abstraction encircling him throughout the novel. His gesture in this later scene of breaking up Omensetter's circle of stones thus symbolically represents his awareness of the dangers of such barriers.

Chapter 5: The Contemporary Meta-Sensibility: A Personal Conclusion

1. Among the works which directly influenced my thoughts about metafiction and man-the-fiction-maker were: Peter L. Berger, *The Sacred Canopy* (Garden City, N.Y., 1967); Ernst Cassirer, *The Philosophy of Symbolic Forms,* trans. Ralph Manheim (New Haven, Conn.: Yale University Press, 1964) and *The Problem of Knowledge,* trans. William Wolgom and Charles Hendel (New Haven, Conn.: Yale University Press, 1950);

Michel Foucault, *The Order of Things,* trans. Richard Howard (New York: The New American Library, 1967); Thomas Kuhn, *The Structure of Scientific Revolutions* (Chicago: The University of Chicago Press, 1962); Susanne K. Langer, *Philosophy in a New Key* (Cambridge, Mass.: Harvard University Press, 1942); W.V.O. Quine, *From a Logical Point of View* (Cambridge, Mass.: Harvard University Press, 1961); Israel Scheffler, *Science and Subjectivity* (New York: Bobbs-Merrill, 1967); Elizabeth Sewell, *The Orphic Voice* (New Haven, Conn.: Yale University Press, 1960); Colin Turbayne, *The Myth of Metaphor* (Columbia: University of South Carolina Press, 1970); and various works by Wittgenstein, Barthes, and Levi-Strauss.

2. See the bibliography.

3. Although I have argued that today's readers are more self-conscious and apt to appreciate nonmimetic forms, the situation with literature is complicated by the apparent declining interest in reading, especially among young people, in favor of other media. Whether or not this decline is permanent and (as educators often claim) ultimately harmful is difficult to gauge, but surely fiction and story-telling will always appeal to our imagination, though they need not be written out in words. The same parents and educators who deplore the fact that Johnny is playing Dungeons-and-Dragons instead of reading *Ivanhoe* may be missing the point that games like these (which include "Boot-Hill" and "Gamma-World" and which will soon be found in video game equivalents) are really do-it-yourself novels, with the narrative elements of a given genre broken down into bits and pieces which the children imaginatively reconstruct. Such reconstructions don't help Johnny learn to read or write, admittedly, but they supply much the same intellectual challenge as reading fiction and may even encourage the creative facility *more* than the more passive activity of reading novels or stories.

4. There have also appeared, of course, a number of more serious metacinematic works whose complexities and artistry are much closer in spirit to the works of Coover, Barthelme, and Gass. A few examples of such films would include Woody Allen's *Stardust Memories,* Karel Reisz's *The French Lieutenant's Woman,* Richard Rush's *The Stunt Man,* Truffaut's *Day for Night,* and (probably still the preeminent metacinematic work of them all), Fellini's *8½.*

5. See Tom LeClair and Larry McCaffery, eds., *Anything Can Happen: Interviews with Contemporary American Novelists* (Urbana: University of Illinois Press, 1982).

6. Alan Wilde, "'Strange Displacements of the Ordinary': Apple, Elkin, and Barthelme, and the Problem of the Excluded Middle," *boundary 2,* (Fall 1981).

7. Ibid.

SELECTED BIBLIOGRAPHY

Metafiction, Fiction and Metaphor-Making, and Postmodernism

Alter, Robert. *Partial Magic: The Novel as Self-Conscious Genre*. Berkeley: University of California Press, 1975.

Auerbach, Erich. *Mimesis: The Representation of Reality in Western Literature*. Trans. W. R. Trask. Princeton, N.J.: Princeton University Press, 1953.

Barth, John. "The Literature of Exhaustion." *Atlantic Monthly*, Aug. 1967, pp. 29–34.

———. "The Literature of Replenishment." *Atlantic Monthly*, Jan. 1980, pp. 64–69.

———. "Tales within Tales within Tales." *Antaeus* 43 (Autumn 1981), 45–64.

Barthes, Roland. *The Eiffel Tower and Other Mythologies*. Trans. Richard Howard. New York: Hill and Wang, 1979.

———. *Image — Music — Text*. Trans. Stephen Heath. New York: Hill and Wang, 1977.

———. *The Pleasure of the Text*. Trans. Richard Miller. New York: Hill and Wang, 1975.

———. *S/Z*. Trans. Richard Miller. New York: Hill and Wang, 1974.

———. *Writing Degree Zero and Elements of Semiology*. Trans. Annette Lavers and Colin Smith. Boston: Beacon Press, 1967.

Bellamy, Joe David. *The New Fiction: Interviews with Innovative American Writers*. Urbana: University of Illinois Press, 1974.

Benamou, Michel, and Charles Caramello. *Performance in Postmodern Culture*. Madison, Wis.: Coda Press, 1977.

Berger, Peter. *The Sacred Canopy: Elements of a Sociological Theory of Religion*. Garden City, N.Y.: Doubleday, 1967.

Black, Max. *Models and Metaphors: Studies in Language and Philosophy*. Ithaca, N.Y.: Cornell University Press, 1962.

———. *The Nature of Mathematics*. London: Kegan Paul, 1933.

Bornstein, George. "Beyond Modernism." *Michigan Quarterly Review* 12 (Summer 1973), 278–84.

Burtt, E. A. *The Metaphysical Foundations of Modern Science*. Garden City, N.Y.: Doubleday, 1954.

Campbell, Joseph, ed. *Myths, Dreams, and Religion*. New York: E. P. Dutton, 1970.

Cassirer, Ernst. *Language and Myth*. Trans. Suzanne K. Langer, New York: Dover, 1946.

———. *Language*. Vol. 1 of *The Philosophy of Symbolic Forms*. Trans. Ralph Manheim. New Haven, Conn.: Yale University Press, 1964.

_____. *Mythical Thought*. Vol. 2 of *The Philosophy of Symbolic Forms*. Trans. Ralph Manheim. New Haven, Conn.: Yale University Press, 1964.

_____. *The Problem of Knowledge*. Trans. William H. Woglom and Charles W. Hendel. New Haven, Conn.: Yale University Press, 1950.

Cope, Jackson, and Geoffrey Green, eds. *Novel vs. Fiction: The Contemporary Reformation. Genre*, special issue 14 (Spring 1981).

Croce, Benedetto. *History: Its Theory and Practice*. Trans. Douglas Ainslie. New York: Russell and Russell, 1960.

DeMan, Paul. *Blindness and Insight: Essays in the Rhetoric of Contemporary Criticism.* New York: Oxford University Press, 1971.

Eliade, Mircea. *The Sacred and the Profane*. Trans. William R. Trask. New York: Harcourt, Brace & World, 1959.

Federman, Raymond. *Surfiction: Fiction Now and Tomorrow*. Chicago: Swallow Press, 1975.

Federman, Raymond, and Carl R. Lovitt, eds. *Current Trends in American Fiction. SubStance*, special issue 27 (1980).

Fiedler, Leslie. *Waiting for the End*. New York: Stein and Day, 1970.

Foucault, Michel. *Madness and Civilization*. Trans. Richard Howard. New York: New American Library, 1967.

_____. *The Order of Things*. New York: Pantheon Books, 1973.

Gado, Frank. *First Person: Conversations on Writers and Writing*. Schenectady, N.Y.: Union College Press, 1973.

Gardner, John. *On Moral Fiction*. New York: Basic Books, 1978.

Gilman, Richard. *The Confusion of Realms*. New York: Random House, 1969.

_____. "The Idea of the Avant-Garde." *Partisan Review* 34 (1972), 382–96.

Graff, Gerald. *Literature Against Itself*. Chicago: University of Chicago Press, 1979.

Grossvogel, David I. *Limits of the Novel*. Ithaca, N.Y.: Cornell University Press, 1968.

Hartman, Geoffrey. *Beyond Formalism: Literary Essays, 1958–1970*. New Haven, Conn.: Yale University Press, 1970.

Harvey, William J. *Character and the Novel*. Ithaca, N.Y.: Cornell University Press, 1966.

Hassan, Ihab. *The Dismemberment of Orpheus: Toward a Post-Modern Literature*. New York: Oxford University Press, 1971.

_____. *Paracriticisms*. Urbana: University of Illinois Press, 1975.

Heisenberg, Werner. *Physics and Philosophy*. New York: Harper and Row, 1958.

Hester, Marcus B. *The Meaning of Poetic Metaphor*. Paris: Mouton, 1967.

Hicks, Walter J. *The Metafictional City*. (Chapel Hill: University of North Carolina Press, 1981.

Hofstadter, Douglas R. *Godel, Escher, Bach: An Eternal Golden Braid*. New York: Basic Books, 1979.

Howe, Irving. *Decline of the New*. New York: Harcourt, Brace, 1970.

Jeans, James H. *The Mysterious Universe*. London: Kegan Paul, 1946.

Johsen, William R. "Toward a Redefinition of Modernism." *boundary 2* 2 (Spring 1974), 539–56.

Kant, Immanuel. *The Critique of Judgment*. Trans. J. H. Bernard. New York: Hafner, 1956.

Kellogg, Robert, and Robert Scholes. *The Nature of Narrative*. New York: Oxford University Press, 1966.

Kenner, Hugh. *The Counterfeiters*. Garden City, N.Y.: Doubleday, 1968.

⎯⎯⎯⎯. *The Stoic Comedians: Flaubert, Joyce, and Beckett*. London: Will Allen, 1964.

Kermode, Frank. *The Sense of an Ending*. New York: Oxford University Press, 1968.

Klinkowitz, Jerome. *The Life of Fiction*. Urbana: University of Illinois Press, 1977.

⎯⎯⎯⎯. *Literary Disruptions: The Makings of a Post-Contemporary American Fiction*. Urbana: University of Illinois Press, 1975.

Kuhn, Thomas. *The Structure of Scientific Revolutions*. Chicago: The University of Chicago Press, 1962.

Langer, Suzanne K. *Philosophy in a New Key*. Cambridge, Mass.: Harvard University Press, 1942.

McCaffery, Larry. "Literary Disruptions: Fiction in a 'Post-Contemporary' Age." *boundary 2* 5 (Fall 1976), 137–52.

⎯⎯⎯⎯. "The Gass-Gardner Debate: Showdown on Mainstreet." *The Literary Review* 23 (Fall 1979), 134–44.

Miller, J. Hillis. *The Form of Victorian Fiction*. Notre Dame, Ind.: University of Notre Dame Press, 1968.

Neff, Emery E. *The Poetry of History: The Contributions of Literature and Literary Scholarship to the Writing of History Since Voltaire*. New York: Columbia University Press, 1947.

Nietzsche, Friedrich. *The Use and Abuse of History*. Trans. Adrian Collins. New York: Liberal Arts Press, 1949.

Nin, Anais. *The Novel of the Future*. New York: Macmillan, 1968.

Olderman, Raymond M. *Beyond the Waste Land*. New Haven, Conn.: Yale University Press, 1972.

Ortega y Gasset, José. *The Dehumanization of Art*. Garden City, N.Y.: Doubleday, 1956.

⎯⎯⎯⎯. *The Modern Theme*. Trans. James Cleugh. New York: Harper and Row, 1961.

Pinsker, Sanford. "*Ulysses* and the Post-Modern Temper." *Midwest Quarterly* 15 (Summer 1974), 406–16.

Poggioli, Renato. *The Theory of the Avant-Garde*. Trans. Gerald Fitzgerald. New York: Harper and Row, 1971.

Popper, Karl. *The Logic of Scientific Discovery*. New York: Science Editions, 1961.

⎯⎯⎯⎯. *Objective Knowledge: An Evolutionary Approach*. New York: Oxford University Press, 1972.

Putz, Manfred. *The Story of Identity: American Fiction of the Sixties*. Stuttgart: Metzler, 1979.

Quine, Willard V. *From a Logical Point of View: Nine Logico-Philosophical Essays*. New York: Harper and Row, 1961.

Richards, Ivot A. *The Philosophy of Rhetoric*. New York: Oxford University Press, 1936.

Robbe-Grillet, Alain. *For a New Novel*. Trans. Richard Howard. New York: Grove Press, 1965.

Rochberg, George. "The Avant-Garde and the Aesthetics of Survival." *New Literary History* 3 (Autumn 1971), 71–92.

Rosenberg, Harold. *The De-Definition of Art: Action Art to Pop to Earthworks.* New York: Horizon Press, 1972.

———. *The Tradition of the New.* New York: McGraw Hill, 1965.

Rosenblum, Robert. *Cubism and Twentieth Century Art.* New York: Abrams, 1966.

Ryle, Gilbert. *The Concept of Mind.* New York: Barnes and Noble, 1949.

Said, Edward. "Contemporary Fiction and Criticism," *TriQuarterly* 33 (Winter 1975), 230–41.

———. "What is Beyond Formalism?" *Modern Language Notes* 86 (1971), 933–45.

Sarraute, Nathalie. *The Age of Suspicion: Essays on the Novel.* Trans. Maria Jolas. New York: George Braziller, 1963.

Scheffler, Israel. *Science and Subjectivity.* New York: Bobbs-Merrill, 1967.

Scholes, Robert. *Fabulation and Metafiction.* Urbana: University of Illinois Press, 1979.

———. "Metafiction." *Iowa Review* 1 (Fall 1970), 100–15.

Sewell, Elizabeth. *The Orphic Voice.* New Haven, Conn.: Yale University Press, 1960.

———. *The Structure of Poetry.* London: Kegan Paul, 1951.

Shattuck, Roger, "After the Avant-Garde." *New York Review of Books,* 12 Mar. 1970, pp. 41–47.

———. *The Banquet Years.* New York: Random, 1968.

Sontag, Susan. *Against Interpretation.* New York: Farrar, Straus & Giroux, 1966.

———. *Styles of Radical Will.* New York: Farrar, Straus & Giroux, 1969.

Spanos, William V. "The Detective and the Boundary: Some Notes on the Postmodern Literary Imagination." *boundary 2* 2 (Fall 1972), 147–68.

Spencer, Sharon. *Space, Time and Structure in the Modern Novel.* Chicago: Swallow Press, 1971.

Steiner, George. *Extraterritorial: Papers on Literature and the Language Revolution.* New York: Atheneum, 1971.

———. *Language and Silence: Essays on Language, Literature and the Inhuman.* New York: Atheneum, 1967.

Sukenick, Ronald. "The New Tradition." *Partisan Review* 39 (1972), 580–88.

Sypher, Wylie. *Rococo to Cubism.* New York: Random House, 1960.

Tanner, Tony. *City of Words: American Fiction, 1950–1970.* New York: Harper and Row, 1971.

———. "Games American Writers Play." *Salamagundi* 35 (Fall 1975), 110–40.

Turbayne, Colin M. *The Myth of Metaphor.* Columbia: University of South Carolina Press, 1970.

Vaihinger, H. *The Philosophy of "As If": A System of the Theoretical, Practical, and Religious Fictions of Mankind.* Trans. C. K. Ogden. New York: Barnes and Noble, 1966.

Valéry, Paul. *Aesthetics.* Trans. Ralph Manheim. New York: Random House, 1964.

———. *The Art of Poetry.* Trans. Denise Folliot. New York: Random House, 1964.

Wasson, Richard. "From Priest to Prometheus: Culture and Criticism in the Post-Modern Period." *Journal of Modern Literature* 3 (1974), 1190–1208.

———. "Notes on a New Sensibility." *Partisan Review* 36 (1969), 460–77.

Wilde, Alan. *Horizons of Assent: Modernism, Postmodernism, and the Ironic Imagination*. Baltimore: Johns Hopkins University Press, 1981.

Wittgenstein, Ludwig. *Philosophical Investigations*. Trans. G. E. M. Anscombe. New York: Macmillan, 1953.

———. *Tractatus Logico-Philosophicus*. New York: Hudson Humanities Press, 1951.

Zavarzadeh, Mas'ud. *The Mythopoeic Reality: The Postwar American Nonfiction Novel*. Urbana: University of Illinois Press, 1976.

Ziolkowski, Theodore. "Towards a Post-Modern Aesthetic." *Mosaic* 2 (Summer 1969), 112–19.

Robert Coover (b. 1932)

I. Novels, Novellas, and Collections of Short Fiction and Plays

The Origin of the Brunists. New York: G. P. Putnam's Sons, 1965 [novel].

The Universal Baseball Association, Inc., J. Henry Waugh, Prop. New York: Random House, 1968 [novel].

Pricksongs and Descants. New York: Dutton, 1969 [stories].

A Theological Position. New York: Dutton, 1973 [plays].

The Public Burning. New York: Viking, 1977 [novel].

"The Water Pourer." Bloomfield Hills, Mich.: Bruccoli Clark, 1972.

"Hair o' the Chine." Bloomfield Hills, Mich.: Bruccoli Clark, 1979.

"After Lazarus." Bloomfield Hills, Mich.: Bruccoli Clark, 1980.

"A Political Fable." New York: Viking, 1980.

"Charlie in the House of Rue." Lincoln, Mass.: Penmaen Press, 1980.

"Spanking the Maid." Bloomfield Hills, Mich.: Bruccoli Clark, 1981.

II. Uncollected Short Fiction and Poems

"One Summer in Spain, Five Poems." *Fiddlehead*, Autumn 1960, pp. 18–19.

"Blackdamp." *Noble Savage* 4 (Oct. 1961), 218–19.

"Dinner with the King of England." *Evergreen Review* 27 (Nov./Dec. 1962), 110–18.

"The Square Shooter and the Saint." *Evergreen Review* 25 (July/Aug. 1962), 92–101.

"D. D., Baby." *Cavalier* (July 1967), 53–56, 93.

"The Second Son." *Evergreen Review* 31 (Oct./Nov. 1963), 72–88.

"The Mex Would Arrive in Gentry's Junction at 12:10." *Evergreen Review* 47 (June 1967), 63–65, 98–102.

"The Cat in the Hat for President." *New American Review* 4 (1968), 7–46.

"Letter from Patmos." *Quarterly Review of Literature* 16 (1969), 29.

"The Last Quixote." *New American Review* 11 (1970), 139–44.

"The Reunion." *Iowa Review* 1 (Fall 1970), 64–69.

"Some Notes on Puff." *Iowa Review* 1 (Winter 1970), 29–31.

"The First Annual Congress of the High Church or the Hard Core (Notes from the Underground)." *Evergreen Review* 89 (May 1971), 16, 74.

"McDuff on the Mound." *Iowa Review* 2 (Fall 1971), 111–20.

"Beginnings." *Harper's,* Mar. 1972, pp. 82–87.

"Lucky Pierre and the Music Lesson." *New American Review* 14 (1972), 201–12.

"The Old Men" and "An Encounter." *Little Magazine* 1 (1972).

"The Dead Queen." *Quarterly Review of Literature* 18 (1973), 304–13.

"Lucky Pierre and the Cunt Auction." *Antaeus* 21 (1974), 13–14.

"The Public Burning of Ethel and Julius Rosenberg: An Historical Romance." *TriQuarterly* 26 (Winter 1974), 262–81.

"Whatever Happened to Gloomy Gus of the Chicago Bears?" *American Review* 22 (1975), 31–111.

"The Tinkerer." *Antaeus* 24 (1977), 111–12.

"The Convention." *Panache* (1977).

"The Fallguy's Faith." *TriQuarterly* 35 (Winter 1976), 79–80.

III. Critical Essays about Robert Coover

Andersen, Richard. *Robert Coover* (Boston: Twayne, 1981).

Angelius, J. W. "The Man Behind the Catcher's Mask: A Closer Look at Robert Coover's Universal Baseball Association." *University of Denver Quarterly* 12 (1977), 165–74.

Berman, Neil. "Coover's *The Universal Baseball Association:* Play as Personalized Myth." *Modern Fiction Studies* 24 (1978), 209–22.

Cope, Jackson I. "Robert Coover's Fictions." *Iowa Review* 2 (Fall 1971), 94–110.

Gregory, Sinda, and Larry McCaffery. "Robert Coover." *Dictionary of Literary Biography Supplement.* Detroit: Gale Research Co., 1982.

Gunn, J. "Structure as Revelation: Coover's *Pricksongs.*" *Linguistics in Literature* 2 (1977), 1–42.

Hansen, Arlen J. "The Dice of God: Einstein, Heisenberg and Robert Coover." *Novel: A Forum on Fiction* 10 (Fall 1976), 49–58.

Heckard, Margaret. "Robert Coover, Metafiction and Freedom." *Twentieth Century Literature* 22 (May 1976), 210–27.

Hertzel, Leo. "What's Wrong with the Christians?" *Critique* 11 (1969), 11–24.

Hume, Kathryn. "Robert Coover's Fiction: The Naked and the Mythic." *Novel* 12 (1978), 127–48.

Kissel, Susan. "The Contemporary Artist and His Audience in the Short Stories of Robert Coover." *Studies in Short Fiction* 16 (1979), 49–54.

McCaffery, Larry. "The Magic of Fiction Making." *Fiction International* 4–5 (Winter 1975), 147–53.

———. "Robert Coover." *Dictionary of Literary Biography.* Detroit: Gale Research Co., 1979, pp. 106–21.

———. "Robert Coover's Cubist Fictions." *Par Rapport* 1 (1978), 33–40.

Schmitz, Neil. "The Hazards of Metafiction." *Novel: A Forum on Fiction* 7 (1974), 210–19.

Scholes, Robert. "Metafiction." *Iowa Review* 1 (Fall 1970), 100–15.

Schulz, Max. "The Politics of Parody; and the Comic Apocalypses of Jorge Luis Borges, Thomas Berger, Thomas Pynchon, and Robert Coover." In *Black Humor Fiction of the 1960s.* Athens: Ohio University Press, 1973, pp. 66–90.

Shelton, Frank W. "Humor and Balance in Coover's *The Universal Baseball Association.*" *Critique* 1 (Aug. 1975), 78–90.

Taylor, Mark. "Baseball as Myth." *Commonweal,* 12 May 1972, pp. 237–39.

Windeapple, Brenda. "Robert Coover's Playing Fields." *Iowa Review* 10 (1979), 66–74.

Wolff, Geoffrey. "An American Epic." *New Times,* 19 Aug. 1977, pp. 48–57.

IV. Interviews

Gado, Frank. "Robert Coover." In *First Person: Conversations on Writers and Writing.* Schenectady, N.Y.: Union College Press, 1973, pp. 142–49.

Hertzel, Leo. "An Interview with Robert Coover." *Critique* 11 (1969), 25–29.

Kadragic, Alma. "An Interview with Robert Coover." *Shanti* 2 (Summer 1972), 57–60.

McCaffery, Larry. "An Interview with Robert Coover." In *Interviews with Contemporary American Novelists,* ed. Thomas LeClair and Larry McCaffery. Urbana: University of Illinois Press, 1982.

V. Bibliographies

Blachowicz, Camille. "Bibliography: Robert Bly and Robert Coover." *Great Lakes Review* 3 (Summer 1976), 66–73.

McCaffery, Larry. "Donald Barthelme, Robert Coover, William H. Gass: Three Checklists." *Bulletin of Bibliography* 31 (1974), 101–06.

————. "Robert Coover." In *Dictionary of Literary Biography.* Detroit: Gale Research Company, 1979, pp. 120–21.

Donald Barthelme (b. 1931)

I. Novels and Collections of Short Fiction or Essays

Come Back, Dr. Caligari. Boston: Little, Brown, 1964 [stories].

Snow White. New York: Atheneum, 1967 [novel].

Unspeakable Practices, Unnatural Acts. New York: Farrar, Straus & Giroux, 1968 [stories].

City Life. New York: Farrar, Straus & Giroux, 1970 [stories].

The Slightly Irregular Fire Engine, or The Hithering Thithering Djinn. New York: Farrar, Straus & Giroux, 1971 [juvenile fiction].

Sadness. New York: Farrar, Straus & Giroux, 1972 [stories].

Guilty Pleasures. New York: Farrar, Straus & Giroux, 1974 [essays].

The Dead Father. New York: Farrar, Straus & Giroux, 1975 [novel].

Amateurs. New York: Farrar, Straus & Giroux, 1976 [stories].

Great Days. New York: Farrar, Straus & Giroux, 1979 [stories].

Sixty Stories. New York: G. P. Putnam, 1981 [stories].

II. Uncollected Short Fiction

"Man's Face." *New Yorker,* 30 May 1964, p. 29.

"Then." *Mother* 3 (Nov.–Dec. 1964), 22–23.

"Philadelphia." *New Yorker,* 30 Nov. 1968, pp. 56–58.

"Newsletter." *New Yorker,* 25 Apr. 1970, pp. 32–33.

"Adventure." *Harper's Bazaar,* Dec. 1970, p. 23.

"The Story Thus Far." *New Yorker,* 1 May 1971, pp. 42–45.

"Natural History." *Harper's,* Aug. 1971, pp. 44–45.

"The Mothball Fleet." *New Yorker,* 11 Sept. 1971, pp. 34–35.

"Alexandria and Henrietta." *New American Review* 12 (1971), 82–87.

"Edwards, Amelia." *New Yorker,* 9 Sept. 1972, pp. 34–36.

"Three." *Fiction* 1 (1972), 13.

"Wrack." *New Yorker,* 21 Oct. 1972, pp. 36–37.

"Over the Sea of Histation." *New Yorker,* 11 Nov. 1972, pp. 40–43.

"A Man." *New Yorker,* 30 Dec. 1972, pp. 26–27.

"Sentence Passed on the Show of a Nation's Brain Damage, etc. Or, The Autobiography of a Crime." *December* 15, nos. 1–2 (1973), 83–94.

"The Inauguration." *Harper's,* Jan. 1973, pp. 86–87.

"You Are Cordially Invited." *New Yorker,* 23 July 1973, pp. 33–34.

"Manfred" [with Karen Shaw]. *New York Times Magazine,* 18 Apr. 1976, p. 87.

"Monumental Folly" [with Edward Sorel]. *Atlantic,* Feb. 1976, pp. 33–40.

"Momma." *New Yorker,* 2 Oct. 1978, pp. 32–33.

III. Articles and Reviews by Donald Barthelme

"A Note on Elia Kazan." *University of Houston Forum* 1 (Sept. 1956), 19–22.

"Mr. Hunt's Wooly Alpaca." Review of *Alpaca* by H. L. Hunt. *Reporter,* 14 Apr. 1960, pp. 44–46.

"The Emerging Figure." *University of Houston Forum* 3 (Summer 1961), 23–24.

"The Case of the Vanishing Product." *Harper's,* Oct. 1961, pp. 30–32.

"After Joyce." *Location* 1 (Summer 1964), 13–16.

"The Tired Terror of Graham Greene." Review of *The Comedians* by Graham Greene. *Holiday,* Apr. 1966, pp. 146, 148–49.

"The Elegance Is Under Control." Review of *The Triumph* by John Kenneth Galbraith. *New York Times Book Review,* 21 Apr. 1968, pp. 4–5.

IV. Interviews and Recorded Remarks

Baker, John F. "PW Interviews: Donald Barthelme." *Publishers' Weekly,* 11 Nov. 1974, pp. 6–7.

Cross, Leslie. "Down in the Village with Donald Barthelme." *Milwaukee Journal,* 4 Feb. 1973, sec. 4, p. 4.

Klinkowitz, Jerome. "An Interview with Donald Barthelme." In *The New Fiction: Interviews with Innovative American Writers,* ed. Joe David Bellamy. Urbana: University of Illinois Press, 1974, pp. 45–54.

McCaffery, Larry. "An Interview with Donald Barthelme." In *Interviews with Contemporary American Novelists,* ed. Thomas LeClair and Larry McCaffery. Urbana: University of Illinois Press, 1982.

O'Hara, J. D. "Donald Barthelme: The Art of Fiction LXVI." *Paris Review* 80 (1981), 180–210.

Schickel, Richard. "Freaked out on Barthelme." *New York Times Magazine,* 16 Aug. 1970, pp. 14–15, 52.

V. Critical Essays about Donald Barthelme

Bocock, Maclin. "'The Indian Uprising'; Or, Donald Barthelme's Strange Object Covered with Fur." *Fiction International* 415 (1975), 134–46.

Couturier, Maurice. "Barthelme's Uppity Bubble: 'The Balloon.'" *Revue Française d'Etudes Americaines* 8 (1979), 183–201.

Farmer, Catherine Dobson. "Mythological, Biblical and Literary Allusions in Donald Barthelme's *The Dead Father.*" *International Fiction Review* 6 (1979), 40–48.

Flowers, Betty. "Barthelme's *Snow White:* The Reader-Patient Relationship." *Critique* 16 (1975), 33–43.

Gillen, Francis. "Donald Barthelme's City: A Guide." *Twentieth Century Literature* 18 (Jan. 1972), 37–44.

Gilman, Richard. "Donald Barthelme." In *The Confusion of Realms.* New York: Random House, 1969, pp. 42–51.

Hiner, James. "I Will Tell the Meaning of Barthelme." *Denver Quarterly* 13 (1979), 61–76.

Hoekzema, Loren. "Two Readings of Lyrical Space: William Gass's *In the Heart of the Heart of the Country* and Donald Barthelme's *City Life.*" Ph.D. diss., Miami University (Ohio), 1976.

Johnson, R. E., Jr. "'Bees Barking in the Night': The End and Beginning of Barthelme's Narrative." *boundary 2* 5 (Fall 1976), 71–92.

Klinkowitz, Jerome. "Donald Barthelme." In *The Life of Fiction.* Urbana: University of Illinois Press, 1977, pp. 73–84.

———. "Donald Barthelme." In *Literary Disruptions: The Making of a Post-Contemporary American Fiction.* Urbana: University of Illinois Press, 1975, pp. 70–87.

Krupnick, Mark L. "Notes from the Funhouse." *Modern Occasions* 1 (Fall 1970), 108–12.

Leland, John. "Remarks Re-marked: Barthelme, What Curios of Signs!" *boundary 2* 5 (Spring 1977), 795–811.

Longleigh, Peter L., Jr. "Donald Barthelme's *Snow White.*" *Critique* 11 (1969), 30–34.

McCaffery, Larry. "Barthelme's *Snow White:* The Aesthetics of Trash." *Critique* 16 (Spring 1975), 19–32.

———. "Meaning and Non-Meaning in Barthelme's Fictions." *Journal of Aesthetic Education* 13 (1979), 16–24.

Malmgren, Carl. "Barthelme's 'The Zombies' and Barthes' *S/Z:* A Cacographic Interpretation of Text." *Journal for Descriptive Poetics and Theory* 3 (1978), 209–21.

Maloy, Barbara. "Barthelme's *The Dead Father:* Analysis of an Allegory." *Linguistics in Literature* 2, no. 2 (1977), 43–119.

Rother, James. "Parafiction: The Adjacent Universe of Barth, Barthelme, Pynchon, and Nabokov." *boundary 2* 5 (Fall 1976), 21–44.

Stott, William. "Donald Barthelme and the Death of Fiction." *Prospects* 1 (1975), 369–86.

Tanner, Tony. *City of Words.* New York: Harper & Row, 1971, pp. 400–06.

Weixlman, Joe, and Sher Weixlman. "Barth and Barthelme Recycle the Perseus Myth." *Modern Fiction Studies* 26 (Summer 1979), 191–209.

Whalen, Tom. "Wonderful Elegance: Barthelme's 'The Party.'" *Critique* 16 (Spring 1975), 44–48.

Wilde, Alan. "Barthelme Unfair to Kierkegaard: Some Thoughts on Modern and Post-modern Irony." *boundary 2* 5 (Fall 1976), 45–70.

VI. Bibliography
Klinkowitz, Jerome, Asa Pieratt, and Robert Murray Davis. *Donald Barthelme: A Comprehensive Bibliography and Annotated Secondary Checklist.* Hamden, Conn.: Shoe String Press, 1977.

William H. Gass (b. 1924)

I. Novels and Collections of Short Fiction
Omensetter's Luck. New York: New American Library, 1966.
Willie Masters' Lonesome Wife. TriQuarterly Supplement 2 (1968). Evanston, Ill., Northwestern University Press, 1968; rpt. New York: Alfred A. Knopf, 1971.
In the Heart of the Heart of the Country. New York: Harper & Row, 1968.

II. Uncollected Short Fiction
"The Clairvoyant." *Location* 1, no. 2 (Summer 1964), 59–66 [part one of "Cartesian Sonata"].
"The Sugar Crock." *Art and Literature* 9 (Summer 1966), 158–71 [part two of "Cartesian Sonata"].
"We Have Not Lived the Right Life." *New American Review* 5 (1969), 7–32 [from *The Tunnel*].
"Why Windows Are Important to Me." *TriQuarterly* 20 (Winter 1971), 285–307 [from *The Tunnel*].
"The Cost of Everything." *Fiction* 1, no. 3 (1972), unpaged [from *The Tunnel*].
"I Wish You Wouldn't." *Partisan Review* 42, no. 3 (1975), 344–60 [part three of "Cartesian Sonata"].
"Mad Meg." *Iowa Review* 7 (Winter 1976), 77–95 [from *The Tunnel*].
"Koh Whistles Up a Wind." *TriQuarterly* 41 (Fall 1977), 191–209 [from *The Tunnel*].
"Susu, I approach you in my dreams." *TriQuarterly* 42 (Spring 1978), 122–42 [from *The Tunnel*].
"The Old Folks." *Kenyon Review,* n.s. 1, no. 1 (Winter 1979), 35–49.
"Summer Bees." *Paris Review* 79 (1981), 231–36 [from *The Tunnel*].

III. Collected Essays
Fiction and the Figures of Life. New York: Alfred A. Knopf, 1970.
On Being Blue. Boston: David R. Godine, 1976.
The World Within the Word. New York: Alfred A. Knopf, 1978.

IV. Reviews
Review of *A Philosophy of the Real and the Possible* by Harry T. Costello. *Philosophical Review* 64 (1955), 513–14.

Review of *The Burning Fountain* by Philip Wheelwright. *Philosophical Review* 65 (1956), 288–91.

Review of *Poetic Discourse* by Isabell Hugerland. *Journal of English and Germanic Philology* 58 (1959), 515–18.

Review of *The Ethical Idealism of Matthew Arnold* by William Robbins. *Philosophical Review* 70 (1961), 428–30.

Review of *The Novels of Henry James* by Oscar Cargill. *South Atlantic Quarterly* 61 (1962), 285–86.

Review of *Ford Madox Ford's Novels* by John Meixner. *South Atlantic Quarterly* 62 (1963), 447–48.

Review of *Our Knowledge of Fact and Value* by Everett Hall. *Philosophical Review* 72 (1963), 518–20.

Review of *What is Remembered* by Alice B. Toklas. *South Atlantic Quarterly* 62 (1963), 620.

Review of *Ford Madox Ford* by Carol Ohmann; *Critical Writings of Ford Madox Ford,* ed. Frank MacShane. *South Atlantic Quarterly* 64 (1965), 421.

Review of *Genoa: A Telling of Wonders* by Paul Metcalf. *New York Times Book Review,* 19 June 1966, pp. 32–33.

Review of *The Absurd Hero in American Fiction* by David Galloway. *South Atlantic Quarterly* 66 (1967), 618–19.

Review of *Harold Monro and the Poetry Bookshop* by Joy Grant. *South Atlantic Quarterly* 67 (1968), 176–77.

Review of *Validity in Interpretation* by E. D. Hirsch. *Criticism* 10 (1968), 75–76.

Review of *The Great American Novel* by Philip Roth. *New York Review of Books,* 31 May 1973, pp. 7–9.

V. Other Publications

"Language and Ethics." In *The Encyclopedia of Morals,* ed. Virgilius Ferm. New York: Philosophical Library, 1956, pp. 289–93.

"Niccolò Machiavelli." In *The Encyclopedia of Morals,* ed. Virgilius Ferm. New York: Philosophical Library, 1945, pp. 305–09.

"Moritz Schlick." In *The Encyclopedia of Morals,* ed. Virgilius Ferm. New York: Philosophical Library, 1956, pp. 524–29.

"Fumbling Sleight of Hand." *New York Times Book Review,* 17 Sept. 1967, pp. 6, 50.

"The Snares of Meaning." *New Republic,* 11 May 1968, pp. 34–35.

"Written with a Hose." *New York Times Book Review,* 22 Sept. 1968, pp. 4–5, 40.

"Fiesta for the Form." *New Republic,* 29 Oct. 1980, pp. 33–34.

"Homage to Ford Madox Ford." *New Republic,* 28 Mar. 1981, pp. 26–32.

"Lament for Our Failure to Improve on Ancient Skills." *Nation,* 2 Aug. 1958, p. 56 [poem].

"The Panther" and "Torso of an Archaic Apollo" by R. M. Rilke. In *North Country* (Grand Forks: University of North Dakota Press, 1975) [translations].

"A Letter to the Editor." In *Afterwords,* ed. Thomas McCormack. New York: Harper & Row, 1969, pp. 88–105.

"Tribute to David Segal." *New York Times Book Review,* 21 Feb. 1971, p. 2 [letter].

"Playwriting in America." *Yale/Theater* 4, no. 1 (1973) [symposium].

VI. Critical Essays about William Gass

Allen, Carolyn J. "Fiction and Figures of Life in *Omensetter's Luck.*" *Pacific Coast Philology* 9 (1974), 5–11.

Bassoff, Bruce. "The Sacrificial World of William Gass: *In the Heart of the Heart of the Country.*" *Critique* 18 (Summer 1976), 36–58.

Busch, Frederick. "But This Is What It Is Like to Live in Hell: William Gass's *In the Heart of the Heart of the Country.*" *Modern Fiction Studies* 20 (Autumn 1974), 97–107.

Caramello, Charles. "Fleshing Out *Willie Masters' Lonesome Wife.*" *Sub-Stance* 27 (1980), 56–69.

Fogel, Stanley. "'And All the Little Typtopies': Notes on Language Theory in the Contemporary Experimental Novel." *Modern Fiction Studies* 20 (Autumn 1974), 328–36.

French, Ned. "Against the Grain: Theory and Practice in the Work of William H. Gass." *Iowa Review* 7 (Winter 1976), 96–106.

Gilman, Richard. "William H. Gass." In *The Confusion of Realms.* New York: Random House, 1969, pp. 69–81.

Hoekzema, Loren. "Two Readings of Lyrical Space: William Gass's *In the Heart of the Heart of the Country* and Donald Barthelme's *City Life.*" Ph.D. diss., Miami University (Ohio), 1976.

Kane, Patricia. "The Sun Burned on the Snow: Gass's 'The Pedersen Kid.'" *Critique* 14 (Fall 1972), 89–96.

McCaffery, Larry. "The Art of Metafiction: William Gass's *Willie Masters' Lonesome Wife.*" *Critique* 18 (Summer 1976), 21–35.

_____. "William H. Gass." In *Dictionary of Literary Biography.* Detroit: Gale Research Company, 1979, pp. 190–96.

_____. "The Gass-Gardner Debate: Showdown on Main Street." *Literary Review* 23, no. 1 (1979), 134–44.

Schneider Richard J. "The Fortunate Fall in William Gass's *Omensetter's Luck.*" *Critique* 18 (Summer 1976), 5–20.

Scholes, Robert. "Metafiction." *Iowa Review* 1 (Fall 1960), 100–15.

Shorris, Earl. "The Well Spoken Passions of William H. Gass." *Harper's,* May 1972, pp. 96–100.

Tanner, Tony. "Games American Writers Play." *Salamagundi* 35 (Fall 1975), 110–40.

_____. *City of Words.* New York: Harper and Row, 1971, pp. 269–72.

VII. Interviews

"In the Heart of William H. Gass," by Joseph Haas. *Panorama, Chicago Daily News,* 1 Feb. 1969, pp. 4–5, 22.

"Fiction Needn't Say Things—It Should Make Them Out of Words: An Interview with William H. Gass," by Carol Spearin McCauley. *Falcon* 5 (Winter 1972), 35–45; rpt. in *The New Fiction: Interviews with Innovative American Writers,* ed. Joe David Bellamy. Urbana: University of Illinois Press, 1975, pp. 32–44.

"Against the Grain: A Conversation with William H. Gass," by Ned French and David Keyser. *Harvard Advocate* 106 (Winter 1973), 8–16.

"A Symposium on Fiction" [Barthelme, Gass, Grace Paley, Walker Percy]. *Shenandoah* 27, no. 2 (Winter 1976), 3–31.

"A Conversation with Stanley Elkin and William H. Gass," by Jeffrey L. Duncan. *Iowa Review* 7 (Winter 1976), 48–77.

"Interview with William H. Gass." *Paris Review* 70 (Summer 1977), 61–90; rpt. in *Interviews with Contemporary American Novelists,* ed. Thomas LeClair and Larry McCaffery. Urbana: University of Illinois Press, 1982.

"A Conversation with William Gass," by Thomas LeClair. *Chicago Review* 30, no. 2 (1977), 97–106.

VIII. Bibliographies

French, Ned. "William Gass Bibliography." *Iowa Review* 7 (Winter 1976), 106–07.

McCaffery, Larry. "Donald Barthelme, Robert Coover, and William H. Gass: Three Checklists." *Bulletin of Bibliography* 31 (July–Sept. 1974), 101–06.

————. "A William H. Gass Bibliography." *Critique* 18 (Summer 1976), 59–66.

INDEX

Abe, Kobo, 21
Abstract Expressionism, 11
Acker, Kathy, 262
Ackroyd, Dan, 256, 258. *See also* The
    Blues Brothers
Allen, Woody, 126, 280n4. *See also Love
    and Death*
Anderson, Sherwood, 18
Andrews, Terry, *The Story of Harold,* 254
Apollinaire, Guillaume, 12
Apple, Max, 263

Bacon, Francis, *Novum Organum,* 9
Barnes, Djuna, 18
Barth, John, 4, 13, 22, 61, 103, 147, 251,
    262; *Chimera,* 4, 6, 16, 19, 254; *Giles
    Goat Boy,* 22; *Letters,* 262; *Lost in the
    Fun House,* 22, 109; "The Menelaid,"
    176; *The Sot-Weed Factor,* 22
Barthelme, Donald, 4, 8, 12, 13, 19, 25,
    61, 69, 79, 151, 152, 160, 169, 183,
    252, 254, 257, 263; "After Joyce," 118;
    "The Balloon," 105-07; "The Big
    Broadcast of 1938," 122, 132-34; *City
    Life,* 22, 100; "City Life," 125; *Come
    Back, Dr. Caligari,* 100, 121, 122-36;
    "Daumier," 105, 107-08, 124; "The
    Dolt," 103, 124; "Florence Green is
    81," 81, 122-25; "For I'm the Boy
    Whose Only Joy Is Loving You," 122,
    134-36; "The Glass Mountain," 108;
    Great Days, 100, 254; "Hiding Man,"
    125-29; "The Indian Uprising," 120;
    "The Joker's Greatest Triumph," 122;
    "Marie, Marie, Hold on Tight," 125;

Barthelme, Donald (*cont.*)
    "Me and Miss Mandible," 104, 122,
    129-32, 134; "Paraguay," 114-15; "The
    Party," 109; "The Photograph," 104;
    "The Player Piano," 99, 122; "Robert
    Kennedy Saved from Drowning," 110,
    111-12, 114; *Sadness,* 99; "See the
    Moon?" 112-14, 124, 140; *Sixty
    Stories,* 254; *Snow White,* 6, 17, 100,
    109, 116-17, 121, 126, 127, 136-50;
    "Subpoena," 103; "To London and
    Rome," 122; "Up Aloft in the Air,"
    122; "Views of My Father Weeping,"
    110-11, 114, 126, 134, 149; "The Vien-
    nese Opera Ball," 122
Bassoff, Bruce, 186, 202, 204
The Beatles, 19, 260; *Sergeant Pepper's
    Lonely Heart's Club Band,* 260
Beckett, Samuel, 6, 13, 18, 100, 109,
    116, 133, 137, 148
Beethoven, Ludwig van, 156
Bellow, Saul, 19
Belushi, John, 256, 258. *See also* The
    Blues Brothers
Bely, Andrew, 21
Black, Max, 165-68
The Blues Brothers, 256, 258; *Briefcase
    Full of Blues,* 256
Body Heat, 257
Borges, J. L., 12, 13, 14, 18, 55, 71, 100,
    147; *Ficciones,* 21, 22
Bowie, David, 256
Brooks, Mel, *Young Frankenstein,* 257
Bugsy Malone, 256
The Burns and Allen Show, 256